SMART MICROGRIDS

Lessons from Campus Microgrid Design and Implementation

SMART MICROGRIDS

Lessons from Campus Microgrid Design and Implementation

edited by

Hassan Farhangi

British Columbia Institute of Technology
Vancouver, Canada

BRITISH COLUMBIA
INSTITUTE OF TECHNOLOGY

CRC Press
Taylor & Francis Group
Boca Raton London New York

CRC Press is an imprint of the
Taylor & Francis Group, an **informa** business

CRC Press
Taylor & Francis Group
6000 Broken Sound Parkway NW, Suite 300
Boca Raton, FL 33487-2742

First issued in paperback 2020

© 2017 by Taylor & Francis Group, LLC
CRC Press is an imprint of Taylor & Francis Group, an Informa business

No claim to original U.S. Government works

ISBN 13: 978-0-367-57451-2 (pbk)
ISBN 13: 978-1-4822-4876-0 (hbk)

Visit the Taylor & Francis Web site at
http://www.taylorandfrancis.com

and the CRC Press Web site at
http://www.crcpress.com

Disclaimer

This book was prepared as the result of research conducted by British Columbia Institute of Technology (BCIT) and its partners. Nevertheless, it does not necessarily represent the views of BCIT, its partners, or the funding agencies that have funded this work. As such, BCIT, its employees, contractors, and subcontractors make no warrant, express or implied, and assume no legal liability for the information in this book; nor does any party represent that the uses of this information will not infringe upon privately owned rights. This book has not been approved or disapproved by BCIT, nor has BCIT certified the accuracy or adequacy of the information in this book. Moreover, the information contained in this book is subject to future revisions. Important notes of limitations include the following: this book is not a replacement for electrical codes or other applicable standards; this book is not intended or provided by BCIT as design specification or as design guidelines for electrical installations; and the book shall not be used for any purpose other than education and training. Persons using this information do so at no risk to BCIT, and they rely solely upon themselves to ensure that their use of all or part of this book is appropriate in the particular circumstance.

Yesterday I was young, so I wanted to change the world.
Today I am wise, so I am changing myself.

Rumi

Dedicated to all those who strive to better the life of others
by being better human beings themselves and who have the
wisdom to strike a balance between progress and keeping
this lonely planet habitable for the future generations.

… and to Sara and Aras

Contents

X CONTENTS

Foreword

This book discusses an applied research initiative conducted at British Columbia Institute of Technology (BCIT) to design and realize a campus-wide smart microgrid as a living laboratory in its Burnaby campus in Vancouver, Canada. BCIT is an institute of higher education, publicly funded to serve the citizens of British Columbia and its partners around the world and to educate and train graduates who are career-ready, are immediately productive in their chosen workplace, and are ongoing assets for their employers.

BCIT was established in 1964 in Burnaby (Greater Vancouver), British Columbia, Canada, as a professional school to train technicians, technologists, and practitioners needed to serve the industry. Since its inception, BCIT has grown substantially to become one of the largest postsecondary academic institutes in Canada. BCIT has five large campuses around Greater Vancouver with many schools and departments, including the School of Business, School of Computing and Academic Studies, School of Construction and the Environment, School of Energy, School of Health Sciences, and School of Transportation. Approximately 18,000 full-time students and 28,000 part-time students enroll and enter BCIT every year. It has more than 1700 full-time and about 500 part-time faculty and staff.

BCIT's technical education currency is assured through applied research. It conducts grant-funded and industry-sponsored applied research and development focused on solving industry's challenges. Bringing together multidisciplinary teams from a range of research areas and technical expertise, BCIT researchers create practical applied research solutions that can be transformed immediately into commercially relevant products, services, and applications. These activities often result in licensing opportunities, spin-off companies, and new start-ups and are primarily motivated by the creation of direct and indirect benefits for students and the public. Applied research provides students with practical learning opportunities and produces outcomes that further enhance the economic success of and employment opportunities for British Columbia.

The Smart Microgrid Applied Research Team (SMART) is a department within the Technology Centre of BCIT. It converges the information technology, communication engineering, electrical engineering, and computing fields to develop technologies and solutions for complex applied research problems in the energy sector. SMART focuses on smart grid and cybersecurity research in collaboration with industry stakeholders.

In 2007, SMART, BC Hydro (British Columbia electric power authority), the government of British Columbia, and the government of Canada began a joint research and development program for designing, constructing, and implementing Canada's first campus-based smart microgrid at BCIT's Burnaby campus to deliver a "path from laboratory to field" through cost-effective solutions for emerging smart grids. As a result of this program, BCIT has amassed a unique technical expertise in delivering cost-effective solutions for smart grid living laboratory design and realization. Capitalizing on its successful track record in developing smart grid technologies and solutions, BCIT strives to share its knowledge and expertise in this area with industry and academic stakeholders in Canada and the world. The present book is an attempt to disseminate and share that unique experience with the world.

Dr. Kim Dotto
Dean, Applied Research
British Columbia Institute of Technology
Burnaby, British Columbia, Canada

Preface

This book is designed as a narrative on how a complex system, such as a microgrid, is designed, implemented, tested, and used. It captures the essence of experiences that our team at British Columbia Institute of Technology (BCIT) has accumulated through eight years of intensive research in this area. As such, the book is meant to reflect our team's thought processes in spec design, technology selection, integration methodology, and realization of various components of the microgrid and its larger system as a whole.

Discussions between BCIT and its partners about the need for a microgrid started in 2007. At the time, the void was felt for an environment with sufficient scale and similar topology to a utility grid to enable our strategic partners to experiment with and qualify technologies, products, and solutions that targeted the utility environment. In that regard, one of the main drivers for the utility's push to set up a microgrid was its initial application as a sandbox where competing technologies and solutions for a smart grid could be evaluated, qualified, and tested.

Nevertheless, the partners soon realized that such an environment could also be used as a platform to develop new technologies and solutions, as well as help with the education of the new generation of workforce, which utilities require to help them realize their smart grid development and rollout plans.

Those early requirements convinced the design team of the merits to spend ample time in the early stages of the initiative to put together a microgrid strategic road map that captured the needs and objectives of partners and stakeholders. The road map enabled the design team to ensure that each component, subsystem, or capability that was implemented in the microgrid enabled and facilitated the emergence of the next set of capabilities and features of the system.

Chapter 1, entitled "Microgrid as the Building Block of Smart Grid," authored by Hassan Farhangi, attempts to introduce the concept of microgrid and its role in the evolution of the legacy grid toward a future smart grid and covers introductory topics such as definitions, architectures, and types of microgrids.

Chapter 2, entitled "Smart Grid System Integration," authored by Hassan Farhangi, introduces models for a smart grid and what it takes to map such models, or parts thereof, within the existing utility grid. The approach in this chapter is to enable the reader to start from an abstract model of a smart grid and quickly move toward what is feasible within the confines of the present legacy grid.

Chapter 3, entitled "Campus Microgrid," authored by Hassan Farhangi, discusses the background of the BCIT microgrid initiative, the drivers behind its development, and the interests and requirements of its stakeholders. An important section in this chapter covers the thought process behind the microgrid road map, the document that drove and oversaw the microgrid initiative from its start to present day.

Chapter 4, entitled "Cogeneration Plants," authored by Minoo Shariat-Zadeh, covers technology fundamentals in the design and implementation of a microgrid's cogeneration plants. The role and the importance of applicable standards are also briefly covered.

Chapter 5, entitled "Electrical Storage System," authored by Eric Hawthorne, provides an extensive overview of electrical storage fundamentals, technology choices. and its integration issues within microgrids. Given the specific nature of experiences the design team has accumulated in storage design and integration, a dedicated section in this chapter is devoted to lessons learned by the design team in developing the BCIT microgrid's electrical storage system.

Chapter 6, entitled "Energy Management System," authored by Janet So, covers one of the most important technologies in microgrid design of the same name. Often regarded as the lynchpin of smart microgrids, the energy management system is the central planning and control system that enables the microgrid to achieve its operational objectives and targets.

Chapter 7, entitled "Microgrid Communication and Control," coauthored by Hassan Farhangi and Kelly Carmichael, provides an overview of a microgrid's communication and data processing requirements, technologies, and networks. The chapter also covers different network domains implemented within the BCIT smart microgrid and their interactions with operational applications of the microgrid.

Chapter 8, entitled "Interconnection," authored by Ali Palizban, covers the critical topic of a microgrid's interconnection with the main grid and the processes involved in ensuring that grid-tied microgrids could safely interconnect with the larger grid.

Chapter 9, entitled "Microgrid Economic, Environmental, and Social Studies," authored by Joey Dabell, covers the very first question that microgrid planners need to answer, which is the economic justification of a microgrid. The chapter also covers the important topic of environmental assessments, which in turn is one of the first major reviews that the microgrid design has to pass before it could be investable. And last but not least, the chapter deals with the need for community outreach and consumer behavior.

Chapter 10, entitled "Microgrid Use Cases, Testing, and Validation," authored by Clay Howey, provides an overview of industry standard use cases, developed by the Electric Power Research Institute, and explains BCIT's preferences for use cases implemented in our test plans and lessons learned in the process.

Chapter 11, entitled "Campus Microgrid Lessons Learned," coauthored by Joey Dabell and Clay Howey, covers a wide variety of experiences and lessons that the BCIT's design team has accumulated in their eight years of design and implementation of the microgrid.

In addition to BCIT's design team, who have authored this book, BCIT's smart microgrid could have not been realized without the generous help, support, and contributions of many executives and researchers, both in industry and in academia, who provided their knowledge, expertise, and guidance to help us move forward. As a research team, we are thankful for their support and contributions and would like to dedicate this book to their generosity and selfless support.

Among these, our sincere thanks go to Dr. Kim Dotto, BCIT's dean for applied research, Dr. Don Wright, past BCIT president Paul Dangerfield, past BCIT vice president for education, and Kathy Kinloch, current BCIT president, who supported our efforts every step of the way, helping us to navigate the organizational complexities at BCIT.

Moreover, many departments and individuals within BCIT supported our work and collaborated extensively with the design team in the process of design and construction of our microgrid. Among these, our special thanks go to Joe Newton and his manager, Nancy Paris.

Furthermore, we would like to offer our sincere appreciations and gratitude to our industry partners, who helped us with guidance, advice, and technology. Among these, our warmest thanks are reserved for Kip Morison, Helen Whittaker, and Giuseppe Stanciulescu of BC Hydro; John Gorjup and Dr. Felix Kwamena of Natural Resources Canada; Dr. Lisa Dignard of CanmetENERGY; Dr. Andrew Vallerand and Rodney Howes of Defence Research and Development Canada; and Jean Lassard of Hydro-Québec.

Last but not least, we have benefited tremendously from our discussions with power system experts, including Dr. Geza Joos of McGill University, Dr. Reza Iravani of the University of Toronto, Dr. Chris Marnay of the Lawrence Berkeley National Laboratory, and Dr. Ali Palizban of BCIT's School of Energy.

Dr. Hassan Farhangi
Editor

Acknowledgments

Over the years, countless individuals, organizations, and entities have provided the Smart Microgrid Applied Research Team at British Columbia Institute of Technology (BCIT) with generous support, funding, and contributions in our quest to establish Canada's very first smart microgrid on the BCIT campus in Burnaby. It may not be possible to list each and every person, and their contributions, in empowering us to achieve our goals. Nevertheless, here is an incomplete list of our partners:

Utilities
- BC Hydro
- Hydro One
- Hydro-Québec
- New Brunswick Power
- Manitoba Hydro

Government
- British Columbia Ministry of Energy and Mines (Innovative Clean Energy Fund)
- Government of Canada (Western Diversification Fund, Natural Resources Canada, Natural Sciences and Engineering Research Council, Defence Research and Development Canada)

Research centers
- CanmetENERGY
- Powertech Labs
- Institut de recherche d'Hydro-Québec

Private sector
- Siemens
- Panasonic
- Tantalus Systems Corporation
- Corinex Communications Corporation
- Schneider Electric
- IBM
- General Electric
- ABB
- Car2Go

Academia
- Simon Fraser University
- McGill University
- University of Toronto
- University of New Brunswick
- University of Alberta
- University of Waterloo
- Ryerson University
- University of Manitoba
- University of British Columbia
- University of Aachen (Germany)

Editor

Hassan Farhangi, PhD, senior member IEEE, PEng, is the director of smart grid research at British Columbia Institute of Technology (BCIT) in Burnaby, British Columbia, Canada, and adjunct professor at Simon Fraser University in Vancouver, Canada. Dr. Farhangi has held adjunct professor appointments at the National University of Singapore, Royal Road University in Victoria, Canada, and at the University of British Colombia in Vancouver, Canada. Dr. Farhangi is currently the chief system architect and the principal investigator of BCIT's smart microgrid initiative at its Burnaby campus in Vancouver, British Columbia, and the scientific director and principal investigator of Natural Sciences and Engineering Research Council's (NSERC) pan-Canadian smart microgrid network (NSERC Smart Microgrid Network or NSMG-Net). He is well published with numerous contributions in scientific journals and conferences on smart grids and has served on various international standardization committees, such as International Electrotechnical Commission (IEC) Canadian Subcommittee (CSC) Technical Committee 57 (TC 57) Working Group 17 (WG 57) (IEC 61850), Conseil International des Grands Réseaux Électriques (CIGRÉ) WG C6.21 (Smart Metering), CIGRÉ WG C6.22 (Microgrids Evolution), and CIGRÉ WG C6.28 (Hybrid Systems for Off-Grid Power Supply). A frequent keynote speaker at various international smart grid conferences, Dr. Farhangi has more than 30 years of experience in academic and applied research in Europe, Asia, the United States, and Canada. Before joining BCIT, he served as the chief technical officer of a number of companies involved in the design and development of systems, components, and solutions for the smart grid. Dr. Farhangi obtained his PhD degree from the University of Manchester Institute of Science and Technology in the United Kingdom in 1982; his MSc degree from the University of Bradford in the United Kingdom in 1978; and his BSc degree from the University of Tabriz in Iran in 1976, all in electrical and electronic engineering. Dr. Farhangi is a founding member of SmartGrid Canada, an academic member of CIGRÉ, a member of the Association of Professional Engineers and Geoscientists of British Columbia, and a senior member of the Institute of Electrical and Electronic Engineers.

Contributors

Kelly Carmichael has 22 years of experience working in the information technology industry. He holds a diploma in computer science from Thompson Rivers University, Kamloops, British Columbia. His information technology work experience ranges from employment in an embryonic entrepreneurial start-up firm all the way up to the large multinational giant IBM. Carmichael has been involved in development projects spanning complex distributed systems all the way to low-level operating system services. He has an interest in the theory and practice of delivering quality, reliable, and maintainable information systems.

Joey Dabell is a project leader at the British Columbia Institute of Technology (BCIT). As a faculty researcher, she functions as a project manager for smart microgrid research, development, and demonstration projects where she coordinates the research, development, and demonstration activities of the multidiscipline Smart Microgrid Applied Research Team. In this role she facilitates collaborations between academic, industry, and community partners; coordinates microgrid-related training and outreach efforts; and participates in business development. Dabell's research interests and activities are at the intersection of microgrid and renewable energy technologies with policy, community outreach, and energy behavior change, particularly as these relate to the socioeconomic and environmental issues leading to 100% renewable energy. She is an active member of BCIT's Sustainability Committee. Dabell received her MET from the University of British Columbia, Vancouver, Canada, in 2009, and her BTech in computer graphics and artificial intelligence programming from BCIT in 1995.

Eric Hawthorne received his MSc degree in computing and information science from Queen's University, Kingston, Ontario, Canada, in 1988. He is a research associate at the Smart Microgrid Applied Research Team within the Centre for Applied Research and Innovation of British Columbia Institute of Technology in Vancouver, Canada. His work focuses on software and systems architecture and renewable energy microgrid energy management systems. He has extensive experience in smart grid applications, systems engineering, and software engineering. He is a coauthor of *97 Things Every Software Architect Should Know: Collective Wisdom from the Experts*. His main research interests are smart grid control systems for renewable energy integration and demand response.

Clay Howey has over 25 years' experience in project management, software development, distributed systems, and data communications. Currently, he is the technical lead on the smart microgrid research initiative at British Columbia Institute of Technology and coordinates the activities of researchers in the areas of energy management, renewable generation integration, substation automation, smart metering, electric vehicles and charging stations, and demand response. Howey also has experience in mobile wireless application development and has expertise in artificial intelligence applications, employing technologies such as expert systems, fuzzy logic, and neural networks.

Ali Palizban received his PhD in electrical engineering from the University of New South Wales, Sydney, Australia. He is currently the program head of the electrical power and industrial control options of the Department of Electrical and Computer Engineering at the British Columbia Institute of Technology's School of Energy. He has worked in the electric power industry consulting engineering firms, academic, and research and development institutions for over 27 years. He is involved in applied research on microgrid design and implementation, substation automation, and voltage/volt-ampere reactive optimization projects. He has published several peer-reviewed papers in electrical power and control systems. He is a member of the Association of Professional Engineers and Geoscientists of British Columbia and a senior member of Institute of Electrical and Electronic Engineers. He is interested in teaching and research in power system analysis and design, control, automation systems, and smart microgrids. He has been directly involved in the design of British Columbia Institute of Technology's microgrid from the early stage of feasibility study, simulation analysis, installation, testing, and final phases of commissioning and operation.

Minoo Shariat-Zadeh received her BSc degree in electrical engineering from the Azad University of Tehran, Iran, in 1995. She is a research associate at the Smart Microgrid Applied Research Team within the Centre for Applied Research and Innovation of British Columbia Institute of Technology in Vancouver, Canada. She functions as a team leader and participant and designs, plans, and conducts smart microgrid projects, renewable energy resource integration, power automation systems, and substation automation systems. She has worked in manufacturing, consulting engineering firms, and research and development for over 19 years. She is a member of the Association of Professional Engineers and Geoscientists of British Columbia. Her main research interests are smart grids, smart microgrids, renewable energies, and control and automation systems.

Janet So is a research analyst in the Smart Microgrid Applied Research Team at British Columbia Institute of Technology. As part of the software team in the smart microgrid research initiative, she has developed applications in areas of energy management system, meter and sensor data acquisition, and demand response algorithms. Her research interests are in smart grid software control systems and demand response. So is an experienced software developer, particularly in web applications. She has worked on a variety of small and large software projects ranging from an e-commerce fashion website to a business intelligent software suite. So holds a BSoftEng from the University of Waterloo, Ontario, Canada.

List of Abbreviations

AC	alternating current
AEPS	area electric power system
AMI	advanced metering infrastructure
AMR	automated meter reading
APS	area power system
a-Si	amorphous silicon
BCIT	British Columbia Institute of Technology
BESS	battery energy storage system
BMU	battery management unit
BOS	balance of system
CAES	compressed air energy storage
CB	circuit breaker
CIGS	copper indium gallium deselenide
CIS	copper indium selenide
CSA	Canadian Standards Association
CSA C22.2 No. 107.1	Standard for General Use Power Supplies
c-Si	monocrystalline silicon
CSV	comma-separated values
CVR	conservation voltage reduction
DAU	data aggregator unit
DC	direct current
DEMS	decentralized energy management system

DER	distributed energy resource
DFIG	doubly fed induction generator
DG	distributed generation
DGTIR	Distributed Generation Technical Interconnection Requirements
DOE	U.S. Department of Energy
DR	demand response
EMS	energy management system
Energy OASIS	Open Access to Sustainable Intermittent Sources
EPRI	Electric Power Research Institute
EV	electric vehicle
FAT	factory acceptance test
FIT	factory integration test
FTP	file transfer protocol
GHG	greenhouse gas
GIS	geographical information system
GOOSE	generic object oriented substation event
GPS	global positioning system
GW	gigawatts (unit of power)
HAWT	horizontal axis wind turbine
HMI	human–machine interface
IEC	International Electrotechnical Commission
IEC 61850	International Electrotechnical Commission standard 61850: Communication Networks and Systems in Substations
IEEE	Institute of Electrical and Electronics Engineers
IEEE 1547	IEEE Standard for Interconnecting Distributed Resources with Electric Power Systems
IEEE 519	IEEE Recommended Practices and Requirements for Harmonic Control in Electrical Power Systems
IT	information technology
kW	kilowatts (unit of power)
kWh	kilowatt-hour (unit of energy)

LAN	local area network
LNG	liquid natural gas
LV	low-voltage
MC	microgrid controller
MCC	microgrid control center
mc-Si	polycrystalline silicon
MDMS	metering data management system
MEM	microgrid energy manager
MEMS	microgrid energy management system
MO	market operator
MS	microgrid switch
MV	medium-voltage
MW	megawatts
NIST	National Institute of Standards and Technology
NOCT	normal operating cell temperature
PCC	point of common coupling
PCS	power conversion system
PIR	project interconnection requirements
PLC	programmable logic controller; power-line communication
PTP	precision time protocol
PV	photovoltaic
R&D	research and development
RD&D	research, development, and demonstration
RESTful	representative state transfer; a web services communication protocol guideline
SAT	site acceptance test
SCADA	supervisory control and data acquisition
SLD	single-line diagram
SOC	battery state of charge (usually as a percentage of capacity)
STCs	standard test conditions
ToU	time of use
UI	user interface
UL	Underwriters Laboratories Inc.

UL 1741	UL Standard for Inverters, Converters, Controllers and Interconnection System Equipment for Use with Distributed Energy Resources
V2G	vehicle to grid
VAR	volt-ampere reactive optimization
VAWT	vertical axis wind turbine
VVO	voltage/volt-ampere reactive optimization
W/kg	watts per kilogram (unit of specific power)
Wh/kg	watt-hours per kilogram (unit of specific energy)
Wh/L	watt-hours per liter
Wi-Fi	wireless local area network
WiMAX	Worldwide Interoperability for Microwave Access

Microgrid as the Building Block of Smart Grid

HASSAN FARHANGI

Contents

Environmental, economic, and political issues in the latter half of the last century have made it challenging for the electric utility industry to continue with the status quo. The rising cost of primary fuels is increasingly challenging the sustainability of generating power out of fossil-based sources in the long run. And given the role that fossil fuels play in electricity generation across the world, the utility industry's baseline costs and carbon footprints are on the rise. At the same time and since tariffs for the sale of electricity to consumers, set by utility commissions across most jurisdictions in the developed world, have not changed, utility companies face reduced revenues and therefore tighter operating budgets.

This means that utilities are unable to invest in the upgrade and modernization of their aging infrastructure, which has well passed its useful life span. An aging infrastructure reduces system reliability and efficiency, which in turn translates into higher technical losses and even lesser revenues for the utilities. And while the supply is under pressure, the demand for electricity increases unabated due to mass electrification of life and economy. It is in this context that the reliability of the largest-ever human-made machine, and the marvel of engineering progress in the last century, i.e., the electrical grid, diminishes to a degree that errors and anomalies in one part of the system cause mass domino failures in the entire network. Blackouts experienced in eastern United States and Canada in 2003, and parts of Europe in the same year, affecting millions of people and costing billions of dollars, are but examples of how critical it is to address the reliability issues of the system sooner rather than later.

Considering the operational and economic challenges that the utilities are facing, the industry has begun looking beyond current technologies toward a future in which such issues would be resolved. That future is called intelligent grid or smart grid. In the smart grid of the future, generation will not follow consumption (as is the case today). In other words, when demand rises, the preferred solution would not be more generation. Rather, the utility will look at gaining more efficiency with their existing assets (i.e., minimizing losses), managing end-user demand (i.e., load control), and partnering with consumers to roll back the load (i.e., conservation). All of these approaches will ensure that consumption follows generation. That is a fundamental change of paradigm. The smart grid of the future will be able to optimize the use of its assets, reduce losses, curtail unnecessary load, and ensure sustainable rationality between what could be economically generated and the load that has to be serviced. And all of that has to be done with proactive commitment to environmental stewardship. The latter requires the industry to invest in renewable sources of energy and facilitate green cogeneration.

The problem, however, is that transition will not be smooth by any stretch of the imagination. In the absence of mature technologies, interoperable standards, and exhaustively qualified solutions, cash-strapped utility companies cannot afford taking the risks involved in upgrading their electricity grid overnight. These companies provide a critical service to society, which cannot be put into jeopardy by rushing through the transition from the legacy grid to a smart grid. Instead, the industry in the developed world is taking steps to modernize the grid through strategic and gradual implantation of fully validated smart grid functions and features into the legacy system.

It goes without saying that these solutions have to be part and parcel of a well-thought-out strategic smart grid road map, which identifies what functions are needed when and how these should be integrated with the larger system at hand. In other words, given the financial resources available to utility companies, the industry in the developed world has already begun adopting technologies for generation diversification, optimal deployment of expensive assets, demand response, energy conservation, reduction of the industry's overall carbon footprint, etc. It is apparent that in this particular case, utilities in the less developed world have a clear advantage compared with their counterparts in the developed world. They do not have a legacy system to worry about. In other words, they could start their smart grid implementation as greenfield projects. Removing the requirement for backward compatibility with the existing grid provides such utilities with a straightforward and a less costly path to a smart grid.

1.1 Introduction to Smart Grid

The existing electricity grid is unidirectional in nature. It is practically built as the required plumbing to transport and distribute power from where it is generated (mainly far from load centers) to where it is needed by consumers (load centers). In other words, the existing grid is essentially a large pipe that connects electricity generators with electrical loads.

This large pipe assumes different forms and uses a variety of complex technologies to ensure highest efficiency in the process of converting the power contained in the primary sources of energy into electricity and subsequently minimal losses in the process of transporting and distributing that energy to the consumers. Nevertheless, the existing electricity system at best converts only one-third of primary fuel energy into electricity without recovering the waste heat, which is mainly a by-product of the combustion process. Almost 8% of its output is lost along its transmission lines, while 20% of its generation capacity exists merely to meet peak demand only (i.e., 5% of the time). In addition to that, due to the hierarchical topology of its assets, the existing electricity grid suffers from domino effect failures.

The next-generation electricity grid, known as smart grid (or intelligent grid), is expected to address the major shortcoming of the existing grid. In essence, a smart grid needs to provide the utility companies with full visibility and pervasive control over their assets and services. A smart grid is required to be self-healing and resilient to system anomalies. And last but not least, a smart grid needs to empower its stakeholders to define and realize new ways of engagement with each other and be proactive in various forms of energy transactions across the system.

To allow pervasive control and monitoring, the smart grid is emerging as a convergence of information technology (IT) and communication technology with power system engineering.

Figure 1.1 depicts the salient features of a smart grid in comparison with those of the existing grid [1]. This side-by-side comparison of the existing grid with a smart grid reveals that these entities use different hierarchies, technologies, and command/control strategies, which are in particular the following:

- The existing grid traditionally uses electromechanical switchgear, while a smart grid will see the replacement of such components with equivalent digital components.
- For the most part, the existing grid relies on limited communication with its field components, capturing few sensory data, status, and alarms from the field and applying limited remote control over some of its gear. A smart grid, on the

Existing grid	Intelligent grid
Electromechanical	Digital
One-way communication	Two-way communication
Centralized generation	Distribution generation
Hierarchical	Network
Few sensors	Sensors throughout
Blind	Self-monitoring
Manual restoration	Self-healing
Failures and blackouts	Adaptive and islanding
Manual check/test	Remote check/test
Limited control	Pervasive control
Few customer choices	Many customer choices

Figure 1.1 Comparison of a legacy grid and a smart grid. (From Farhangi, H., *IEEE Power & Energy Magazine*, 8, 18–28, 2010. © 2010 IEEE. With permission.)

other hand, is characterized by the flow of extensive sensory data from across its network, supplemented with two-way communication, command, and control of its major assets and subsystems. Such pervasive control allows a smart grid to detect failures much faster and take immediate and appropriate actions to "heal" the situation without the need for operator intervention.

- Failures in the existing grid normally create a domino effect, causing major blackouts. A smart grid, in contrast, boosts its system reliability by quickly isolating and islanding faults and therefore protects the rest of the system from inevitable interruptions that may happen due to component failures, system malfunctions, and/or environmental conditions.
- The existing grid is characterized by large generators, often placed far away from load centers. In contrast, a smart grid facilitates cogeneration and integration of renewable sources of energy into its network. In other words, a smart grid has a much more diverse generation portfolio than the existing grid.
- The existing grid delivers power to a termination point and as such has no interactions with what lies beyond that termination point. In contrast, a smart grid empowers all those who are involved in energy transactions across its network to play a role in improving the service, boosting its efficiency, and reducing its load. In the short term, this involves consumers, while in the long term, this may potentially involve consumers and their intelligent appliances.

1.1.1 Increasing Capabilities

Given the fact that the roots of power system issues are typically found in the electrical distribution system, the point of departure for grid overhaul is firmly placed at the bottom of the chain. This is the area that traditionally has seen very little investment by utility companies. In other words, while the existing electricity grid has incorporated many modern technologies and increasing complexity in its power plants, control centers, and transmission infrastructure, the same cannot be said about the distribution system.

As Figure 1.2 demonstrates, utilities have begun investing in distribution automation as the precursor to achieving increasing capabilities over time. The expectation is that investments in the distribution network shall enable utilities to employ the required applications (e.g., energy management, outage restoration, distribution automation), in their back-office environment. Although the scenario seems straightforward, the difficulty is in choosing the right end-to-end communication and command and control technologies, as well as the analytic technologies required to manage the inordinate amount of data (also known as big data) that will be generated in the process. This is an iterative exercise, in which each target application will determine the nature, volume, and frequency of data it needs to function.

These parameters are what communication engineers require to design and implement an appropriate end-to-end communication plumbing. Such plumbing is quite expensive in terms of cost, installation, and commissioning and is therefore expected to serve the utility for many years to come. However, the absence of much needed clarity of the requirements of future utility applications makes it almost impossible to have full confidence in the ability of the chosen communication technologies, protocols, and standards to be able to meet all

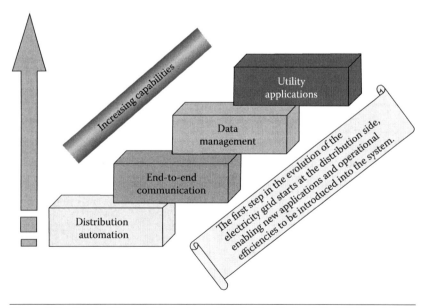

Figure 1.2 Smart grid's capability development trends. (From Farhangi, H., *IEEE Power & Energy Magazine*, 8, 18–28, 2010. © 2010 IEEE. With permission.)

the functional requirements of a utility's future smart grid capabilities and applications. That is one of the major impediments that could potentially slow down the emergence of the smart grid and the flow of utility investments to realize it.

1.2 Smart Grid Evolution

Given the role the electricity grid plays in the day-to-day life and economic activities of societies, it is hard to imagine that it will undergo a fundamental change in the short term. This notion is further accentuated when one considers the level of development and maturity of the technologies required to build a smart grid's relatively complex functions and capabilities. As such, it is understandable if utilities adopt a gradual and phased approach to incorporating the smart grid's capabilities and functions into their existing networks.

It goes without saying that in addition to satisfying the utilities' cost–benefit requirements, such capabilities and functions have to pass the litmus test of technical/operational maturity, upstream/downstream interoperability, and backward compatibility with the legacy grid.

Within the context of these new capabilities, communication and data management play an important role. These basic ingredients enable the utilities to place a layer of intelligence over their current and future infrastructure, thereby allowing the introduction of new applications and processes in their business.

1.2.1 Convergence

As Figure 1.3 depicts, the convergence of communication technology and IT with the power system, assisted by an array of new approaches, technologies, and applications, allows the existing grid to traverse the complex, yet staged, trajectory of architecture, protocols, and standards toward the smart grid. In other words, the fusion of communication technologies and information technologies into power systems, allows each utility to determine the appropriate smart grid system architecture that fits their service requirements, asset mix, and generation portfolio.

Consequently, no two utility companies may adopt the same architectural approaches to building their smart grid. Each utility,

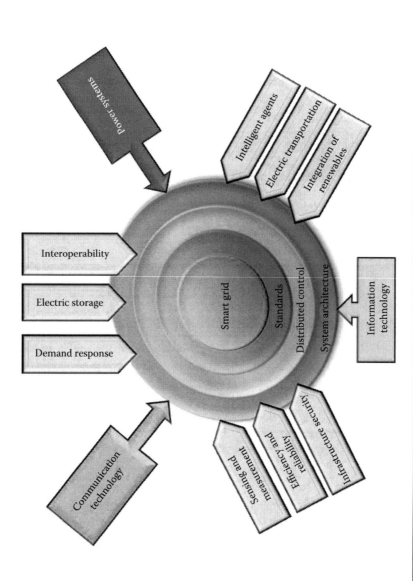

Figure 1.3 Convergence of disciplines in a smart grid. (From Farhangi, H., *IEEE Power & Energy Magazine*, 8, 18–28, 2010. © 2010 IEEE. With permission.)

influenced by their jurisdictional territory, service parameters, business targets, and peculiarities of their legacy grid, will determine the mix and scope of smart grid functionalities that they will develop, the time frame for their rollout, and their integration methodology and development road map. These are the required parameters that will determine the topology of the new system, the command and control technologies it requires, and therefore the protocols and standards needed to ensure their seamless integration.

While emphasizing the core technologies of communication, information, and power systems as the basis of any and all smart grid systems, Figure 1.3 captures an array of smart grid functions as an example of what utilities will have to consider in their quest to gradually transform their legacy electricity grid toward their desired smart grid systems.

In practice, however, technological innovations, or lack thereof, will determine the pace of that transformation. Nevertheless, as the backbone of the power industry, the electricity grid is now the focus of research and development of new technologies. Utilities in North America and across the world are taking solid steps toward incorporating these new technologies in many aspects of their operations and infrastructure.

1.2.2 Transformation Pyramid

As discussed, each utility will have to define and plan its own journey through this complex process. At the core of this transformation is the need to make more efficient use of current assets and infrastructure. Figure 1.4 shows a typical utility pyramid, where asset management is at the base of smart grid development. It is upon this base that utilities build the foundation of the smart grid through careful overhaul of their IT infrastructure, communication technologies, and circuit topology. Therefore, each utility shall have to start with a fully developed business case meant to justify the required investments and then move through a process of upgrading its fundamental assets with the capabilities required to support the desired functionalities in the short, medium, and long term.

Making such detailed analysis involves an iterative process in which top-down and bottom-up analysis need to be done to determine, specify, and size up the constituent technologies required to

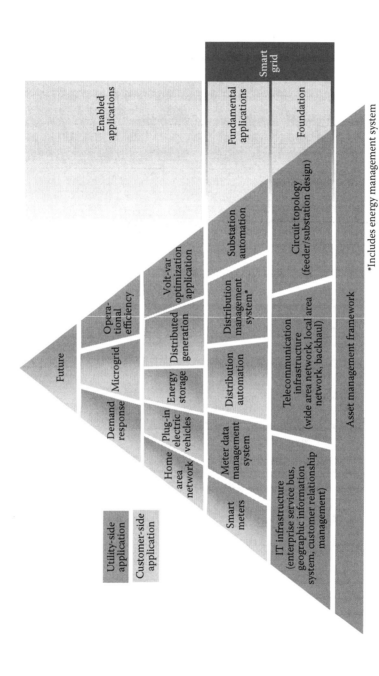

Figure 1.4 Smart grid priority pyramid. (From Farhangi, H., *IEEE Power & Energy Magazine*, 8, 18–28, 2010. © 2010 IEEE. With permission.)

build such a pyramid. Without a doubt, this involves lateral and vertical integration among various smart grid capabilities and functions, some of which may not even be on the radar screen of the utility yet.

As an example, Figure 1.4 shows that the fundamental business objective of the utility in question is asset management. In other words, the utility has to have a well-developed business case that demonstrates that a smart grid would be able to boost the productivity and efficiency of its current assets. Given the typical value of such assets, that justification is often used carefully in the North American power industry.

Having established the required foundation, the utility can now plan for the next layer of sophistication to be introduced into its system. As Figure 1.4 shows, the foundation layer includes new automated substations and feeders, end-to-end telecom networks, and the required enterprise applications, such as geographical information system (GIS) and customer relationship management. The smart grid's fundamental applications, such as substation automation, distribution automation, and smart metering infrastructure (advanced metering infrastructure [AMI]), can then be built on top of this foundation.

It goes without saying that if the foundation technologies and fundamental applications are not designed with the forward-looking view and consideration of the requirements of future smart grid applications, the pyramid can never be cost-effectively completed. In other words, the smart grid's foundation and fundamental applications could either enable or impede (depending on how well they are designed) future integration of a wide variety of more complex applications with a fully operational system.

As discussed, the organic growth of this well-designed layer of intelligence over utility assets enables the smart grid's fundamental applications to emerge. It is interesting to note that, although the foundation of a smart grid is built upon a lateral integration of these basic ingredients, a smart grid's capabilities will be built upon vertical and lateral integrations of the upper layer applications. As an example, a critical capability such as demand response may not be feasible without tight integration of smart meters and home area networks. Similarly, distributed generation, including renewables, cannot be integrated into the system without energy storage.

Knowing where a utility needs to be, we now need to determine where we are and as such map out the path that will get us there.

1.2.3 *Mapping the Path to Smart Grid*

As discussed earlier, utility companies across the globe are at different stages of infrastructure and workflow developments. At the same time, depending on diverse business, technological, and operational parameters, each utility may adopt a different mixture of the smart grid's functions and technologies to meet its investment objectives. That means that neither the point of departure nor the ultimate destination would be exactly the same for all utility companies. In other words, each utility will have to determine its own trajectory for transition from its legacy grid to the smart grid. Moreover, no two smart grid implementations by different utilities may be exact replicas of each other.

Having said that, the mechanics involved in mapping out the path to the smart grid is almost universal. It involves understanding the peculiarities and shortcomings of the legacy system, and planning for interim solutions, within the confines of the utility companies' constraints and objectives. The mapping process starts with a strengths, weaknesses, opportunities, and threats analysis of the suitability, or lack thereof, of the status quo to meet the utility's business objectives. Such an analysis should determine what the gaps are, what is needed to address those gaps, what are the priorities, and therefore, given the known constraints, what functionality needs to be introduced and where.

Figure 1.5 shows the hierarchical nature of the legacy grid, where silos of generation, transmission, and distribution are separated by hidden boundaries of command, control, and monitoring. The legacy grid's architectural hierarchy has evolved over many decades and has served the industry well. The basic premise in this topology is "load following." In other words, each utility has to figure out the "peak load" that each of its feeders has to serve, size up the bulk components in substations that serve those feeders (e.g., transformers, switchgear), and aggregate those loads to determine the peak generation and transmission capacity that is required to serve those loads. The system operates around the notion of load forecasting, which determines how much generation needs to be attached to the system to service the "forecasted" loads and how much transmission capacity needs to be engaged to bring the generated power from power plants to load centers.

As such, the legacy grid is relatively intelligent as it has to react within fractions of cycles to changes in voltage and frequency, the

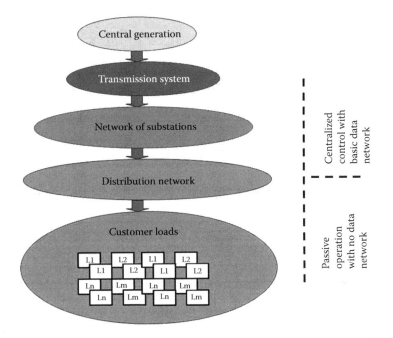

Figure 1.5 Legacy grid's hierarchical structure. (From Farhangi, H., *IEEE Power & Energy Magazine*, 8, 18–28, 2010. © 2010 IEEE. With permission.)

two measurements that demonstrate whether or not the system generation capacity is adequate for servicing the loads. To keep the variations in system frequency and voltage within acceptable bands, much intelligence has already been implanted into the system. However, the main control parameter in this hierarchy is the amount of generation that the system can engage at any given point in time to ensure voltage and frequency stability. Such intelligence requires centralized control through a basic supervisory control and data acquisition network, capable of data, command, and control transactions.

As Figure 1.5 demonstrates, the legacy grid has no control over the loads it needs to serve. As such, the only information it has on whether or not the engaged generation is sufficient to meet the actual load requirement is the variation in system frequency and voltage. That is the reason why in the past century, the notion of a load-following electricity grid saw no need to match the investments that were done in generation and transmission silos with those done at the distribution network. While the former saw the introduction of multitudes of monitoring, analytics, data networking, and command and control functions, the distribution network was left struggling with very little monitoring, command and control at the low-voltage substations, and an antiquated electromechanical metering system at the termination points (i.e., the customer premises).

However, as the load continued its unabated growth, the utilities soon realized that they could no longer keep the safety margin of the system within permitted operational guidelines. Slight anomalies, either human made or nature caused, were blamed for major blackouts across the globe. Erosion of the system's safety margins, combined with mass electrification and therefore rising demand, compounded with rising cost of production and stagnant revenues, took away the utility companies' financial ability to expand the only parameter at their control to meet the demand, i.e., more generation capacity.

Moreover, environmental concerns related to the negative impact of greenhouse gas emissions as by-product of fossil fuels, combined with the utilities' inability to build more transmission lines to transport the extra power from generation centers to load centers, forced the industry to change its fundamental paradigm from load following to "generation following." In other words, given the inability of utility companies to bring more generation capacity on board to serve the rising demand, the industry had no choice but to entertain the paradigm shift from "generation follows demand" to "demand follows generation." That is how the concept of the smart grid was born.

In contrast to the legacy grid, smart grid advocates generation following. To do that, utility companies need to have an accurate and real-time measure of the constantly changing load that they need to serve. Having real-time information about the load would enable the utilities to adopt various measures to curb the load in line with their existing generation capacity. Such measures could range from financial incentives (time of use, maximum demand penalties, lower tariffs for off-peak use, etc.) to outright load shedding (i.e., service disconnect). It goes without saying that the adoption of any or all of such measures is regulated by regulatory bodies in each country, and utilities do not have a free hand in imposing such measures at will.

Moreover, the need to have accurate and real-time information about the load means that the first step that utility companies need to take is to upgrade their distribution network. Figure 1.6 suggests

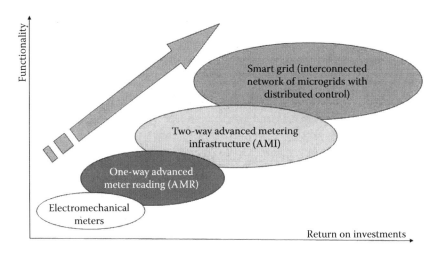

Figure 1.6 Smart grid's return on investment. (From Farhangi, H., *IEEE Power & Energy Magazine*, 8, 18–28, 2010. © 2010 IEEE. With permission.)

that the first stage in smart grid development should begin with replacing the old antiquated electromechanical meters with smart meters, capable of two-way communication and control within a much larger intelligent infrastructure, called AMI. Here such meters are capable of reporting consumption levels, alarms, events, and other power system quality parameters in real time. Such information could be used by the upper analytic tools within the utility back-office network to decide how to price the service and/or how to control those loads.

It should be noted that in early stages of smart metering developments, many utilities toyed with the idea of one-way advanced meter reading (AMR) technologies, where the meter was expected to send the subscriber's consumption information to a utility headend at predetermined intervals. As such, these meters were equipped with one-way communication technologies, which meant that they were not able to receive and react to commands from utility headends.

However, the AMR technology was short lived, as utilities soon recognized the need to use smart meters for demand response, load control, and service configuration. As such, the industry required smart meters to be capable of two-way communication, resulting in AMI becoming the mainstream smart metering technology. As such, AMI is regarded as the first stage in transition to smart grid, where the move toward intelligent entities (known as smart microgrids), interconnected with a system of distributed supervisory command and control, facilitates the emergence of the smart grid.

As Figure 1.7 demonstrates, AMI enables the next set of capabilities within the smart grid space to materialize. The figure suggests that the development of smart grid in any given utility will most likely traverse through two distinct, yet interrelated stages, known as AMI and smart grid. As discussed earlier, the AMR phase was a historical anomaly that will not be discussed further. Instead, we will focus on technologies and capabilities that characterize the two most prominent stages of this evolution, namely, AMI and smart grid.

The diversity and specification of technologies and their resulting capabilities in each stage will be determined by the strategic road map of the utility and their priorities. For instance, the AMI subsystem could be implemented as a means to automate the utility's billing function only, or it could be designed as a platform to extend the reach of upper-layer tools in the utility's back office into the far corners of the distribution network through establishment of two-way communication, distributed command and control, and smart sensor networks at the utility's termination points. The decision to limit or expand the capabilities of the AMI system therefore depends to a large extent on the cost–benefit analysis that each utility has to conduct prior to committing to such expensive developments.

Figure 1.7 shows the expected return on investment for technologies in various stages of smart grid development. For example, the availability of AMI data, in one-way transactions, automates the billing system. In other words, if the utility needs to automate their billing environment only, a one-way communication system with such meters would have been sufficient. In such a scenario, demand response, load shedding, or other load control functions would not be possible as the AMI system is incapable of receiving and implementing commands from the utility headend. In contrast, a two-way communication capability with these meters would now enable the utility to develop some level of control over the service. Demand response, outage detection, and restoration would become feasible.

Through AMI, the utility can now allocate maximum demand restrictions on each customer, and it can detect if the service is down or what the conditions of the meter were prior to an outage (last gasp events) and the status of the network that feeds the service. Such

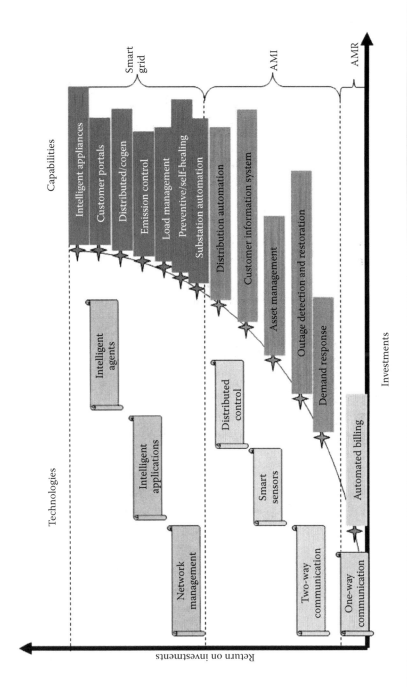

Figure 1.7 AMI-driven smart grid capabilities. (From Farhangi, H., *IEEE Power & Energy Magazine*, 8, 18–28, 2010. © 2010 IEEE. With permission.)

information is critical for detection and timely restoration of outages. The combination of smart meters status, alarms, and last gasp messages with the utility's GIS tools provides a potent platform for feeder automation, outage detection and restoration, and asset management. Similarly, the utility's customer relationship management (customer information system) tools will greatly benefit from access to real-time AMI data, providing consumers with valuable information about their service, load profile, and consumption habits. AMI enables an informed consumer to play a proactive role in managing their own carbon footprint.

Moreover, the ability to communicate with the customer and remotely connect or disconnect their service enables the customers and the utility to engage in different service contracts. For instance, one customer can opt to be on a prepayment contract, allowing the utility to monitor their paid-up credit and warn them if the credit is about to fall below an agreed upon level. The service could then be disconnected by the utility if no further payments are made. This type of service contract is ideal for rental and short-stay accommodations. Remote control of service saves the utility from the cost of dispatching trucks and crew to connect and disconnect a service when renters move in and out of rental homes.

In contrast, the exact same system could be used as a postpayment metering system, in which the customer will get regular electricity bills showing their consumption details on a regular basis. To reduce the cost of meter readings, many utilities practiced quarterly, biannual, or even annual meter readings while issuing customers with monthly "estimated bills." AMI saves the utility the cost of meter readings and errors in actual reads and provides the customers with accurate, on-demand billing data. Moreover, given advanced capabilities for tamper detection built into such meters, utility companies have a higher level of confidence that electricity theft and tampers could be detected and dealt with in real time.

While AMI is all about putting new measurement hardware and communication systems at the termination points of the system, the next set of smart grid capabilities emerge as the result of tight integration between back-office tools with field components and edge devices. Figure 1.7 shows that capabilities such as substation automation, distributed generation, and intelligent homes could emerge only when technologies such as network management, intelligent applications, and distributed control are integrated with the utility's downstream field components and edge devices.

Consequently, one may argue that given the size and the value of utility assets, the emergence of the smart grid will more likely follow an evolutionary trajectory rather than a drastic overhaul. The smart grid will therefore materialize through strategic implants of distributed control and monitoring systems within and alongside the existing electricity grid. The functional and technological growth of these embryos over time helps them to emerge as large pockets of distributed intelligent systems across diverse geographies. This organic growth shall allow the utilities to shift more of the old grid's load and functions on to the new grid and as such improve and enhance their critical services.

These smart grid embryos shall facilitate distributed generation and cogeneration of energy. They will also provide for the integration of alternative sources of energy and management of the system's emissions and carbon footprint. And last but not least, they will enable utilities to make more efficient use of their existing assets through demand response, peak shaving, and service quality control.

However, the problem that most utility providers across the globe face is how to get to where they need to be as soon as possible, at the minimum cost, and without jeopardizing the critical services they are currently providing. Moreover, what strategies, and what road map, should such utilities pursue to ensure that they achieve the highest possible return on the required investments for such major undertakings. And as is the case with the adoption of any new technology, the utilities in the developing world have a clear advantage over their counterparts in the developed world. The former have fewer legacy issues to grapple with and as such may be able to leap forward without the need for backward compatibility with their existing systems.

1.3 Definition of Microgrids

The notion of gradual transition to the smart grid through strategic implantation of intelligence within and across parts of the legacy grid is introduced in the previous section. Such embryonic entities include the most basic components of the electricity grid, i.e., power plants and loads, in close proximity. The power supplied by local power plants may or may not be sufficient to meet the demand. As such, these embryos may need to cover the shortfall from the larger grid, if one is available. Due to the close proximity between load centers and power sources, no transmission assets would be required. Such an entity, regarded as a scaled-down version of the electricity grid, is called a microgrid. Microgrids may also incorporate various degrees of local command and control. The degree of sophistication of the overarching command, control, and protection in such systems may identify them as smart microgrids.

The academic and scientific literature contains many definitions of microgrids. Although there are subtle differences between these definitions, they share a fundamental premise: a microgrid is an interconnected system of loads and local generation that can operate independently of the power grid (islanded) or is attached to it (grid-tied). Currently, study groups have been convened by Institute of Electrical and Electronics Engineers, International Electrotechnical Commission, and International Council on Large Electric Systems to refine and standardize such definitions from a wide variety of per-spectives and different stakeholder requirements.

It goes without saying that different stakeholder communities attach different attributes to such definitions. Those concerned about climate change insist that microgrids incorporate renewable sources of generation. In contrast, those concerned about energy surety and reliability insist on microgrids to have access to firm power. In that regard, given the unpredictable nature of renewable sources of energy, the latter category insists on storage to be a component of microgrids to assist with removing some of the uncertainties associated with renewable sources of generation.

There are also those who are concerned with cyber security who emphasize the inclusion of various layers of defense in the microgrid against intrusion, cyberattacks, and malware. And last but not least, those concerned about "total cost of ownership" insist on efficiency and optimization to be the hallmarks of microgrids.

The fact of the matter is that all or some of these attributes are what differentiate different types of microgrids from each other. We will discuss this in detail in Section 1.5. For now, it should be empha-sized that an interconnected system of loads and generators does not necessarily need to be intelligent. In other words, a truly scaled-down version of the legacy grid in which no intelligence is incorporated into the system to make it generation following rather than load following could still be regarded as a microgrid, albeit unintelligent. In contrast, a smart microgrid is a collection of local loads serviced solely, or jointly, by local generation and the larger grid and equipped with a layer of intelligence to achieve desired load management, optimum efficiency, minimum cost, and maximum reliability.

What sets smart microgrids apart from the legacy microgrids is the presence of various pockets of intelligence, incorporated into power generation, load control, load classification, energy management, access authorization, etc. It goes without saying that the level and sophistication of such intelligence defines the presence and/or absence of some of the differentiating attributes discussed earlier in this section. It should be noted that from this point onward, we will use the terms *microgrid* and *smart microgrid* interchangeably. In other words, our focus in the rest of this book will be on microgrids that have sufficient built-in intelligence, qualifying them as smart microgrids.

1.4 Architecture of Microgrids

As discussed earlier, a smart grid is defined as a grid that accommodates a wide variety of generation options, e.g., central, distributed, intermittent, and firm. It empowers the consumer to interact with the energy management systems to manage their energy use and reduce their energy costs. A smart grid is also required to be a self-healing system. It should predict looming failures in the immediate horizon and take corrective actions to avoid or mitigate system problems. A smart grid also uses IT to continually optimize its capital assets while minimizing operations and maintenance costs.

However, given the gap between where we are today and where we need to be down the road, one can immediately appreciate that the larger problem is the rollout of a highly distributed and intelligent management system, with enough flexibility and scalability capable of not only managing the system's growth, but also accommodating ever changing technologies in communication, IT, and power systems.

On the other hand, given the fact that nearly 90% of all power outages and disturbances have their roots in the distribution network, the move toward the smart grid has to start at the bottom of the chain, i.e., in the distribution system (including metrology and distribution substations). One should note that although AMI is regarded as the first step toward that eventuality, upgrading the metering system without comparable upgrades to distribution substations, edge devices, and distribution networks will not be conducive to systemic development of the smart grid.

Moreover, the argument was made that with rapid increase in the cost of fossil fuels, coupled with the inability of utility companies to expand their generation capacity in line with the rising demand for electricity, the focus on grid modernization has moved toward introducing technologies that can help with demand side management and revenue protection. That clearly means that the next logical step of grid modernization has to leverage the existing infrastructure and implement its distributed command and control strategies over its backbone to enable concurrent materialization of two concepts: energy conservation and distributed generation. Utilities hope that through energy conservation, while facilitating cogeneration, the stress level on their assets could be reduced, enabling them to defer the investments necessary to build more generation and transmission capacity.

It goes without saying that deregulation of the electric utility industry, environmental concerns associated with central power plants, the volatility of energy cost, and rapid technological developments of distributed energy resource (DER) units have resulted in a significant proliferation of DER units in the utility power systems. Recent trends indicate continued penetration of DER units in power systems, at both medium- and low-voltage levels. The latter has been the main reason for justifying investments on microgrids. It is in that light that a microgrid is defined as a cluster of loads and DER units capable of operating either independently or as a slave to the larger grid.

Figure 1.8 shows the basic building blocks of a smart microgrid. At a minimum, these should include various sources of local generation (including renewable sources of energy), various types of loads (exhibiting different load profiles), and networked intelligence. The latter includes the components required to implement the necessary command and control functions in the microgrid. This highly simplified block diagram emphasizes the fact that the basic components of a smart microgrid are integrated through two independent, yet

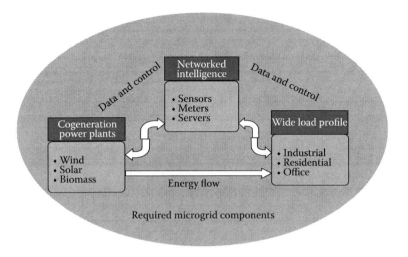

Figure 1.8 Smart microgrid basic building blocks. (From Farhangi, H., *IEEE Power & Energy Magazine*, 8, 18–28, 2010. © 2010 IEEE. With permission.)

interrelated, highways. One is the traditional one-way energy flow interconnection, which transports power from local power plants to microgrid loads. Another is a two-way data and control highway that collects sensory, alarm, and status information from across the microgrid to be made available to an energy management system, the output of which is channeled to the microgrid components in the form of commands and configuration settings and/or parameters.

It should be noted here that depending on the size of the microgrid, command and control functions could be centralized or distributed. In other words, the complexity of the microgrid and the required throughput and frequency of the data and commands that have to be exchanged between different components in the microgrid may make the choice of a distributed control strategy more compelling than a centralized one.

1.5 Types of Microgrids

Given the role that microgrids play in enabling utilities to gradually introduce smart grid technologies into their distribution system, one could recognize the need for controlled interconnection of microgrids into a much larger system, commonly called supergrid. In this regard, each microgrid is assumed capable of managing its own loads based on the DER sources available to it while meeting interconnection requirements (synchronization, protection, power quality, etc.) with the larger grid. Here one needs to emphasize the term *interconnection* rather than *integration* as each microgrid is empowered to determine its own degree of centralized control and management in response to external stimuli by following its own set of operational objectives and requirements. Figure 1.9 demonstrates interconnected microgrids, each with its own set of loads, DER units, and command and control components. Each microgrid is optimized to deliver a set of unique deliverables and functionalities for the objectives for which it is designed.

A quick review of the literature reveals that there is not yet a universally converging consensus among experts on the definition of microgrids. Some attempt to classify microgrids based on their size; some take its interconnection, or lack thereof, with the larger grid as a point of differentiation; and yet others take the application for which the microgrid is designed to serve as its definition.

Nevertheless, and from a size-agnostic point of view, one could see three different types of microgrids emerging in the industry today. These are, in no particular order, the following:

1. Urban microgrids: These are smart microgrids with various loads and DER resources, which are primarily identified as grid-tied microgrids, capable of operating in an islanded mode, if and when required. The need to operate in grid-tied mode imposes certain restrictions and requirements on such microgrids. They need to meet all codes, standards, and interconnection requirements put in place to protect the larger grid and preserve its power quality integrity. Various applications for urban microgrids include microgrids for campuses, gated communities, and mall/shopping centers.

2. Remote microgrids: These are smart microgrids that operate exclusively off-grid. Similar to urban microgrids, they have their own set of DER sources and various types of loads. However, due to the fact that they operate independently of the larger grid, they do not need to comply with the requirements and restrictions faced by urban microgrids. In contrast to urban microgrids, which have grown in numbers in the

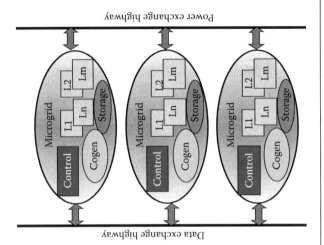

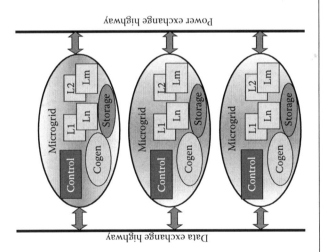

Figure 1.9 Interconnected smart microgrids. (From Farhangi, H., *IEEE Power & Energy Magazine*, 8, 18–28, 2010. © 2010 IEEE. With permission.)

last few years due to intensive public and private investments, remote smart microgrids are not yet common. Lack of investments into remote microgrids may be due to multitudes of economic, technological, and political reasons. Nevertheless, there are numerous remote communities, remote settlements, and island communities in many parts of the world that are prime candidates and could take advantage of smart microgrid technologies and systems. An example of such legacy microgrids are First Nations communities in Canada, where power generation is mostly done through diesel generators.

3. Agile microgrids: Also known as temporary microgrids, these are microgrids designed to be set up, configured, and dismantled based on changing operational requirements. Examples of such microgrids are distribution systems for forward operating bases of the military, seasonal events, disaster recovery operations, and field hospitals. What differentiates this type of microgrids from the other two is the agility, configurability, and flexibility of its operation.

Detailed discussions about the characteristics and specifications of different types of microgrid are outside the scope of this book. As such, in the subsequent chapters of this book, our focus will be on urban smart microgrids, as the microgrid built on the campus of British Columbia Institute of Technology in Vancouver is an urban microgrid. Consequently, from now on whenever we talk about smart microgrids, we mean an urban smart microgrid with the main characteristics noted earlier (i.e., grid-tied and capable to operate in islanded mode).

1.6 Interaction between Smart Microgrids

Preceding discussions have shown that the only type of microgrid that could be regarded as the constituent component of smart grid is an urban microgrid. That is simply due to the fact that not only are urban microgrids designed to operate in an islanded mode, but also they are required to be capable of interconnecting with their neighboring microgrids as well as the larger grid as the building block of a much larger system (supergrid). It goes without saying that neighboring microgrids, of any type, could potentially interact with each other.

However, the interaction of multiple microgrids introduces operational challenges related to fast transients produced as a result of switching of generation and/or load assets, as well as slow transients as a direct result of scheduling of generation assets. Consequently, to ensure the safety and security of interconnection, one of these microgrids have to impose its interconnection parameters (e.g., frequency, voltage level) on the others. And in the absence of the larger grid, whose operational parameters will drive interconnections, one cannot guarantee safe and secure operation of such interconnected microgrids.

In other words, the presence of the grid is the most critical prerequisite for the integration of smart microgrids into an eventual supergrid. It should also be noted that poorly designed and constructed microgrids could have serious adverse impacts on the stability of the larger grid with which they are connected. In particular, each microgrid has to put provisions and assets (e.g., storage) in place to firm up the intermittent power generated by its DER units (e.g., solar and photovoltaic) units. Furthermore, the microgrid has to shield the larger grid from issues related to diverse response times of the particular generation units it uses to control commands and fault scenarios. Moreover, given a microgrid's relatively low inertia, the microgrid is responsible for dealing with its susceptibility to large excursions from the initial operating conditions.

As Figure 1.10 stipulates, what that essentially means is that the major role that the supergrid of the future will play would be to impose global service quality parameters on all interconnected microgrids in its network. Those global parameters shall ensure successful interconnection and energy transactions between different microgrids in that network. Not only shall such parameters regulate the electrical boundaries of the microgrids, but also they will impose operational and performance parameters to facilitate transactions. In other words, the regulation and the quality of service issues will determine the success of such interconnected smart microgrids.

The question now becomes about what impact could or should such parameters have in the design, architecture, and implementation of smart microgrids. In other words, could smart microgrids be further classified based on their level of "interconnectability?" The answer to that rhetorical question is affirmative. In fact, urban microgrids are

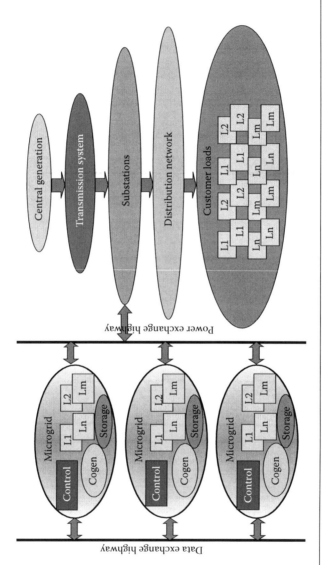

Figure 1.10 Transition from a legacy grid to a smart grid. (From Farhangi, H., *IEEE Power & Energy Magazine*, 8, 18–28, 2010. © 2010 IEEE. With permission.)

designed to be interconnectable. Without interconnectivity with the larger grid, the smart microgrid concept reduces to integration and limited control of DER units with loads they serve. Such microgrids could therefore not be regarded as the building blocks of the smart grid.

To be qualified as a component of a smart grid, microgrids have to incorporate technologies that enable them to monitor, diagnose, protect, and comply with the operational parameters and quality requirements of a much larger system through coordinated command and control and power management. Provided that the microgrid meets the aforementioned requirements, it could be defined as a cluster of DERs that are locally controlled and behave, from the perspective of the main electricity grid, as a generator and/or as a load.

The other important consideration for the implementation of smart microgrids is the economic justification of the investments required to build them and operate them. That issue is not often a straightforward calculation. Depending on the objectives for which the microgrid will need to be designed, many parameters have to come together to justify such investments. For example, in one instance the main objective would be to lower the cost of electricity, in which case one has to ensure that local power generation could be achieved cost effectively and within environmental constraints. Or the issue may be the reliability of the supply from the main grid, in which case one has to complement the energy from the main grid with firm and reliable energy produced locally. All in all, access to cost-effective, environment-friendly, and reliable sources of energy locally will be the cornerstone of microgrid design.

One should emphasize that in jurisdictions such as British Columbia, where more than 90% of the energy produced is from renewable sources (primarily hydro) and where the cost of energy is kept low as a result of regulatory pressure, it would be difficult to justify investments on urban microgrids. Factors that may have a deterministic impact on the feasibility of setting up microgrids in such jurisdictions may include, among other things, contribution to the energy supply and energy security, the supply power quality, and environmental impacts. Furthermore, in certain instances, the need for ancillary services may take the center stage. These include provisions for reactive power generation, voltage regulation, reserve, and black start capability.

Having said that, the availability of low-cost liquid natural gas (LNG) or shale gas across North America may trigger feasibility studies to construct microgrids in fast-growing suburbs where the main grid may not be able to support population and economic growth without major upgrades to its generation and transmission capacity. Given that building new megapower plants and punching transmission corridors into built-up urban areas may not be feasible, urban smart microgrids, powered with local LNG/shale gas power plants, may be an optimum solution to support suburban growth.

In contrast to LNG and shale gas, the cost associated with power generation out of renewable sources, such as wind, solar, and biomass, has not gone down sufficiently enough to enable such sources to compete cost effectively with fossil fuel-based generation, unless greenhouse gas emission consideration could impose otherwise.

It goes without saying that even if microgrids could be economically justified, the inclusion of technologies required to facilitate and regulate the interconnection of microgrids and the management of the energy flow between them will become further points of contention. Such technologies would add to the construction and operational cost of microgrids, and unless a clear strategy, a road map, and justification for their interconnection are available, the additional cost of incorporating those technologies into the microgrid will become a major question mark.

It goes without saying that experiences accumulated as a result of research and development into microgrids can add tremendous value to the utility industry's playbook and determine, inform, and qualify the next needed steps, developments, and investments by stakeholders in removing obstacles against the integration of microgrids, and therefore the emergence of the supergrid, in the not too distant future.

Reference

1. Hassan Farhangi, The path of smart grid, *IEEE Power & Energy Magazine*, Vol. 8, No. 1, pp. 18–28, Jan. 2010.

2

SMART GRID SYSTEM INTEGRATION

HASSAN FARHANGI

Contents

The security of the electrical power supply, energy efficiency, the environment, and the economy have encouraged political leaders, scientists, and the public to recognize the need for major overhaul of the power industry in such diverse areas as technology, business model, standards, regulatory issues, consumer psychology, and education.

It is therefore not surprising to see that smart grid–related blogs, newsletters, and conferences have endured numerous debates and discussions around the issue of grid overhaul through "integration" of smart grid capabilities and functions into the existing grid. However, it seems that debates on the approach, methodology, and sequence of what needs to be done are not informed by a holistic view of system integration and a methodology for developing integration maps based on a utility's smart grid strategic road map. This means that in the haste of "getting it over and done with," numerous projects get started without a clear strategy and road map for smart grid system integration.

Faced with diverse technological, organizational, and business issues adversely affecting their bottom line, utility companies are contemplating immediate changes (and/or upgrades) to their technologies, business processes, and organizations. However, at the same time, the realities of insufficient resources, regulatory impediments, and technological issues have prevented the development of concrete plans and concerted actions in this regard.

A closer look at mainstream discussions within the utility industry reveals that despite the consensus on the need to change, there is no agreement across the board in any given utility on the smart grid road map and integration map. The absence of industry-wide standards and blueprints for smart grid integration has further compounded the issue. That means that smart grid development plans in most utilities are bound to be driven by the silo mentality of the constituent parts of the utility organization, according to which the generation folks tend to push for expanding generation capacity through integration of renewables, while the transmission folks opt for expanding transmission capacity through automation, and last but not least the distribution folks plan for integration of new assets, technologies, and intelligence on the downstream side of the network.

Furthermore, and given the fact that each group has traditionally been exposed to certain vendors and technology providers for their respective silos, groups tend to regard the technologies and solutions offered by those vendors as the answer to much larger system-wide problems, problems that by default transcend the confines of a single silo in a utility environment. This means that the adopted solutions in each silo tend to be meaningful within that silo and may not integrate with solutions adopted by other silos for a cohesive system-level solution to a utility's system-level problems.

The situation is further complicated by the diversity of views, interests, and approaches advocated by vendors and technology providers in the field. Influenced (and often constrained) by their core competencies and technologies, each vendor defines the problems, and therefore the solutions, influenced and informed by their technologies and products. One should not be surprised to hear different suppliers put different spins on basic concepts such as distribution automation and demand response. The irony is that they are mostly sincere in what they are advocating. The issue is whether their prescription is the holy grail of what is needed to solve the utilities' smart grid integration puzzle. This seems to be a reenactment of Rumi's story "Blind Men and the Elephant." Everyone has their own understanding of what this creature is based on what part of it they have managed to touch. The absence of sight (and/or light) has convinced each and every one of the righteousness of their belief, undermining the fact that smart grid's system-wide issues require all its constituent parts to work together and materialize a collective strategy of what needs to be done. In Rumi's words, "If each of us held a candle there, and if we went in together, we could see it."

Nevertheless and despite the diversity of views that industry pundits may have, resulting in no clear path forward, the electricity grid may find it difficult to sustain the status quo. It has no better option than to change and adopt different modalities and functions consistent with the realities of the sector. That is why at the national level in North America, the U.S. administration, as well as Canada's federal government, has introduced major funding programs to support development work required to facilitate the rollout of a smart grid, a constituent component of both nations' critical infrastructure, which needs to be more reliable, efficient, and capable of exploiting and integrating different sources of energy.

However, the gap between where the industry is today, and where it needs to be tomorrow, is quite wide. The electricity grid in North America, and across the world, has not witnessed a systemic adoption, and planned integration, of new technologies, business processes, tools, and standards in its major operations. In particular, the power distribution arm of the utility industry in North America has seen very little, if any, improvement in socioeconomic approaches to energy distribution, consumption, and conservation. The electricity system continues to operate as a one-way system, in which primary fuels are converted into electricity and pushed down the transmission pipes and into distribution plumbing without having real-time information on consumer loads and demand, consumption patterns, and distribution power quality.

The electricity grid of the future, or the smart grid, is expected to turn the electricity grid into an integrated power and information highway, where stakeholders (consumers and producers alike) are empowered to engage in a variety of service transactions. Conservation, reduction of the industry's carbon footprint, diversity of supply, integration of renewable sources of energy, distributed resources, and cogeneration will be the hallmark of the smart grid.

Moreover, given the scale of what needs to be done, the overhaul of the North American electricity grid can materialize only through public and private partnership. A quick review of the goals of this partnership charts an exciting path forward, a path marked by the need for interdisciplinary and multidisciplinary work into not only technology but also consumers' behaviors, business processes, enterprise organizational issues, utility revenue models, interoperability standards, system topologies, system integration, etc. The nature, scope, and dimensions of such work require a North American effort and an integrated approach to ensure mobilization of diverse technological and scientific talent across North America to address the most pertinent issues that will determine the quality of life for this generation and the next across the globe.

2.1 Utopian Vision

As is customary in the real estate industry, the precursor to the start of every development project is an artist's impression of the final product. The smart grid, as envisaged by many, is not immune to such perceptions. That is what one can see in Figure 2.1. The figure is essentially a utopian vision of what the smart grid is desired to be, a collection of diverse sources of energy, integrated with low-emission power plants, hydropower stations, and energy storage facilities, interacting and communicating through superbandwidth communication technologies. This wishful picture assumes that all assets, domains, actors, and technologies coexist in full harmony and under transparent protocols, harmonized standards, and compatible topologies. Unfortunately, that is far removed from the reality of the situation we are dealing with today in North America and across the globe.

As discussed, the point of departure between the path to the smart grid and the particular set of smart grid capabilities that each utility may want to achieve would not be the same across all jurisdictions. Having said that, and regardless of a utility's current baselines, operational priorities, and organizational abilities for devising smart grid system integration maps, the ideal way to approach smart grid system integration is to analyze each smart grid capability in terms of its core decision making and "data-customer/command-supplier" interface requirements. That analysis will identify to which domain such functions would belong, which layer they will have to reside in or be attached to, and what their data processing, command and control, interface protocol, and communication requirements would be.

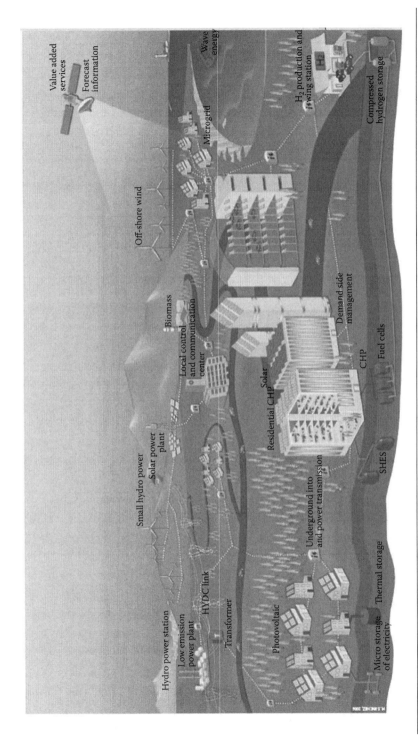

Figure 2.1   Utopian vision of the smart grid. (Courtesy of GreenEvolution Project, Moscow, Russia, www.greenevolution.ru.)

The reality is, of course, that the smart grid cannot and will not be a greenfield exercise. The smart grid will materialize through incremental improvements of an already existing fully operational machine. In other words, the smart grid will emerge from coordinated and well-planned introduction of new technologies, capabilities, and components into the existing grid, without jeopardizing its integrity and availability. And to do that, we need to chart a clear and pragmatic path from the realities of today's grid to the desired grid of tomorrow.

2.2 Conceptual Model

To demonstrate the complexity of such interactions within the framework of the smart grid, the National Institute of Standards and Technology (NIST) produced a much more realistic view of the smart grid [1]. Shown in Figure 2.2, the smart grid of the future is represented as a collection of domains (where specific transactions take place) and actors (who initiate and perform those transactions) and networks (which comprise pathways required to connect actors and assets).

The NIST's conceptual model attempts to provide a more refined view of smart grid, a view that lies somewhere between the two extremes of utopian impressions of the smart grid and a utility integration map. Its significance is in the fact that it does not distance itself from the reality of the utility situation on the ground. The model takes the hierarchical architecture of a utility's existing system, comprising bulk generation, transmission, and distribution, and adds on top of those domains new domains, networks, and actors which individually and collectively embody the new capabilities, features, and functions, dubbed as intelligent grid or smart grid.

Moreover, the NIST's conceptual model does not prescribe or advocate any particular system topology and integration map. All it does is define a placeholder for new actors, and their associated domains and networks, who could potentially initiate and/or participate in new transactions and involvements with the utility system. New actors could reside in the markets domain, buying and selling bulk energy, or they could play the role of a regional transmission operator, selling transmission capacity, or they could act as a service provider, helping end customers achieve energy conservation. If empowered, actors in

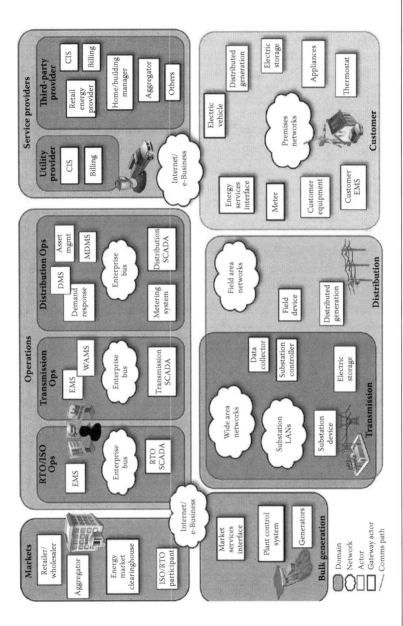

Figure 2.2 Smart grid conceptual model. CIS: customer information system; ISO: independent system operator; RTO: regional transmission organization; SCADA: supervisory control and data acquisition; WAMS: wide area monitoring system. (From NIST Smart Grid Interoperability Framework.)

the four new domains, namely, markets, operations, service providers, and customers, could each provide the legacy grid (comprising generation, transmission, and distribution) with unprecedented capabilities and functions. Applicable regulatory regimes in each jurisdiction will facilitate or impede the roles that such actors may be able to play. For instance, regulations may not allow the utility, or a third-party service provider, to engage customer-owned appliances for the purpose of load reduction or curtailment. Similarly, privacy issues in most jurisdictions may not be conducive for data mining features applied to customer's consumption data.

Nevertheless, the NIST's conceptual model provides a realistic view of the constraints associated with the current legacy system, as well as a pragmatic array of new features and function that, if allowed, could add tremendous value to the existing grid. At the same time, the model has traces of prescribed strategies for the evolution of the exiting grid. For example, in addition to projecting the fact that bulk generation will be with us for the foreseeable future, it incorporates distributed generation functions within both the medium-voltage (MV) and low-voltage (LV) domains. And given the fact that most probably the predominant source for distributed generation shall be renewable sources, which are intermittent in nature, the model incorporates electric storage in both the MV and LV domains.

The next level of refinement in such a model requires accurate specification of use cases. Although no standard definition of use cases is yet available, use cases generally capture the narrative of transactions that could be implemented within such an environment. For example, a third-party billing services provider may need to initiate a use case to gather consumption data from a utility's smart metering system, gain access to contractual agreements between the energy service provider and the customer, and also obtain the applicable rates and tariffs for each time slot within the billing period. Given the fact that such a use case involves multiple actors, multiple domains, and multiple networks, the use case has to describe clearly which actor initiates the transaction, who the recipient(s) of the transaction are, and what type of data and/or command will be exchanged between the actors and when and for what purpose. The narrative account of each transaction enables the system designers to identify the exact specification of what communication technologies, what command and control algorithms, and what type of processing would be required to execute the intended use case. The collection of such use cases enables the utility to finalize its functional mapping of smart grid features and functions into its existing legacy grid infrastructure.

As mentioned, each use case attempts to describe what actors, assets, and tasks are required to realize specific functions. Figure 2.3 is yet another attempt to map select smart grid functions onto the existing legacy grid and identify what assets are required for each function. It shows, for example, that demand response and dynamic pricing are functions that require the involvement of a utility's upstream assets (including generation, transmission, control infrastructure, communication technologies) down to downstream assets (including receiving stations, distribution substations, smart meters) all the way to customer loads. It goes without saying that in each and every one of such functions, different use cases could be defined to capture various operational aspects, as subsets of those functions. Furthermore, the significance of this representation is that it provides a high-level view of data/communication requirements for each function. This means that, for example, the data type, throughput, and response time required for transactions associated with the asset management function will be quite different from the requirements defined by the transactions associated with "self-healing."

2.3 Functional Mapping

Figure 2.4 is an attempt to take the smart grid functions in Figure 2.3 and map these across different layers of a fully integrated smart grid system [2]. In such an approach, smart grid functions are seen as cutting across multiple layers of utility structures, including but not limited to corporate, engineering, field operations, and distribution systems. This approach turns a utility's traditional silo structures on its head, as this approach traverses organizational boundaries for efficient and cost-effective realization of target smart grid functions. What is critical in this approach is not how a particular function needs to be realized, but where it belongs as an entity providing other entities in its vicinity with services for which it is designed. Association with a given layer would then determine the performance metrics of the assets that are needed to support the efficient operation of that capability.

Moreover, the layered approach attempts to identify the nature of each layer in terms of the dominance of data processing and

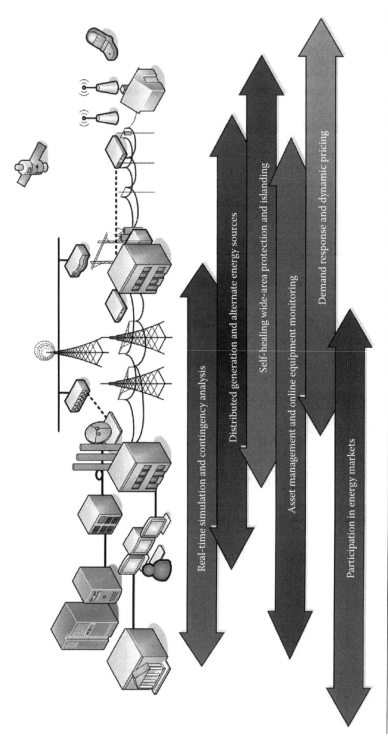

Figure 2.3 Smart grid capabilities mapped to the legacy grid. (Courtesy Erfan Ibrahim, EPRI smart grid R&D overview, Electric Power Research Institute [EPRI], Palo Alto, California.)

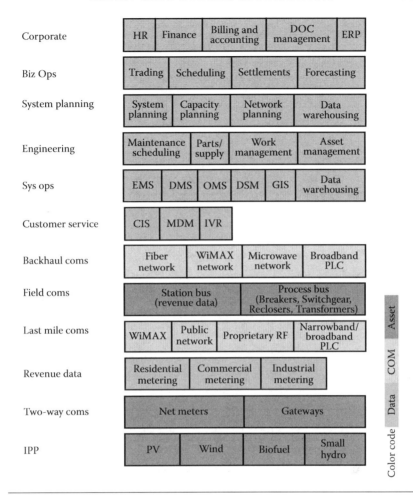

Figure 2.4 Layered integration of smart grid functions. DMS: distribution management system; DOC: documents; DSM: demand side management; ERP: enterprise resource planning; IVR: interactive voice response. (From Farhangi, H., *IEEE Power & Energy*, 12, 52–66, 2014. © 2014 IEEE. With permission.)

communication technologies versus the utility's traditional assets. This does not necessarily mean that a layer that is dominated by data processing does not depend on communication technologies or other existing utility assets. By its nature, each smart grid capability may have to rely on all three constituent components of the smart grid, i.e., power systems, telecommunication, and IT.

Furthermore, the layered approach embeds within it the notion of the temporal and spatial requirements of each layer. More stringent requirement for access to real-time data would place a layer closer to layers that produce such data and vice versa. In other words, the proximity of the layers to each other is directly proportional to their interface and data/command exchange requirements. As an example, the energy management system (EMS) and VVO/CVR (VVO: voltage/volt-ampere reactive optimization [VAR]; CVR: conservation voltage reduction) layers have to be in close proximity to each other and to the field assets, with which they would have a direct, real-time, and unimpeded data exchange relationship. The same is not true for the billing layer, which could be placed further away from the field assets and has no need for real-time connections to these.

It goes without saying that not all functions within each layer need to be integrated at the same time. Each utility could choose one or more functions from each layer and decide when and how they need to be realized. However, regardless of the integration plan for each function, what is critical is to understand which layer it would belong to and as such what its data processing, command and control, interface protocol, and communication requirements would be. This would ensure that the architecture of the system, the communication topology, the adopted technologies, and the associated protocols are chosen in such a way that they would lend themselves to future integration of new functionalities and capabilities. That would be the only way to ensure that the gradual transition to the smart grid could be managed without excessive reengineering and expensive overhauls.

As discussed, each utility's enterprise function places a particular set of requirements on different layers of the system in terms of its vital specs, such as data structures, protocols, security regime, latency, throughput, and, last but not least, interactions with the actual assets. In reality, of course, applications could and should reside where their function is required; i.e., some may exist within a substation, and some in the utility back office or on the enterprise bus. Nevertheless, and regardless of which environment they are attached to, each application has to have the ability to communicate seamlessly and efficiently with relevant system nodes as and when required. For instance, an asset management application has to communicate with all relevant assets assigned to it from different domains of generation, transmission, and distribution.

As an example, a utility that intends to first roll out its smart meters, with the intention of subsequently integrating an asset management application over its vital system assets, has to ensure that the advanced metering infrastructure (AMI) system it is integrating will lend itself well (as a set of distinct assets) to seamless integration with the asset management application that it will be rolling out in the future. It goes without saying that it would not be acceptable to have patchworks of individual asset management tools for different categories of assets. In other words, no utility would be happy using an asset management tool for its smart meters, another for its relays, switches, reclosers, and protection components and yet another for its transmission equipment. As such, one would expect that a major requirement for the selection of any AMI solution would be its ability to interface with existing or future smart grid functionalities, enabling on-demand or event-based reporting of health, configuration, settings, and maintenance schedule of all AMI assets, including meters, headends, and communication equipment. Similarly, a utility that is planning to implement dynamic pricing and time-of-use tariffs in the future has to ensure that its AMI system is capable of handling and/or relaying such real-time information with the system's relevant points of termination.

The approach advocated in Figure 2.4 is unfortunately not the norm. One may suspect that the majority of utilities will attempt to integrate smart grid functions with their operations, starting at two extreme ends of the system hierarchy, i.e., at the bottom of the chain through rollout of AMI systems and at the top of the chain through adopting and integrating new enterprise bus functions. That approach is understandable and very much in line with the current constraints of the utility's assets and organizational structures. In fact, the early attempts to modernize the system had to take into account the realities of a highly compartmentalized system and operational hierarchy, tasked with delivering a critical service to their customers while meeting the challenges most utilities are grappling with.

Figure 2.5 depicts the approach utilities in general have taken in their integration of smart grid functions. The point of entry of new functions into the hierarchical structure of the utility system has been at the interface with customers (e.g., smart meters), plus their associated support functions within the enterprise bus (e.g., metering data management system [MDMS]). Patches of plumbing to connect the two ends of the function (e.g., the required communication system to support the capture and exchange of data for the purpose of billing and revenue management) is thus inserted within the appropriate information and communications technology layer of the system.

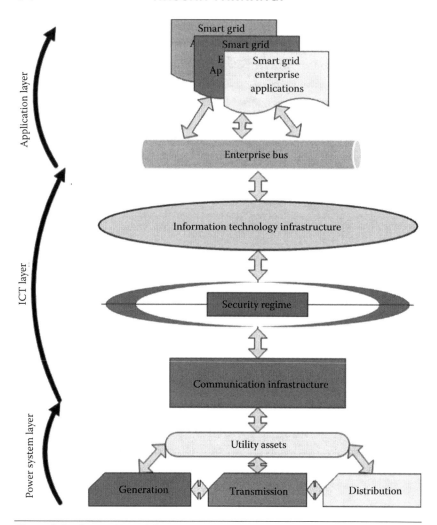

Figure 2.5 Smart grid capabilities over the utility's existing infrastructure. (From Farhangi, H., *IEEE Power & Energy*, 12, 52–66, 2014. © 2014 IEEE. With permission.)

The question that utilities have not answered here is what other smart grid capability should the chosen AMI technology support? The current integration of AMI systems across many jurisdictions in the world assumes a disjoint utility network (assuming such networks exist at the lower layers of the distributions system, which is not often the case), parts of which could conveniently be bypassed. As shown in Figure 2.6, what typically happens in such installations is that smart meters are grouped into a local area network type of association (as meshed or otherwise) and exchange their data/command

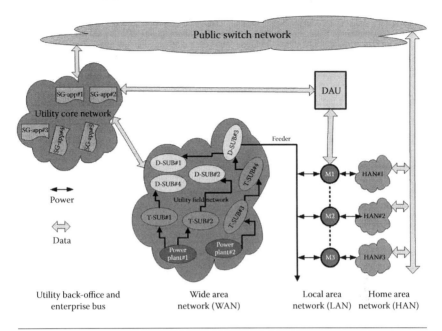

Figure 2.6 Early implementations of AMI technology. (From Farhangi, H., *IEEE Power & Energy*, 12, 52–66, 2014. © 2014 IEEE. With permission.)

(through radio-frequency or power-line communication [PLC] links) with a data aggregator unit (DAU), which is installed on a pole top in their vicinity. The DAU would then employ a dedicated communication link (often proprietary wireless protocols) to exchange such aggregated data/commands with an MDMS within the utility enterprise bus. This means that the specification of the constituent components of the system is therefore optimized to ensure data exchange between smart meters and their associated MDMS residing within the utility's core network. Not only is the AMI system as such oblivious to anything that happens in between, but also it has no provisions to handle or carry any other information or data, however critical or important such data may be for other smart grid functions to be rolled out in the future. This simply means that important sensory data and information produced at the downstream side of the network, which may be critically required by middle layers of the system, bypass such layers and end up in the upper layers of the system for a specific function and/ or purpose (e.g., billing) and as such do not contribute and/or enable future smart grid functions that may benefit from access to such data.

The problem is that even if the utility desires and/or plans to have all its smart grid layers across its networks, fully conversing and exchanging data and commands, it has to deal with the larger impediment of having no standards and protocols to support seamless communication and data exchange across system layers. A closer look at Figure 2.7 demonstrates the multitude of standards and technologies that compete to dominate each layer of a typical utility smart grid system. The reality of the situation is that today, components across different domains, even those within the same domain, use incompatible technologies and standards for integration and communication. That makes it almost impossible to integrate different layers of the system without major overhauls or redesigns of the network.

Having given up on the industry to put its own house in order, user groups across many domains have sprung up with the mandate of harmonizing these disparate standards. The spaghetti diagram in Figure 2.8 demonstrates the complexity and tediousness of this exercise.

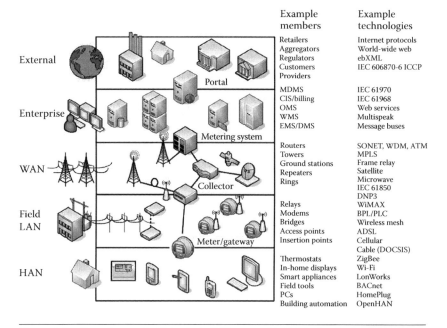

Figure 2.7 Competing smart grid standards. ADSL: asymmetric digital subscriber loop; BACnet: communications protocol for building automation and control; BPL: broadband powerline; DNP3: distributed network protocol; DOCSIS: data over cable service interface specification; ebXML: eXtensible markup language; MPLS: multiprotocol label switching; OMS: outage management system; SONET: synchronous optical networking; WDM: wavelength division multiplexing; WMS: widea-area monitoring system. (Courtesy of ZDNet, CBS Interactive, San Francisco, California, http://www.zdnet.com.)

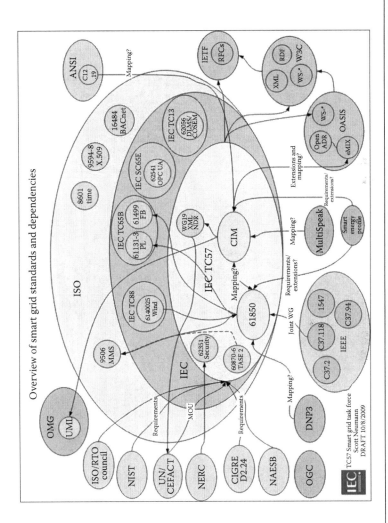

Figure 2.8 Smart grid standards harmonization map. CIM: common information model; DLMS: device language message specification; DNP3: distributed network protocol; IETF: internet engineering task force; NAESB: north american energy standards board; NERC: north american electric reliability corporation; OGC: open geospatial consortium; OMG: object management group; UML: unified modeling language; W3C: world wide web consortium. (Courtesy of IEC, Geneva, Switzerland.)

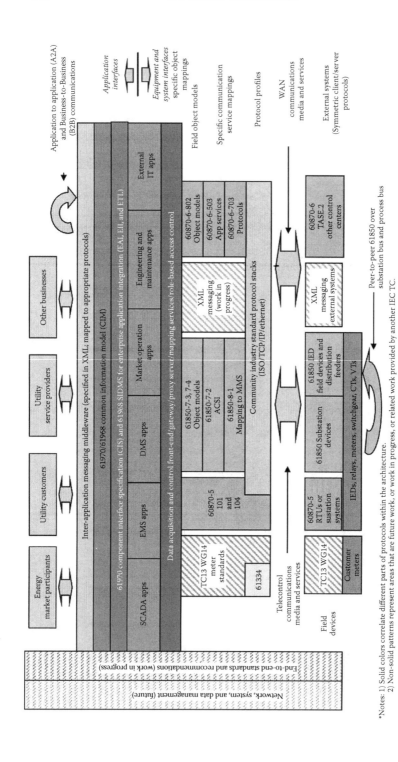

Figure 2.9 IEC TC57 architecture. EII: enterprise information integration; ETL: extract-transform-load; RTUs: remote terminal units; SIDMS: system interfaces for distribution management systems. (Courtesy of IEC, Geneva, Switzerland.)

*Notes: 1) Solid colors correlate different parts of protocols within the architecture.
2) Non-solid patterns represent areas that are future work, or work in progress, or related work provided by another IEC TC.

Among these, the International Electrotechnical Commission's (IEC) TC57 architecture, shown in Figure 2.9, may have the best chance of success as it commands larger participation by the community and a much more extensive repository of different standards that could be upgraded and/or improved to fit the bill.

Having said that, no one can predict with any certainty when and how such harmonization efforts would yield the desired results. Until then, all claims made to justify investments in AMI systems, exemplified in Figure 2.10, would be questionable. Nevertheless, given such impediments against systemic system integration, one would certainly hope that the utilities' quest for the modernization of their infrastructure would not come to a screeching end because utilities would no doubt attempt to integrate further smart grid functionalities based on their particular priorities and road map. And at this point, it seems that such integration has to be done on a case-by-case basis.

To illustrate this issue further, let us discuss the implementation issues of a typical smart grid function that many utilities regard as a priority. One such function that several utilities intend to implement in short order is VVO and CVR. The Department of Energy's (DOE) recent studies on energy conservation across the United States

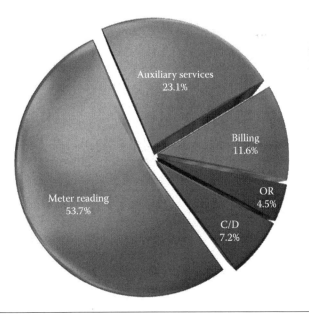

Figure 2.10   AMI investment justification pie chart. OR: outage restoration. (Courtesy of Pacific Gas and Electric Company, San Francisco, California.)

indicated that CVR functions integrated across less than half of U.S. feeders could potentially yield more than 2% demand reduction in the U.S. electrical system. In fact, it has been suggested that many utilities regard VVO/CVR as a priority to realize on critically congested feeders of their system. Claims have been made that the return on investment of VVO/CVR integration is 6 to 1 with a payback period of 2–3 years. That is a great incentive to regard investment in advanced VVO/CVR as the next item on the integration map of many utilities after AMI.

Prior to AMI, the VVO/CVR function in distribution substations (if it existed at all) used a statistical aggregated profile of the feeder load to determine the settings and configurations of cap banks, tab changers, voltage regulators, etc., to correct the feeder's power factor and also ensure compliance of voltage gradient across the entire feeder from substation to the last customer with American National Standards Institute/Institute of Electrical and Electronics Engineers (IEEE) requirements. Given the fact that no real-time information of the actual voltage samples across the feeder was available, the settings and configurations for such VVO/CVR assets were either ineffective or inefficient.

The advent of AMI changed that situation. Engineers in charge of planning for new VVO/CVR functions saw the opportunity of using real-time voltage, current, and power factor (V/I/PF) sample values from smart meters at each customer node to build a realistic and accurate real-time view of the load profile across any given feeder and as such optimize VVO/CVR settings based on accurate voltage gradient across the feeder, the climatic conditions, and time of use. Such an approach was named adaptive real-time VVO/CVR.

To implement adaptive real-time VVO/CVR, two approaches were considered. One relied on capturing the smart meters' sensory data through an interface with MDMS in the back office and then running VVO/CVR algorithms on powerful enterprise servers by using the network model of the distribution system and finally transferring the new settings to the field VVO/CVR assets through the supervisory control and data acquisition (SCADA) system. In other words, VVO/CVR functions are split into a client–server configuration, with the server operating in the back office and relying on MDMS databases to continuously calculate new settings for VVO/CVR clients in the field and transfer new configurations to such assets through the SCADA system. This approach is called centralized VVO/CVR control.

Centralized VVO/CVR control seemed quite attractive at first as the availability of accurate network models, combined with adequate processing power on the enterprise bus and access to the MDMS system could result in highly effective settings for VVO/CVR assets. However, further studies by researchers at British Columbia Institute of Technology (see Figure 2.11) indicated that VVO/CVR functions could be a lot more efficient (and less costly) if on-demand sample values of V/I/PF from bellwether smart meters could be made available much more frequently than what current AMI systems are capable of providing through their MDMS interface [3]. This required VVO/CVR algorithms to be processed locally within each substation, by using local sensory data associated with each individual feeder. This approach is called decentralized VVO/CVR control.

Although research on decentralized VVO/CVR algorithms is ongoing, early results indicate that a decentralized approach is more efficient and cost effective for such applications. The difficulty in realizing a decentralized VVO/CVR control strategy is that, although it requires the AMI system to supply it more data more frequently, as a substation-based function, it has no direct access to the AMI system. This means that such data have to be extracted from the MDMS system (on the enterprise bus) and transported down to the substation through the SCADA system. The issue there is that current AMI systems (which directly interface with an MDMS system in the back office) are not typically designed to supply such magnitude of real-time data from the field to the MDMS without the risk of network congestion. Secondly, most SCADA systems are incapable of transferring such massive amounts of time-sensitive information from the back office to the field devices without depriving other critical functions of access to their allocated bandwidth. And, thirdly, given the fact that the VVO/CVR function is feeder bound (i.e., its required inputs and outputs are all local), there is very little rationale in involving upper-layer enterprise functions for its operation.

This example is a clear indication of how critical the smart grid integration map would be to the realization of a smart grid. If a utility's integration map fails to accommodate access to time-sensitive data for upper-layer-based smart grid functions, utilities would either have to

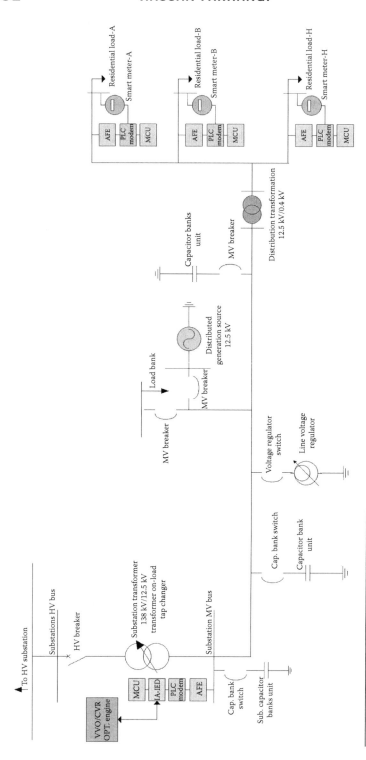

Figure 2.11 AMI-based VVO engine. AFE: analog front end; HV: high voltage; MCU: micro controller unit. (From Farhangi, H., *IEEE Power & Energy*, 12, 52–66, 2014. © 2014 IEEE. With permission.)

give up implementing future smart grid functionalities or expose their valuable assets (in this case communication systems) to hauling time-sensitive data back and forth across various layers of their information and communications technology hierarchy and therefore risk system inefficiency and "by-design" failure.

Another example of the criticality of forward-looking smart grid integration maps is the requirement to achieve tighter and more meaningful interfaces with customer-based assets. It is believed that in the not too distant future, substation-based VVO/CVR functions need to extend their reach beyond smart meters and include a level of coordination (or even command and control of) customer-side generation assets and loads.

As depicted in Figure 2.12, such assets would include rooftop photovoltaic (PV) MDMS interface [4]. In fact, recent reports about the negative impact of uncoordinated rooftop solar cells on the stability of feeders' voltage levels are quite discouraging. The unpredictable and intermittent behavior of such distributed generation assets could not entirely be mitigated with utility field assets (e.g., cap banks). And even if such costly assets could effectively be used to help stabilize voltage levels, their useful life span (and health) could be considerably compromised through these frequent anomalies (e.g., voltage levels pushing outside the American National Standards Institute band due to a customer's rooftop PV system's intermittent generation).

The severity of voltage stability issues with electric cars in their vehicle-to-grid (V2G) mode may be far less in comparison with those of rooftop PV systems, but it is still an issue for which utilities need to allocate adequate provisions. Although electric car manufacturers may not enable V2G functionality for their cars in the foreseeable future due to their concern on the cost of battery warranties, utilities need to plan and be ready for such issues should V2G become a reality.

What is interesting is that both the aforementioned threats could be converted into opportunities for a utility if appropriate provisions are made into the utility's smart grid integration map to take advantage of the availability of such downstream assets and integrate them with substation-based future EMSs. Depicted in Figure 2.12, the EMS system incorporates various command, control, and processing functions by using global system attributes and local feeder data to

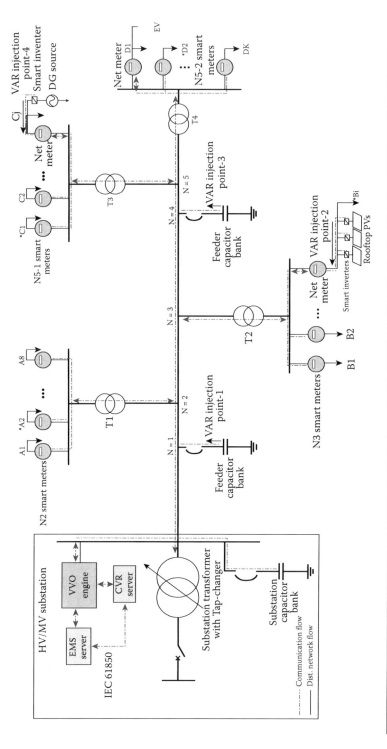

Figure 2.12 AMI-based VVO engine with distributed resources. DG: distributed generation. (From Farhangi, H., *IEEE Power & Energy*, 12, 52–66, 2014. © 2014 IEEE. With permission.)

configure *all* of its assets (inside and outside the substation) to achieve its energy management goals.

Obviously, the requirement that such level of integration places on the AMI system is even more serious than the previous example. Here the AMI system should work as the conduit of communication and coordination between substation-based EMS engine and customer-owned cogeneration resources, placed behind the meter. As such, it would be critical to ensure that smart grid integration maps require AMI systems to support such functionalities without major engineering and overhaul. As discussed earlier, a forward-looking smart grid integration map is critical for the realization of the smart grid. And given the cost involved in integrating new technologies and functionalities into the existing grid, the smart grid integration map could prove to be the savior or the Achilles' heel of a utility's smart grid program. In making that judgment, every utility has to review the operational requirements of its medium- and long-term smart grid functions and determine if its smart grid integration map supports seamless transition from where they are to where they would like to be in the future.

In addition to the examples that were discussed at length earlier, other smart grid capabilities, which several utilities consider implementing, may be considered as a litmus test to ascertain the suitability of a utility's smart grid integration map in supporting the following:

- Distributed generation: As discussed earlier, concerns over cogenerator synchronization, VAR control, voltage stability, etc., have convinced the utilities of the necessity to find ways of achieving a level of integration (notwithstanding regulatory impediments in various jurisdictions across North America) between feeder assets and behind-the-meter customer-owned equipment. Given the fact that the point of common coupling between the utility and the customer is the smart meter, such level of integration has to be facilitated by the utility's smart grid integration map.
- Sensor networks on the LV side of the distribution system: Although such sensory data on the LV side (such as phase measurement units) have not yet been established as a critical requirement, one should assume that should that become a necessity, the AMI infrastructure could be the primary means

to support such real-time data through an auxiliary channel and transport that to the substation. The alternative to using the existing AMI assets for such data would be to construct a dedicated low-latency communication system with a universal communication protocol and mission-critical availability/resilience, together with secure and intrusion-resistant multi-tier access, to be the carrier of such data for upper layers of the system. And that could be quite costly.

Again, irrespective of the chosen architecture for the implementation of sensor networks, a utility's smart grid integration map has to include provisions for supporting additional data networks going forward:

- Customer-side EMS: EMSs on the customer side of the distribution systems are often regarded as "killer apps," enabling accurate, reliable, real-time, and end-to-end energy management functions. Given the trend to design distribution substations as "energy Hubs," in charge of achieving cost-effective management of power and services transactions between prosumers (producers/consumers), it is paramount to move away from a broadcast-based global utility pricing/tariff signaling system to a real-time substation-based local pricing signal. Since the price of gas is never the same across all gas stations in a town, so could be the price of electricity across different substations in a given jurisdiction, or in a town. In other words, every substation should be able to price its services based on a host of local parameters (such as load congestion, demand profile, available energy from the grid and from prosumers). And in that case, a utility's smart grid integration map should facilitate the required integration between the energy hub (the substation) and its termination points (prosumers).

The central theme in all of the examples discussed earlier is the need to have a forward-looking smart grid integration map that empowers utilities to add incremental functionalities to their existing grid, if and when required, without the need to redo any of their previous investments. Given the examples discussed earlier, which cannot by any stretch of the imagination be comprehensive, the utilities have to be extremely careful about the initial investments that they are making in this regard. And that does not appear to be always the case, as some of the choices that have already been made in the early stages of that process are not encouraging.

As an example, the prevalent AMI model, implemented in many jurisdictions across North America, relies on local data collection units (often referred to as DAUs) as the primary interface between smart meters and MDMS applications in the back office. In such a model, either the local distribution substation would be totally disconnected from the AMI system that monitors the customers feeding off its feeders or, if there is any communication between the smart meters and the substation equipment, the data have to go through the round-robin of being captured by DAU locally, passed on to its appropriate MDMS in the remote back office, handed over to the SCADA headend in the back office, and then find their way through the SCADA network from the back office down into the substation.

It goes without saying that such long delays in data/command communication would make it almost impossible to efficiently run any number of smart grid capabilities that rely on distributed command and control and as such require local analytics and decision making. Such applications are by default substation resident, with a stringent need to have unimpeded access to real-time data from smart meters, sensors, and other termination points associated with that substation. In other words, smart meters should ideally be the substation's over-the-fence intelligent electronic devices, fully engaged in real-time data and command exchange with substation-resident functions, failing which they could be regarded only as an interim solution to automate billing and revenue management and nothing more.

Finally, a utility's smart grid integration map has to support the realization of the utility's integrated network domains, as depicted in Figure 2.13, which emphasizes the need for a distributed command and control system (using a system of intelligent agents) running across multiple domains of the utility network, providing end-to-end communication and data exchange between all utility assets. And in that regard, no smart grid asset should be planned as an outlying function, divorced from the utility's existing and planned functionalities. And if that is the case, one could seriously doubt the business justification for such expensive assets, or the utility's ability to roll out cost-effective and efficient smart grid capabilities.

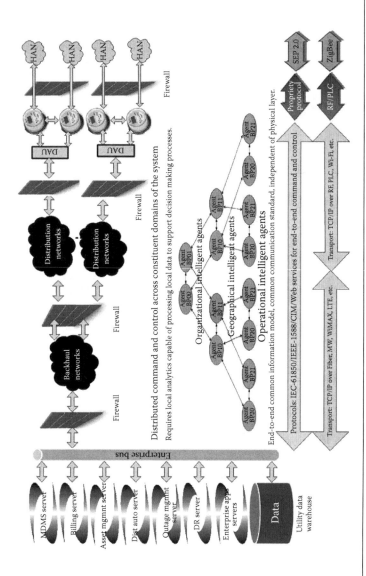

Figure 2.13 Smart grid distributed command and control. LTE: long term evolution; TCP/IP: transmission control protocol (TCP) and the Internet Protocol. (From Farhangi, H., *IEEE Power & Energy*, 12, 52–66, 2014. © 2014 IEEE. With permission.)

2.4 Energy Hub Paradigm

The utility industry has come to the conclusion that the move to the smart grid has to start at the bottom of its hierarchical system, where over the past century very little, if any, modernization has taken place. The distribution part of utility infrastructure is essentially the same as what it was at the early stages of the electrification in North America. What is notable is that the majority of anomalies and failures that the system has had to deal with have had their roots in the distribution system as well. At the core of the North American distribution system, substations have traditionally played the role of a point of common connection—that is, they housed the protection, switching, and metering functions of the utility company. However, in the context of smart grid, distribution systems need to evolve into foci where services, loads, and stakeholders meet to ensure efficient energy transactions across target jurisdictions. Therefore, at the core of the move toward a green economy is the need to develop the innovative technologies and solutions required to transform the legacy grid's aging distribution substations.

To realize that vision, significant research on new and innovative substation command and control, data collection, and decision support systems would be required. Utilities, in collaboration with researchers and the private industry, need to find forward-looking solutions and technologies for the following:

- Efficient delivery of electricity services to consumers and the industry
- Integration of alternative and renewable sources of energy in the energy mix
- Empowerment of consumers to assume their rightful role as a stakeholder to manage their carbon footprint

That requires a major paradigm shift in the role of today's distribution substations from an unintelligent point of common connection with consumers into a vibrant energy hub capable of the following:

- Optimizing the utilization of committed substation assets in line with the required service delivery

- Allowing substations to integrate renewable sources of energy, community storage, and cogeneration in its energy portfolio
- Facilitating energy transactions among all stakeholders through innovative communication mediums and protocols

2.5 Energy Hub Vision

The U.S. DOE's 2035 vision of the electricity grid of the future identifies the need to develop innovative technologies and solutions for the following three areas of the electricity grid:

1. Optimized utilization of assets and increasing system efficiency
2. Large-scale integration of clean energy sources (80% by 2035)
3. Allowing 100% customer participation in energy transactions

To achieve that vision, the DOE advocates significant departure from the utility's hierarchical architecture, positioning distribution substations as energy hubs. The impact of that approach is significant, as substations could no longer operate as a "flow-through" layer in service/energy delivery, but have to be a hub where available system energy and user demand are corroborated, service needs are rationalized, and stakeholders are engaged.

To realize that vision, significant research on new and innovative substation command and control, data collection, and decision support systems would be required. In particular, an environment is required to develop the following technologies:

1. Development of intelligent optimization and conservation systems for efficient delivery of services to consumers
2. Development of command and control technologies for substations operating as an energy hub
3. Development of cost-effective communication technologies for customer-resident EMSs

While item 1 focuses on developing the intelligence required within the substation to optimize asset commitment in relation to required services, item 2 attempts to extend the required command and control strategies for integration with over-the-fence components, such as cogenerators, storage components, and loads. And, last but not least, item 3 attempts to develop the required protocols for a communication medium that is native to such components (e.g., PLC).

As an example, the integration of these three technologies would enable the energy hub (i.e., the substation) to capture a real-time view of the available energy in the hub (through PLC with cogeneration and storage components), as well as building a real-time load profile (through PLC with smart meters and customer-resident EMSs) and decide what assets are required to optimally provide the required services.

The availability of real-time information from the immediate service territory of distribution substations could significantly increase their service reliability, lower their cost, and prolong the life of their assets. Real-time attributes of this nature can help develop a new generation of highly efficient and optimized VVO and CVR engines. The DOE's recent studies on energy conservation across the United States indicated that CVR functions implemented across less than half of U.S. feeders could potentially yield more than 2% demand reduction on the U.S. electrical system.

Shown in Figure 2.14, the energy hub of the future is a critical component of the smart grid, where legacy substations are transformed into semiautonomous energy management entities, with their own set of energy resources (e.g., feed from the grid, local renewable generators, local storage) and static and dynamic loads (e.g., clusters of fast direct current charging stations, as well as residential, commercial, and industrial loads) managed by a wide variety of highly specialized resident intelligence, allowing the energy hub to determine the following:

- Which termination points will be served from which source of energy and at what cost
- What level of service quality will have to be associated with each customer
- Decide in the event of supply shortage, or contingencies, which loads should be shed and which loads should be kept alive

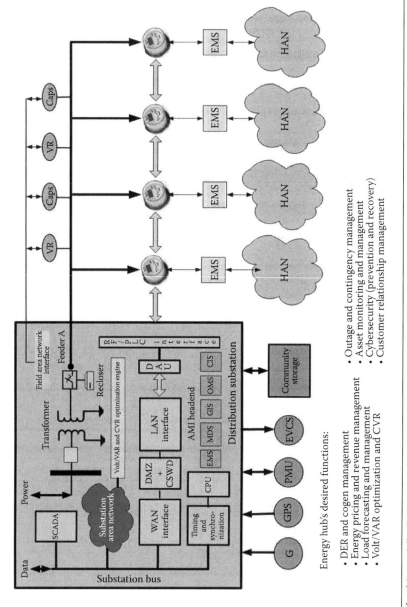

Energy hub's desired functions:

- DER and cogen management
- Energy pricing and revenue management
- Load forecasting and management
- Volt/VAR optimization and CVR

- Outage and contingency management
- Asset monitoring and management
- Cybersecurity (prevention and recovery)
- Customer relationship management

Figure 2.14 Advanced distribution substations (energy hubs). (From Farhangi, H., *IEEE Power & Energy*, 12, 52–66, 2014. © 2014 IEEE. With permission.)

- Keep close watch on the health of its assets, prevent and minimize outages, and schedule the necessary maintenance based on system stress and load requirements
- Price its own services based on its cost components (i.e., load congestions, age of assets, cost of energy resources, etc.) and therefore manage the resulting revenues

The last point mentioned purports to the idea of spot pricing for electricity. The advocates of this type of energy pricing draw parallels between gas stations and substations and argue that since the price of gas is not the same across all gas stations in any given jurisdiction, so should the price of electricity be across different substations within the utility network. Although this may not be realizable in the short term, all indications are that utility cost framework may dictate the implementation of such pricing strategies in the not too distant future.

References

1. NIST Special Publication 1108R2, NIST Framework and Roadmap for Smart Grid Interoperability Standards, Release 2.0, National Institute of Standards and Technology, United States Department of Commerce.
2. Hassan Farhangi, A roadmap to integration, *IEEE Power & Energy*, Vol. 12, No. 3, Jun. 2014, pp. 52–66.
3. Moein Manbachi, Hassan Farhangi, Ali Palizban, Siamak Arzanpour, Real-time adaptive optimization engine algorithm for integrated Volt/VAr optimization and conservation voltage reduction of smart microgrids, CIGRÉ Canada Conference, Montreal, Quebec, Canada, Sept. 2012.
4. Moein Manbachi, Hassan Farhangi, Ali Palizban, Siamak Arzanpour, Impact of V2G on real-time adaptive Volt/VAr optimization of distribution networks, IEEE EPEC Conference, Halifax, Nova Scotia, Canada, Aug. 2013.

3

CAMPUS MICROGRID

HASSAN FARHANGI

Contents

As discussed earlier, a campus microgrid is essentially a grid-tied or an urban microgrid. Other than large industrial complexes, most urban centers in North America host one or more university campuses, organized in the form of a small suburb, with its own facilities, layout, and infrastructure. Most such campuses receive their electricity from one or more medium voltage feeds from the local utility company. In that regard, campus microgrids are grid-tied microgrids with a diverse and variable load profile. Usually, campus microgrids incorporate residential load profile (i.e., dormitories), industrial load profile (workshops, labs, etc.), and last but not least, commercial load profile (i.e., offices, classrooms, etc.). From that perspective, a campus microgrid cannot be studied without taking into account its relationship with the larger grid, of which it is simply a component.

3.1 Lay of the Land

In the face of a rising demand for electricity amid increasing costs and environmental concerns related to greenhouse gas emissions as a result of fossil fuel consumption, utility companies desire to find ways to better manage the demand and integrate renewable sources of energy into the mainstream power system. For example, BC Hydro is attempting to meet 50% of all its future growth in electricity demand through energy conservation. Ontario's Hydro One has been steadily progressing toward the implementation of an intelligent grid to serve 1.3 million customers by deploying a standards-compliant communications infrastructure.

However, the main barrier to moving forward for these and other power suppliers is the current antiquated nature of the utility's electricity grid. Designed to cater to a centralized power generation, transmission, and distribution system, the grid is inherently incapable of accommodating new technologies and solutions. It is the last remaining sector providing a critical service to customers without having real-time feedback about how its services are utilized by its users. The electricity grid has traditionally operated as an open-loop system where no real-time data have been captured for such things as instantaneous demand, consumption profiles, or system performance. This open-loop system cannot store energy nor can it integrate renewable (and thus intermittent) sources of energy, such as wind, solar, biomass, and wave/tide. The grid for the new millennium has to be built around notions such as system-wide visibility, pervasive control, diversification of sources of energy (including intermittent renewables), operational efficiencies, and energy conservation.

Built in the last century, Canada's electricity grid is a one-way hierarchical system whereby the power is dispatched based on historical consumption data rather than to meet the real-time demand. As such, the system is overengineered (by design) to ensure a so-called safety margin and as such withstand maximum peak loads, which might not be present at all times. This means that the system's expensive assets are not efficiently used at all times.

However, the massive electrification of life all over the world, and the rising demand for electricity, has quickly eroded that safety margin, thus exposing the system to operational failures. In other words, in the absence of that safety margin and when the demands exceed the forecasted levels, the system simply fails, resulting in brownouts and blackouts. Such circumstances have come about much faster for the developing world, which have experienced rampant rolling blackouts across many jurisdictions in Asia and Africa.

Nevertheless, electric power generation, transmission, and distribution are supported by an electricity grid, which forms the backbone of a typical power network. A grid may reference a subnetwork, such as a local utility's transmission grid or distribution grid, a regional transmission network, or a whole country's or entire continent's electrical network. Regardless of the size, the extent, and the complexity of such grids, they share the same hierarchical (and often silo) structure in terms of constituent components of the network. Such grids are essentially designed to be load following. Worst still, there are no real-time data to indicate what the real load would be at any given point in time. As such, statistical assumptions about the size of the load to be served have to be made by each grid operator. And given the fact that such assumptions become invalid over time, the need for a paradigm shift to transition the grid from load following to generation following becomes critical.

3.2 Drivers and Inhibitors

Current centralized grid systems all over the world experience significant power loss through inefficiencies. They are also being challenged by increasing demand, rising costs, tightening supply, declining reserve margins, and need to minimize environmental impacts. At no time in its century-long history has the North American utility industry had to confront so many diverse and concurrent challenges, as it does now. In the last few decades, electrical power providers have faced one or more of the following challenges:

- Aging infrastructure (more than 70% of the utility assets in the United States are over 25 years old)
- Reliability (recent blackouts in California, Northeast United States, and Eastern Canada)
- Security (researchers have proven that the U.S. electrical grid is prone to attacks)
- Market dynamics (various jurisdictions are moving toward industry deregulation)
- Rates and pricing (need to implement multitariffs, time of use, smart metering, etc.)
- Distributed generation (need to allow access to the grid by independent power producers [IPPs] and co-gens)
- Efficiency and optimization (need for demand response and peak control)

- Rising energy costs (related to rising oil prices and security of supply)
- Conservation (need to conserve the planet's limited sources of energy)
- Mass electrification (meeting increasing demands for electricity)
- Renewable energy (integration of renewable sources of energy into the grid)
- Green energy (minimizing the industry's carbon footprint)

As emphasized, the stakeholder community has long come to the realization that the given challenges cannot be addressed within the confines of the legacy grid. In other words, at the core of the current crisis is the inability of the legacy electrical grid to respond to such challenges without a major technological overhaul of its infrastructure, systems, and components.

The problem however is not proving that an overhaul of the grid is a necessity. That is almost an undisputable given or fact. The stakeholders, including the utility companies, the governments, and the public, have come to the conclusion that such a transition from legacy grids to smart grids is not only necessary but also vital to sustain and promote economic growth and quality of life in the new millennia. The issue rather is how to overhaul the system, without impacting the critical services that it is currently providing for the larger population. The analogy of building a race car while competing in an actual race does not seem far-fetched.

In other words, the need to modernize the system, add new components, subsystems, and operational technologies, without having any adverse impact on its day-to-day operation seems to be impossible. What accentuates the problem is the realization of the fact that most utility companies, if not all, are cash strapped and not in a position to commit to large expenditures in this area without justifying the immediate paybacks in terms of additional revenues or services.

To further complicate the matter, one should also note that the absence of mature technologies, protocols, and standards in the smart grid sector is certainly not helping the situation. The fact of the matter is that the majority of technologies advocated for use in smart grids, including information and technology and communication technologies, have their roots elsewhere in the industry. These were designed in a different era and with different applications, specifications, and reliability requirements in mind. To port those technologies over into the smart grid sector amounts to almost repurposing and/or redeveloping such technologies. And with redevelopment comes the issue of the validation and the qualification of these new and improved (or repurposed) technologies. And that is another major issue involved in the further development of smart grids, which is how can such technologies be validated and/or qualified as utility grid ready without incorporating these in actual utility-scale networks. Can utilities take the risk of adopting such technologies based on test bench or lab validations? Those are further inhibitors that slow down the desired transition from the legacy grid to the smart grid.

3.3 Stakeholders and Partnerships

In July 2008, the Government of British Columbia, in Canada, through its Innovative Clean Energy (ICE) fund provided funding to a consortium of Canadian companies, led by the British Columbia Institute of Technology (BCIT), to set up Canada's very first smart microgrid on the Burnaby campus of BCIT. In November 2009, the Government of Canada, through the Western Diversification Fund, provided the project with matching funds for BC's Innovative Clean Energy fund. The project received further investments from CanmetENERGY-Natural Resources Canada (NRCan) and from BC Hydro.

At an overall investment of more than $30 million for over 5 years, BCIT began the process of designing and developing a scaled-down version of the smart grid; i.e., a smart microgrid to enable utility companies, technology providers, and researchers from across Canada to work together to develop, test, and qualify architectures, protocols, configurations, and models of the evolving intelligent grid with the intention of charting a "path from lab to field" for innovative and cost-effective technologies and solutions for North America's evolving smart electricity grid.

BCIT's smart microgrid was designed as a research, development, and demonstration (RD&D) platform where existing and future technologies in telecommunication, smart metering, cogeneration, smart distribution, and intelligent appliances were employed to develop and qualify the most robust, cost-effective, and scalable solutions required to facilitate and nurture the evolution and emergence of the smart grid in one form or another.

To widen the private sector participation in the initiative, BCIT assembled a consortium of industry partners, referenced here as BCIT microgrid private industry consortium, to help with the design and the implementation of BCIT's smart microgrid. BCIT microgrid private industry consortium, composed of local and international technology companies at the forefront of technology development in this field, covered a wide array of hardware, software, and system technologies required for the realization of a smart grid. The validation and the qualification of architectures, models, and protocols developed were guided, supervised, and validated by partnering utility companies who acted as the end customers of the developed technologies and solutions.

Canada's first smart microgrid infrastructure was implemented at BCIT's main campus in Burnaby. It enabled high-tech companies, end customers, and researchers to work together to develop and qualify various system architectures, configurations, interface protocols, and grid designs to meet national and global priorities for cogeneration, efficient transmission and distribution of electricity, load control, demand response, advanced metering, and integration of clean energy sources into existing and future grids.

3.4 RD&D Road Map Design

Utilities in North America have had their fair share of challenges in taking the first step on their path to smart grid, namely, large rollouts of smart metering projects across their distribution circuits. The reaction of the public to the utility companies' push to implement smart metering programs took many in the industry by surprise. In addition to consumer associations' open call to disband the idea, many jurisdictions saw the introduction of symbolic resolutions, passed by county and municipal councils, banning smart meter installation. In response to such backlash from customers, many North American utilities have had either to slow down the smart metering rollouts or to devise opt-out programs, while investing in information campaigns to reach their customers.

Unrelated to the form or the shape that the consumer backlash manifested itself (e.g., complaints about health effects of radio-frequency [RF] radiation, concerns over privacy and security of customer data, or perceived imminent rise in the cost of energy), one could see that such concerns were primarily attributed to misinformation and an absence of buy-in for this new technology on the part of utility customers.

What is interesting is that very few, if any, utilities attempted to answer the more fundamental question of why their customers should embrace this new technology with open arms. What was in this new technology for them to be a willing participant in this process? Would smart meters reduce utility bills? Would it provide customers with more reliable service? Would smart metering protect the customers' vital information and personal data? What would the short- and long-term impact of smart metering be on customer engagement? What is next after smart metering? What future functionalities and capabilities would be enabled through these smart meters that would be beneficial to customers?

In fact, not only very little attempt was made to answer these valid questions adequately and convincingly, some utilities added fuel to the fire by suggesting that smart meters would help with customer behavior change or load control through time of use and dynamic pricing. Such suggestions, without a well-formulated plan to prove to the customers that such behavior change would not and should not happen at the cost of their convenience, or at their expense, reinforced public perceptions that smart metering was nothing but a quick money-grab exercise by cash-strapped utilities, trying to fill their budget holes at the expense of rate payers.

The question that arose here was why would utilities not confront such misconceptions head on and communicate with their customers about the merits of smart metering? Why would they not portray smart metering as the first step toward smart grid integration, and all the unprecedented capabilities that smart grids will afford their customers? Why would they not attempt to convince their customers that smart grid shall effectively empower them to be an active stakeholder and player in their energy/service transactions?

Although there could be many reasons for such disconnect between utilities and their customers, some speculated that either utilities have not yet managed to develop the required smart grid strategic road map, or even if they did, there could have been very little consensus across their organizations on the integration plan and a realistic schedule required to implement it. Regardless of the root cause of this, the pundits saw this as the utilities' failure to formulate the right communication plan to help their system, organization, staff, infrastructure, assets, and ultimately customers navigate collectively and as one, through this uncertain, yet exciting, transition toward a new set of service transactions, energy paradigms, and fundamentally different roles and responsibilities.

It goes without saying that no utility has ever discounted the need for a smart grid strategic road map and, subsequently, a smart grid integration map, prior to committing such large investments in their assets and infrastructure. Therefore, the question is not the existence of such blueprints but simply their role in driving (and informing) the major technology investment commitments that the utilities are making today. The litmus test for that is to ask a series of questions to ascertain how conducive each investment is toward a seamless transition from a less-intelligent grid to an intelligently integrated smart grid.

As discussed earlier, the need for the development of a strategic road map for smart grids was recognized early on by many practitioners and planners in the utility industry. The work began on identifying the utilities' business and corporate objectives and goals, recognizing the most critical issues and impediments in reaching those goals, and devising a plan on how to address them. Figure 3.1 depicts an early attempt by a group of experts from BCIT and BC Hydro, who collaboratively worked over a period of several months to formulate an RD&D road map for their joint smart microgrid initiative on BCIT's Burnaby campus [1]. This collaborative effort took into consideration what each party was hoping to achieve from the joint project, the modalities of their respective development efforts, the realities on the ground, and the resources and the technologies needed to achieve those goals over a 5-year period.

As demonstrated in Figure 3.1, the BCIT/BC Hydro smart microgrid road map recognized the following five development streams across the full spectrum of the microgrid initiative:

- Stream 1: Energy Management System (EMS)—Stream 1 aimed to develop successively evolving versions of an open architecture, standard compliant EMS tool, with increasing

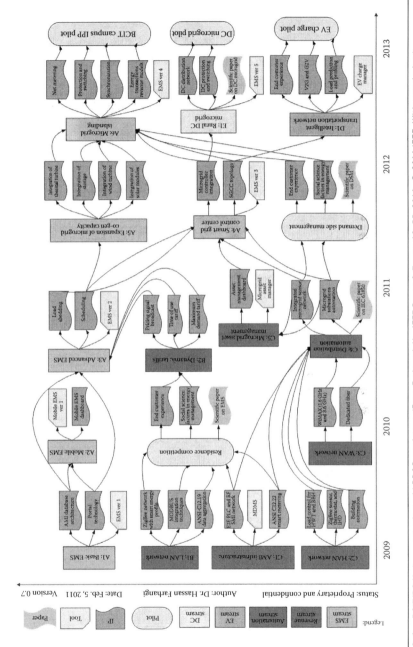

Figure 3.1 BCIT/BC Hydro smart microgrid RD&D road map. (From Farhangi, H., *IEEE Power & Energy*, 12, 55, 2014. © 2014 IEEE. With permission.)

functionality and features. Indicated as the A stream, it aims to develop the following applications:

- A1: EMS Ver 1 has built-in static tariffs, utility portal, and consumer portal.
- A2: Mobile EMS has built-in static tariffs, scalable portals, and mobile device dashboard technology.
- A3: EMS Ver 2 has dynamic tariffs, utility pricing signals, and consumer-initiated load shedding and scheduling.
- A4: EMS Ver 3 is integrated with a microgrid controller, implementing a distributed command and control architecture.
- A5: A5 is focused on the integration of renewable sources of energy (wind and solar) with local co-gen sources and the development of solutions for energy storage, net metering, synchronization, and protection/switching.
- A6: EMS Ver 4 is capable of accommodating consumer choices of electrical power generation sources and implementing various revenue models for energy transactions.

- Stream 2: Revenue Data Exchange—Stream 2 developed solutions for revenue data capture and aggregation over a wireless local area network (LAN), compliant with ANSI-C12.19. Indicated as the B stream, it incorporated the following activities:
  - B1: The LAN consists of the ZigBee network with smart energy profile and Modbus termination/integration.
  - B2: B2 is an ongoing project with NRCan, aiming at initiating and broadcasting utility pricing signals across the distribution network based on the time of use and the maximum demand/load considerations.

- Stream 3: Microgrid Automation System—Stream 3 aimed to integrate home area networks, LANs, and wide-area networks into an end-to-end command and control system. Indicated as the C stream, it attempts to develop the following:
  - C1: An advanced metering infrastructure consists of programmable logic controller (PLC)- and RF-equipped smart meters, retrofitted to become compliant with ANSI C12.22.

- C2: A home area network consists of load control devices for hot water tanks and baseboard heaters, as well as ZigBee sensors, thermostats, and in-home displays.
- C3: A WiMAX network (1.8 GHz) consists of base stations and WiMAX clients to be installed on campus substations to gather real-time data from the health and the conditions of campus electrical assets.
- C4: The distribution automation focuses on upgrading and equipping BCIT's substations with remote monitoring and control gears and sensors. WiMAX clients were required to facilitate full real-time visibility over the operation of BCIT's substations.
- C5: The development of a microgrid asset management tool integrates intuitive dashboard technology for asset maintenance and control.

- Stream 4: Intelligent Transportation System—Stream 4 focused on the development and the integration of electric vehicle (EV) charging infrastructure. Indicated as the D stream, it aimed to develop the following application:
  - D1: EV charging infrastructure allows grid-to-vehicle and vehicle-to-grid modes of operation.
- Stream 5: Rural and Direct Current (DC) Microgrids— Stream 5 aimed to investigate the complexities associated with the design and the realization of off-the-grid and rural microgrids. Indicated as the E stream, it aimed to develop the following application:
  - E1: Cost-effective rural microgrid blueprint using DC as the backbone of electrical distribution and consumption.

Furthermore, each stream aimed to validate the developed solutions through a real-life extensive pilot. Five pilots were planned:

- Pilot 1: Residence Competition—The presence of a LAN, together with our EMS Ver 1, allowed us to hold a competition among our residences, encouraging students to conserve energy. The competition was successful and was widely covered in the media. This pilot aimed to log and document the end customer's experiences with EMSs and understand the social science factors that needed to be considered in the

design of EMS systems. Such pilots need to be repeated with
EMS Ver 2 and Mobile EMS Ver 1.

- Pilot 2: Demand Side Management—With the aid of a fully
integrated end-to-end EMS, an EMS Ver 3 pilot was planned
with the intention of logging and documenting the end customer's experiences with an EMS that may be perceived as
intrusive. We needed to understand the social science factors
that should be considered in designing an EMS that may be
allowed by the consumer to go beyond the smart meter and
attempt to control predetermined appliances at home.
- Pilot 3: EV Charge Pilot—Having a network of smart meters
at the charging points for EVs on the campus allowed us to
determine end customer experiences and use the patterns of
EVs, as well as the complexities involved in predicting and
profiling mobile loads of this nature.
- Pilot 4: Rural and DC Microgrids—Given the fact that the
access to rural communities would have been difficult in the
early stages of this development, we planned to convert a
single building on the campus as a DC nanogrid and understand the issues involved in DC distribution networks, protection, and switching. Subsequently, we planned to leverage
the accumulated knowledge on the DC grids and expand the
pilot to a real completely off-the-grid rural community.
- Pilot 5: BCIT as an island-able IPP—Pilot 5 was planned as a
comprehensive pilot, whereby all the know-how, components,
and solutions developed around the campus microgrid could
be put to test through the EMS Ver 4. Important issues for
IPPs such as net metering, protection, switching, synchronization, and the economics of running a successful IPP could
be examined and investigated.

As Figure 3.1 demonstrates, the road map highlighted the need for
several constituent streams, each informing as well as enabling the
other streams along the way. For example, the EMS stream included
several layers of sophistication (and therefore features), based on the
availability of certain assets and capabilities provided by other parallel streams, such as advanced metering infrastructure (AMI), communication infrastructure, and load/asset management. The interplay

between these functionalities, made possible by the integration of their respective technologies, would enable stepwise jumps in the range of capabilities that the initiative was expected to provide.

BCIT/BC Hydro's smart microgrid initiative reinforced the notion that smart grid integration consisted of several concurrent streams, designed to introduce intelligence (and thereby command and control) into strategic areas of the system, providing capabilities and functionalities that transcends the silo legacy architecture of the system. The nature of these capabilities and their intended reach would determine which assets and/or subsystems have to be integrated to materialize the target functionality.

By default, smart grid integration does not always have to be end to end for *all* capabilities. Different smart grid functions require different assets to be integrated, with different capabilities and different requirements. As such, a smart grid integration map has to closely follow the utility's strategic road map and the intended smart grid functionalities that need to be enabled in each stage of the development.

In practice, however, smart grid integration has taken many twists and turns. It is doubtful that North American utilities would follow similar modalities and approaches for smart grid integration. Rather, it is logical to assume that each utility has taken a different path toward implementing their smart grid plans.

Given the fact that the electricity distribution network in almost all jurisdictions across North America had long been overdue for a major overhaul, the utilities' first step in smart grid integration began with limited rollouts of a one-way automated meter reading, followed by major investments in two-way AMI. As discussed, the overwhelming justification for the investments in AMI was its enabling role in facilitating the move toward the eventual realization of smart grid functions. That understanding convinced many utilities in North America to plan for major smart metering investments. Many projects were announced, and pilots sprang up across the continent. And in the absence of a well-formulated smart grid integration plan, specifying how smart metering would lead to smart grid, pilot project evaluations focused on the requirements for smart metering, rather than on its forward compliance with future smart grid functions, and as such, most pilots were perceived to be successful, resulting in substantial investments in smart metering projects.

However, as the full cost of the ownership of AMI systems became clear, and given the regulatory constraints, and in the absence of clear revenue models, utilities found it increasingly difficult to justify the AMI capital expenditure. Added to less-than-convincing cost-benefit models for AMI, the consumers' backlash against smart metering slowed down AMI rollouts in many jurisdictions across North America. The absence of clear smart grid road maps, and the utilities' less-than-convincing arguments in favor of smart metering, prompted many experts in the field to express doubts about the AMI rationale, questioning whether or not smart grid was being integrated backward. Some suggested that the return on investments would be more palatable if the distribution substations were automated first. Others pointed to the need to start right at the top, upgrading the utilities' enterprise applications in the back-office and on the enterprise bus before attempting to invest at the bottom of the chain.

The fact of the matter was that all those questions were quite valid. And the reason why such doubts were being expressed was the absence of the utilities' smart grid integration map, demonstrating how the AMI was going to be leveraged to gradually upgrade the functional capabilities of the grid. The January 2010 issue of the Institute of Electrical and Electronics Engineers' *Power & Energy Society* magazine featured an early attempt to demonstrate the linkages between technologies and capabilities along the path from smart metering to smart grid. That stipulation, captured in the previous chapter, argued that AMI would have to be perceived as an enabling platform for two-way communication and distributed command and control among all previously unmonitored and uncontrolled components of the distribution system. It further emphasized that the protocols, the topology, and the architecture of AMI systems had to be designed as a forward-looking source of sensory/status/alarm information capable of allowing future (and yet to be developed) smart grid capabilities to reach (and be integrated with) the downstream side of the utility system. In other words, the specification of the AMI system had to take into account the communication, the data/command exchange, and the access requirements of future applications of smart grids.

What this further demonstrated was the notion that smart grid integration could be broadly divided into two categories: one that operates in local domains using global system attributes, such as demand response or outage detection, which require access to real-time local data with local analytics and local decision-making processes; and another that operates over multiple domains, requiring wide-area situational data awareness, overview of the system constraints as a whole, and its operational objectives, such as management of distributed energy resources, self-healing, outage prevention, etc. While the former group is enabled through a well-designed forward-looking AMI system with appropriate latency, throughput, availability, and resilience requirements, the latter relies on a well-designed and optimally integrated network of distributed systems with suitable security, scalability, and access protocol specification, enabling efficiently distributed command and control through multilayer, multitier, and multiagent systems.

In other words, one needed to emphasize the fact that smart grid integration is built upon forward-looking information, command and control architectures, capable of meeting the functional and operational requirements of a gradually evolving smart grid system, with incremental needs for higher levels of performance, scalability, and resilience without the need for costly departures from its original design and implementation. It goes without saying that once in place, the utilities would find it almost impossible to undo their committed investments (AMI, substation automation, etc.) and upgrade their assets to enable new smart grid functionalities. And that would mean that the cost and the pain associated with the transition from legacy grids to smart grids would to a large extent be dependent on the suitability of the utilities' smart grid integration map to support that transition.

The irony is that there is an element of truth in every approach that has been put forward on how to build a smarter grid. This diversity of views could only be attributed to the fact that without a doubt there is more than one way to integrate a smarter grid. Depending on a variety of potentially conflicting, and yet interacting, drivers (priorities, regulations, legacy assets, organizational/process issues, etc.), different utilities may choose different points of departure on their long journey toward smart grid. And consequently, the trajectory that each utility may take in integrating their system with different smart grid functionalities, even if similar starting points are adopted, may prove to be quite unique and dissimilar compared to others.

However, regardless of where that starting point is, it is crucial for utilities to spec out their journey (as much as they possibly could, given all the unknowns) in such a way that subsequent moves toward other areas of the system could be seamlessly realized and without the need to substantially change/upgrade the assets which are already rolled-out. As an example, if after an AMI rollout the plan is to take substation automation as the next area for investment, the utility should ensure that the subsequent downstream moves to implement demand curtailment or load shedding, as well as upstream moves to implement asset management or self-healing, could be realized without having to change or upgrade the investments incurred for substation automation and AMI.

Moreover, the fact that the "specifications of various parts of the system" need to be taken into account to ensure the seamless integration of components, assets, and functions in both spatial and temporal domains, emphasizes the notion that the sphere of influence of Smart Grid capabilities varies considerably across different doamins. Some span through upstream layers of the system, involving enterprise functions, utility operations, and revenue management (e.g., contingency management, asset management, energy market participation), while others traverse through local downstream layers of the system, involving field and prosumer-facing assets (e.g., demand response, load management). It is the latter group that places a heavy burden on the AMI system, as it requires close integration and tight operational linkages to AMI system components, protocols, and technologies. A poorly designed and implemented AMI system would prove to be inhibitive for the efficient implementation and/or correct operation of such downstream smart grid functions.

3.5 Microgrid Implementation

Like any other strategic planning document, a smart grid road map has to be regarded as a living document, subject to change, modifications, and improvements. By default, such long-term plans determine one's immediate actions while being informed by the results of the actions completed. In our case, the first two years of the implementation went according to the plan. However, at the start of the third year, discussions between BCIT and BC Hydro pointed to the need to move the integration of EV charging stations with the microgrid from year 4 to year 3. Moreover, the decision was made to push out the DC microgrid indefinitely as our technology partners and end customers were as of yet unwilling to commit to R&D investments in this area.

Other than those two changes, the BCIT/BC Hydro smart microgrid RD&D road map was successfully completed with the completion of the OASIS subsystem, which combined the last two major tasks of setting up an island-able microgrid with EV charging stations as some of the loads it would serve. It should also be noted that the project was completed by the end of 2014, rather than its completion target of the end of 2013.

BCIT's Burnaby campus, upon which the RD&D road map was implemented, is one of the largest postsecondary academic campuses in Vancouver. As Figure 3.2 shows, BCIT's Burnaby campus resembles a small neighborhood, containing over 50 buildings, tucked between Canada Way to the north and Deer Lake Parkway to the south. The campus houses classrooms, administration buildings, workshops, food outlets, student services, and dormitories.

The sheer size and the diversity of activities required BCIT's Burnaby campus to cater to a variety of different electricity consumption profiles ranging from heavy industrial machinery for instructional purposes in the workshops to office-type consumption in classrooms, along with a residential-type profile in dormitories. This microgrid enables utility providers, technology providers, and researchers to work together to facilitate the commercialization of architectures, protocols, configurations, and models of the evolving smart grid. The ultimate goal is charting a path from lab to field for innovative and cost-effective technologies and solutions for Canada's evolving smart electricity grid.

BCIT's smart microgrid is a test bed where communication technologies (RF and PLC), smart metering (single phase [1P] and three phase [3P]), cogeneration (thermal turbine, solar, and wind), and smart appliances are integrated to qualify the merits of different solutions, showcase the capabilities, and accelerate the commercialization of locally developed technologies and solutions for the smart grid.

BCIT's smart microgrid is constructed using locally developed technologies, components, and devices supplied by Canadian

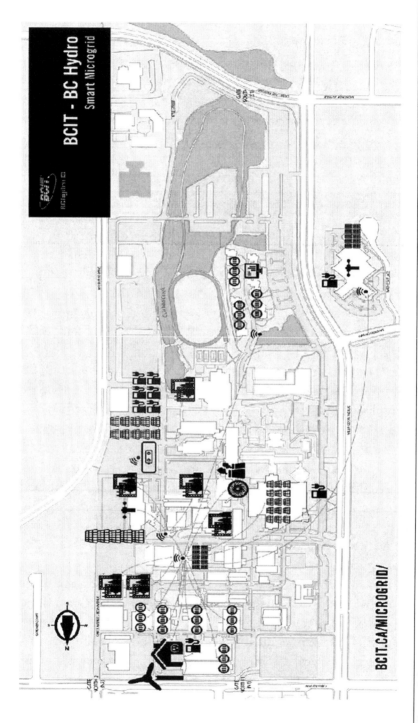

Figure 3.2 BCIT's Burnaby campus in Burnaby, British Columbia, Canada. (Courtesy of BCIT, Burnaby, BC, Canada.)

technology companies. The validation and the qualification of architectures, models, and protocols is guided, supervised, and scrutinized by BC Hydro and other Canadian utility companies.

BCIT's smart microgrid enables Canadian high-tech companies, Canadian end customers, and Canadian engineers to work together and verify various system architectures, configurations, interface protocols, and grid designs to meet Canada's priorities for cogeneration, efficient transmission, and distribution of electricity, load control, demand response, advanced metering, and integration of clean energy sources into the existing and future grids. BCIT's smart microgrid helps utility companies, such as BC Hydro, to qualify technologies for remote monitoring and control of cogeneration plants in terms of their carbon footprint, output quality, and efficiency.

It is also important to note that the utility industry is no longer interested in experimenting with end-to-end proprietary technologies and solutions supplied by a single company. Utilities continue to have painful memories of being constrained by proprietary solutions supplied by large monopoly companies, constraining the pace and the scope of the technical innovations to what such vendors chose to supply. Utilities would like to see smart grid RD&D centers to be built with an open topology and architecture, using the most innovative, cost-effective, and standardized technologies available in the open market.

As such, BCIT's smart microgrid is built with a forward-looking open and nonproprietary architecture, using the best of the breed technologies available from Canadian and international high-tech companies. For instance, the current AMI built on a BCIT campus utilizes smart metering technologies from different vendors.

BCIT's smart microgrid also enables first nations and other remote communities in Canada to become power producers leveraging the available renewable sources of energy (e.g., run-of-the-river, solar, wind, beetle-infested timber) and to operate such plants with acceptable environmental and commercial standards.

In addition to helping the Canadian power industry to begin to address some of Canada's clean energy priorities, BCIT's smart microgrid helps Canadian high-tech companies to demonstrate and showcase the capabilities of their technologies and solutions to end customers and open up the North American and international markets to Canadian-made technologies.

The key deliverables of this project over its three consecutive phases are the following:

1. Construction of a smart microgrid test bed to verify the following:
   a. Provisioning methods for smart termination points (meters, data aggregators, appliances, sensors, controls, etc.)
   b. Innovative electrical distribution system including smart substations
   c. Innovative network architecture and topology for smart grid
2. Operational analysis and qualification of the following:
   a. Resilience, reliability, security, and scalability
   b. Data collection and distributed command and control methods
   c. Consumer behavior and their participation in energy conservation efforts
3. Qualification of interface protocols and models to ensure the following:
   a. Interface with the utility back-office tools (billing, load management, service provisioning, outage restoration, etc.)
   b. Seamless end-to-end deployment, operation, and maintenance
   c. Easy and intuitive human interface for operators and customers

The sheer size and the diversity of activities requires BCIT's Burnaby campus to cater to a variety of different electricity consumption profiles ranging from heavy industrial machinery for instructional purposes in the workshops to office-type consumption in classrooms along with a residential-type profile in dormitories.

In addition to such diverse usage patterns, the campus includes cogeneration power plants. There is an existing photovoltaic (PV) tower, capable of generating up to 8 kW of electricity, as well as three smaller PV systems elsewhere on the campus with a total generation capacity of around 14 kW. Newer PV modules are also installed on the roof of BCIT's new gateway building. These new solar modules are capable of generating 17 kW of power for the campus. A cogeneration plant, consisting of a multifuel boiler and turbine, capable of delivering 250 kW of power, has already been installed on the campus. Furthermore, one vertical axis wind turbine, capable of generating 5 kW of power, has been installed near one of the central buildings. Last but not least, 250 kW of solar canopies, feeding into 500 kWh of lithium ion battery storage, have been installed on one of the large parking lots on the campus.

As shown in Figure 3.3, BCIT's smart microgrid is an integration of four entities: cogeneration plants, campus loads, meshed network, and core intelligence [2].

1. Cogeneration plants
    a. Intelligent thermal turbine

    A key component of BCIT's smart microgrid is its intelligent thermal turbine. The plant allows smart sensors to monitor the load demand to bring the cogeneration plant online to supply part of the required power to the BCIT microgrid during peak consumption periods. The cogeneration control system is equipped with smart sensors, integrated with the BCIT's microgrid core intelligence to achieve the desired system response. The nominal capacity of this plant is 250 kW.

    b. Solar photovoltaic stations

    The BCIT Burnaby campus is already equipped with four solar PV cogeneration systems. An 8 kW grid-tied PV tower is located at the east side of the campus (in front of Building SE1). This tower has four sides, each with a 2 kW PV capacity. Inverter and monitoring systems are installed inside the tower. The interfaces to monitor the energy production are available as well. A 2 kW grid-tied PV system is installed on the east roof side of the AFRESH home, located at the north side of the campus (next to Building NE3). It generates electricity for the AFRESH building. AFRESH is an acronym for accessible and affordable, flexible, resilient, energy efficient, sustainable, and healthy. As shown in Figure 3.4, the AFRESH home is a housing demonstration project built on the BCIT campus. AFRESH's energy-efficient features include a solar installation, geothermal (geoexchange)

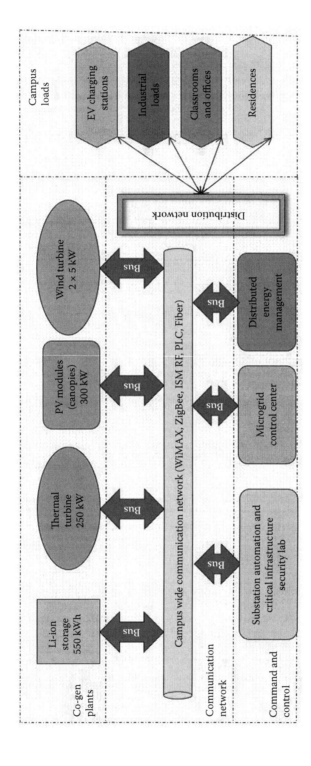

Figure 3.3 BCIT/BC Hydro smart microgrid topology. (From Farhangi, H., Campus based smart microgrid at British Columbia Institute of Technology in Vancouver, Canada, *CIGRE*, 3, Bologna, 2011. With permission.)

Figure 3.4 Net-zero home on BCIT campus. (Courtesy of BCIT, Burnaby, BC, Canada.)

heating, a fuel cell, smart meters, a plug-in hybrid/EV charging stations, and an inverter, storage, and control installation. Moreover, two 1.4 kW grid-tied PV systems, as a curtain wall, are installed on the facade of a technology place (Building SE 19), a multitenant building owned and operated by Discovery Parks, that is located on the BCIT campus. The fourth PV system is a 1 kW grid-tied PV system installed on Building NE25.

As mentioned, 250 kW of PV canopies is installed on Parking Lot 7, feeding into a 500 kWh storage and power conversion systems. The output (measured in real time by our EMS tool hauling the data from their attached net meters) is fed into one of the distribution substations nearby. Moreover, the output of the power conversion systems also drives a number of local EV charging stations, as well as other shedable loads.

Planned islanding is demonstrated by enabling the EV charging station to operate fully detached from BC Hydro using the lithium ion battery pack. The batteries could be charged from a BC Hydro feeder to a maximum charge of not exceeding the total amount of electricity generated by all PV modules across the campus.

This setup has enabled us to demonstrate the viability of load shifting through the utilization of renewable sources of energy meeting the incremental load placed on the grid by up and coming applications such as EV charging stations.

c. Wind turbine

As previously discussed, a vertical axis wind turbine is installed next to the AFRESH home. It feeds its output into the AFRESH's circuits through a local panel and some lead acid battery packs.

2. Campus loads

Four different buildings, with a variety of consumption profiles, were selected to be equipped with smart terminations.

a. The BCIT machine shop houses large computer numerical control machines and heavy equipment mainly used for instructional purposes.

b. The BCIT welding shop contains numerous transformers and welding equipment, used for training.

c. Building NE1 contains several circuits supplying classrooms, cafeterias, offices, etc. Residences are BCIT student dormitories.

d. Campus loads provide a rich set of service profiles prevalent in most urban settings. We have particularly focused on the power usage pattern, the frequency, the types of loads, and the applications that these buildings provide.

3. Meshed network

As shown in Figure 3.5, the BCIT smart microgrid network integrates the following seven components [3]:

a. Smart meters are capable of measuring multitudes of consumption parameters (e.g., active power, reactive power, voltage, current, demand) with acceptable precision and accuracy. Smart meters are chosen to be tamper proof and capable of storing the required data for a number of billing cycles. These meters are supplied by a wide variety of different manufacturers.

b. Smart displays are capable of measuring consumption profiles and displaying those in an easy-to-understand form with end customers.

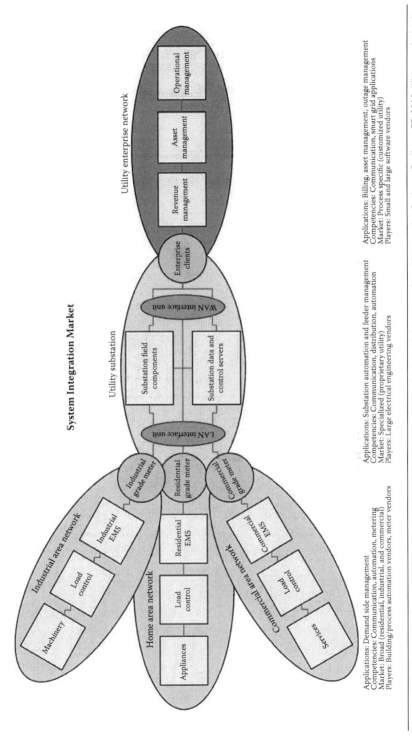

Figure 3.5 BCIT/BC Hydro smart microgrid network domains. (From Farhangi, H., *Smart Grids from a Global Perspective*, Springer, Berlin, p. 77, 2016. With permission.)

c. Communication modules enable each meter to communicate with its adjacent meters or with mobile/stationary data aggregators. Communication technologies such as low-cost RF, PLC, and ZigBee have been used.

d. Access and networking middleware allows the setup and the management of a secure meshed network comprising smart components in the same neighborhood, together with their assigned data aggregator.

e. A data aggregator unit is capable of exerting command and control over a meshed network of slave meters. The aggregator is capable of accessing each and every node in its assigned network.

f. Smart appliances control is capable of exerting command and control over smart appliances to adjust/control their performance and service level based on user and/or utility requirements.

g. Aggregator application software allows the authentication and the handshake with each node in the network. It is capable of identifying each termination, querying them, exchanging data and command with them, and storing the collected data for scheduled and/or on-demand transfer to utility servers.

BCIT's smart microgrid adopts an open architecture to allow the experimentation and the adoption of other transport technologies as and when they become available.

4. Core intelligence

BCIT's microgrid control center (MCC) enables data aggregators to be networked with the utility control centers in a variety of different configurations, network topology, and architectures. The wide-area network is emulated using BCIT's MCC's routers, switches, firewalls, and servers. MCC's servers are equipped with a selection of back-office utility tools to communicate with data aggregators, exchange command/control data, and act as an interface between smart grids and the utilities' back-office software tools such as billing and accounting.

This test bed setup enables technology providers to demonstrate the capabilities of their products. It also helps the utilities to experiment with various architectures, configurations, and protocols and see how a larger system can be constructed using such technologies. With this self-contained power grid, we can demonstrate how to effectively set up and operate a large-scale smart power grid to help better conserve and control energy usage across British Columbia and Canada.

The system is designed in such a way as to

- Ensure the integrity of time-sensitive data (event-based and/or schedule-based)
- Ensure the reliability and the security of communication channels
- Parse data and make sense of what is important (which needs immediate attention) and what is not (which will be used for statistical reporting and archiving)
- Mirror critical databases of substations
- Present data in a useful and visual way (graphical outputs, interactive, query-based)
- Develop predictive models of events and real-time responses
- Manage distributed control to prevent cascading failures or for the graceful degradation of user services based on service priorities
- Real-time wide-area control to manage generation and prevent overprovisioning
- Have context-dependent models and control of components to achieve robustness, fault-tolerance, or graceful performance degradation
- Verify and qualify large-scale distributed real-time embedded systems
- Develop support for the integration and the control of alternative and cogeneration plants

To achieve each of the objectives, we worked with our partners to arrive at the most suitable system architecture and topology. In doing so, we were guided by the requirements and the constraints specified by our end customers, such as BC Hydro. Also, to be as cross-platform agnostic as possible, we use Java as our main development language.

The rest of this book will delve into the individual components of BCIT's microgrid. As Figure 3.6 demonstrates, we have come a long way in meeting the targets and the deliverables set by our road map (refer to Figure 3.1). Given the fact that road maps are generally statements of intents, desires, and plans, it is remarkable that what was designed, built, and commissioned bears a close resemblance to the picture that our road map painted early in the process. A detailed comparison between our early understandings of what was needed to be done in 2007 to what was ultimately achieved in 2015 is a testimony to the time well spent in achieving consensus across the board and involving all stakeholders, to ensure that what was designed stayed relevant to the needs and the priorities of the community of the stakeholders. Close collaboration with the industry ensured that BCIT's microgrid design team understood the industry priorities by trying to push the envelope in terms of the development of approaches, technologies, and solutions that addressed the critical issues which the sector as a whole was facing.

Nevertheless, our work is far from over. What has so far been done is simply a baseline for the design of a microgrid. The design team appreciates the fact that microgrids are not projects; they have

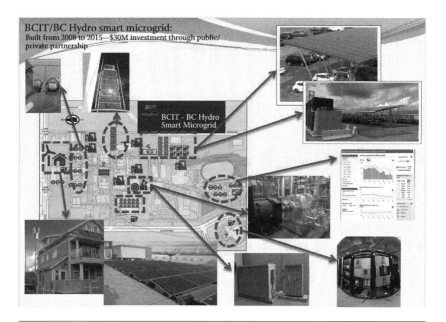

Figure 3.6 Overview of the microgrid's major assets commissioned on BCIT Burnaby campus.

a beginning but no end. Microgrids should be regarded as an ongoing initiative, focused on constantly raising the bar and pushing the envelope on energy conservation, sustainable development, energy workforce training and education, and last but not least minimizing campus carbon footprint.

References

1. Hassan Farhangi. A roadmap to integration. *IEEE Power & Energy*, Vol. 12, No. 3, p. 55, June 2014.
2. Hassan Farhangi. Campus based smart microgrid at British Columbia Institute of Technology in Vancouver, Canada. *CIGRE*, p. 3, 2011.
3. Hassan Farhangi. Cyber security vulnerabilities: An impediment against further development of smart grid. *Smart Grids from a Global Perspective*. Edited by Anne Beaulieu et al., Springer, Berlin, p. 77, 2016.

4

COGENERATION PLANTS

MINOO SHARIAT-ZADEH

Contents

As discussed, a smart grid may incorporate distributed generation (DG) and cogeneration of energy through solar or wind resources. These may operate in parallel with the legacy grid, as well as independent of it for extended periods, often depending on the source of power and the availability of energy storage systems.

This chapter begins with a review of solar power generation and solar photovoltaic (PV) technology and applications. It explores the technical considerations involved in the selection and the integration of solar PV systems within DGs.

Moreover, a case study will be described: the solar PV system of the Energy OASIS microgrid at the British Columbia Institute of Technology (BCIT) in Burnaby, BC, Canada. The requirements and the specifications of that system will be reviewed. This includes the project specifications, the design requirements, and the equipment selection considerations. The chapter then continues with a review of wind power generation, technologies, and applications. A case study on a vertical axis wind turbine (VAWT) installation at BCIT will also be described.

4.1 Solar Installations

Solar energy is what could be converted of the sun's radiation through either passive or active means to do useful work as light, thermal energy (heat), or electric power. Two active, and more common, solar technologies are solar collectors and solar PV. Solar collectors employ electrical or mechanical equipment to provide water heating or air ventilation.

Solar PV technology is used to generate electricity. This chapter focuses on the solar PV power and technology, a technology that uses PV materials and devices to directly convert sunlight into electricity.

- Solar PV systems applications: The mainstream applications of solar PV power systems could be mapped into three main categories: large solar power plants integrated with the grid at the transmission level; medium solar power plants integrated within microgrids at the distribution level; and last but not least small rooftop PVs integrated with customer side assets. Notwithstanding their point of common coupling (PCC) with the grid, PV installations conform to similar topology and setup, with differences in the capabilities of their power conversion interface, availability or lack of storage, ancillary services, etc.
- Solar PV systems main components: A solar PV system consists of solar PV modules (panels) that directly convert solar radiation into electricity through the PV effect. Solar PV modules must be mounted on a structure. This is required in order to provide solar panels with the protection and the structural support they need and keep them oriented in the correct direction. The mounting systems may be at a fixed tilt and attached to the ground or on sun-tracking frames. As shown in Figure 4.1, the balance of system (BOS) normally refers to the other electrical components of solar PV systems, other than the solar PV panels, and may include protection and safety

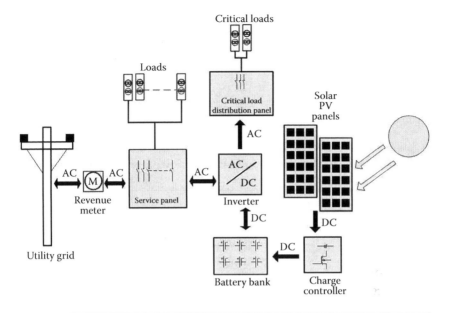

Figure 4.1 Example of a grid-connected solar PV system including battery energy storage system.

devices, power conditioning equipment, and inverters. Power conditioning equipment provides DC electricity to the DC loads. When required, inverters are employed to convert DC electricity generated by the solar PV modules into alternating current (AC). AC can then be used as connection to public electricity grids or be distributed to support local AC loads. In grid-tied applications, interconnection with a public utility is required. PCC (also known as point of interconnection or point of delivery) is the point where the utility's distribution system and the DG installation interconnect. For overhead service connections, the PCC is typically at the weather head. For underground service connections, the PCC is at the revenue meter base. The PCC may also include breakers, switches, and protection devices and equipment. Usually the utility is responsible for design, construction, maintenance, and operation of all facilities on the utility side of the PCC, while the DG plant is responsible for design, construction, inspection, maintenance, and operation of all facilities on its side of the PCC. Most off-grid applications include some sort of energy storage and require storage charge/discharge controllers.

4.1.1 Solar PV Project Development

The development of a typical solar PV project can be broken down into many stages, including conceptual study, feasibility study, and design and construction.[1] This section introduces the considerations that owners and stakeholders for DG plants need to take into account when planning a solar PV project.

For instance, a typical scope for a feasibility study of such projects includes, but is not limited to, creation of a detailed site plan, detailed site assessment, assessments of solar resources, environmental characteristics, assessment of technology options, and system design constraints.

The development phase will then take the project from the feasibility stage through to completion and may include the selection of solar PV modules, the preparation and submission of permit applications, the tendering process, the selection and ranking of contractors, the purchasing and procurement processes, the installation, the testing, and the commissioning. An overview of the different phases involved in the realization of typical solar PV projects is provided here:

- Conceptual study: Assuming that an opportunity for the design and the construction of a solar PV installation is identified, this stage focuses on clarifying the objectives of the project and how this system should function to meet its performance requirements.
- Feasibility study: This stage will provide stakeholders with an early assessment of the potential for the solar PV project and the high-level requirements of the project, outlining what could be achieved at what cost and at what time frame. The study should provide stakeholders with enough information for them to make the appropriate commitments required to realize the solar PV project. Such feasibility study may include the following components:
  - Site assessment: The first step in evaluating the potential of solar electricity is a site assessment. Accurate and comprehensive site assessments are critical for the success of solar PV projects. Through site surveys, the professionals responsible for the design, the installation, the commissioning, the operation, and the maintenance of the system will be able to capture the information required to

develop technical specifications and financial proposals. Site surveys will help correctly budget for and design the system. An efficient site survey will ensure the success of the project. There are tools and applications that can be used to make sure all the information is collected during a site visit.

- Shading: Solar PV modules are extremely sensitive to shading. PV cells within a PV module are typically connected in a series. The amount of current flowing through a module may be limited by the weakest point in that module such as a shaded spot. In addition, the shaded spot will heat up to the point that it may become damaged since it would be acting like a resistor, stopping the flow of the current. Therefore, when evaluating potential locations to mount solar PV arrays, a shading analysis needs to be performed. This will identify when and where shading will occur taking the seasonal variations into consideration. In most cases, the ideal location for a solar array is a higher structure such as building roofs or solar parking canopies. Currently, there are several tools and applications that professionals use to determine the most economical and efficient PV array location and position. Such tools can be employed to create an accurate solar site analysis through combining site-specific shading data with the published global weather data. Such data can be applied to architectural, engineering, solar, and ecological applications.
- Geotechnical investigation: When it comes to the installation of a cost-effective support structure, the selection of the foundation for the mounting structure is critical and depends on the type of the mounting system. A proper investigation of the subsurface condition must be carried out to avoid the selection of the wrong foundation type and materials. An inadequate geotechnical survey can later lead to costly changes to design and procurement, which in turn may delay the project completion date.
- Estimate irradiation/insulation: It is important to understand how much sunshine a specific site receives on a regular basis. The usual figure of merit is peak sun hours

per day. For example, the data retrieved from the Natural Resources Canada's website indicates that Vancouver receives an average of 3.7 sun hours per day. The same source reveals that Phoenix has a daily average of 6.9 sun hours.[2]

- Orientation: Solar PV modules will produce the most energy when the sun is shining directly onto them, through a 90° angle. However, this is not always possible, and a correction factor must be applied for the projects that are not at the perfect tilt. Properly aiming the modules with an appropriate tilt will maximize the solar energy that the PV array collects. Although there are some general rules, for example, a tilt angle equal to the latitude of the site will maximize yearly performance; however, that is not all. There are other considerations such as a tilt that can lower the impact of snow accumulation in winter or a tilt that maximizes the seasonal performance of a solar PV system. This needs to be carefully analyzed and assessed.

- Soiling: Soiling refers to the accumulation of dust, dirt, leaves, and bird droppings on the solar PV modules. Dirt and dust particles can degrade the output of a solar PV panel by as much as 6% over the period of a year. This should be considered when selecting a proper site and solar PV modules and developing an effective inspection and maintenance plan.

- Proximity to electrical services: Another consideration when determining a suitable site for a solar PV system is its proximity to other electrical components of the system. This may include point of delivery, main distribution panel, and loads. Close proximity to other components of a solar PV system will reduce the wire losses and voltage drops, which in turn results in the installation of smaller conductors and reduced cost of procurement and implementation.

4.1.2 Technology Fundamentals

A number of solar PV cells interconnect to compose a solar PV module (or panel). Solar PV modules are the most critical components of a solar PV system. There are a wide range of PV cell technologies in the market today using different types of material, such as the following[3,4]:

- Wafer-based crystalline silicon technology is the most prevalent technology and is classified as either monocrystalline silicon (c-Si) or polycrystalline silicon (mc-Si). Monocrystalline cells are extremely thin wafers of silicon, cut from a single silicon crystal. Solar cells in monocrystalline panels are slices cut from pure drawn crystalline silicon bars. The entire cell is aligned in one direction, which means that when the sun is brightly shining on them at the correct angle, they are extremely efficient. These panels work best in bright sunshine with the sun directly shining on them. They have a uniform blacker color because they absorb most of the light. Monocrystalline cells are also the most efficient type of c-Si cells. Higher efficiency means space efficiency. With a higher output, less space is needed to achieve the desired capacity. Monocrystalline panels have a life expectancy exceeding 25 years. They have better low-temperature performance than mc-Si cells. Today, monocrystalline cells are known to be the most commercialized solar PV technology. However, they are the most expensive of all solar cells.

  Polycrystalline panels are made up of silicon offcuts, which are constructed to form blocks and create a cell made up of several pieces of pure crystal. The individual crystals are not necessarily all perfectly aligned together, which means there may be losses at the joints between them, and they are not quite as efficient as c-Si cells. However, this misalignment can help in some circumstances, because the cells work better under light at all angles and in low light. Typically, mc-Si solar PV cells operate at a lower efficiency than c-Si cells due to the fact that the material has a lower purity. Polycrystalline modules are less space efficient as well. Another drawback of mc-Si modules is that their heat tolerance is less than that of c-Si panels, which means they do not perform as efficiently in high temperatures. Polycrystalline panels may be better suited to the duller conditions, although the difference is marginal.

- Thin-film technology is characterized by the slimness of the PV cell. Unlike wafer-based crystalline silicon cells, which have light-absorbing layers that are traditionally 200–350 μm thick, thin-film solar cells have light-absorbing layers that are just 1 μm thick. Thin-film solar cells are made by depositing several layers of a light-absorbing semiconductor onto a substrate-coated glass, metal, or plastic. The semiconductors do not have to be thick because they absorb energy from the sun very efficiently. As a result, thin-film solar cells are lightweight, durable, and easy to use. There are three main types of thin-film solar cells, depending on the type of semiconductors used: amorphous silicon (a-Si), cadmium telluride (CdTe), and copper indium (gallium) di-selenide (CIS/CIGS). Each has its own advantages and drawbacks. For instance, amorphous silicon (a-Si) cells are well understood since they are trimmed-down versions of the traditional silicon wafer cells. They are best for smaller applications and less than ideal for larger-scale applications, due to the significant degradation in their power output when exposed to the sun. The newest generation of thin-film solar cells uses thin layers of either cadmium telluride (CdTe), copper indium selenide (CIS), or copper indium gallium di-selenide (CIGS) instead of silicon that is used in traditional solar cells.

Wafer-based crystalline silicone technology and thin film technology could be compared from a variety of angles. For example, traditional crystalline silicon-based solar panels require a complex and time-consuming manufacturing process that drives up their per-watt cost. On the other hand, nonsilicon thin-film solar cells are much easier to manufacture and therefore less costly.

As discussed earlier, c-Si cells enjoy high efficiency, high stability, and high reliability. Other benefits include lower installation cost and high resistance to heat. The c-Si panels also withstand the severe conditions associated with space travel. Longevity is another plus and when it comes to recycling, silicon seems to be more environmentally friendly. On the downside, c-Si cells have higher initial costs, and they are considered to be more expensive than other solar components. Moreover, c-Si modules are very fragile and need a firm mounting structure. They also have a lower absorption coefficient. On the other hand, thin-film cells are more flexible and easier to handle since they are available in thin wafer sheets. Thin-film cells are less expensive but with lower efficiency, which can offset the price advantage. Thin-film technologies may not be considered for larger applications since they have more complex structure and require more space and unique installation skills.

Researchers in the solar PV industry tend to look for ways to improve the efficiency and the cost effectiveness of solar PV cells. Concentrating PVs, which are mostly used in larger utility-grade applications, organic solar cells, and advanced inorganic thin films are some of the emerging and novel solar PV technologies that are under investigation with a potential for higher efficiency and lower cost than c-Si and thin films.

- Solar PV module performance measurements: The performance of a solar PV module is measured with peak watt ratings (Wp or kWp). A set of laboratory tests called standard test conditions (STCs) create uniform test conditions that make it possible to conduct uniform comparisons of PV modules by different manufacturers. These conditions define the performance at an incident sunlight of 1000 W/m^2, a cell temperature of 25°C (77°F), and an air mass (atmospheric density) of 1.5 kg/m^3. However, STC conditions are not typical in the real world. When operating in the field, solar PV modules typically operate at higher temperatures and at somewhat lower insulation conditions. In order to determine the power output of the solar cell, it is important to determine the expected operating temperature of the PV module. Therefore, a different procedure, called normal operating cell temperature (NOCT), has been adopted. NOCT incorporates more reality into the conditions by assuming 800 W/m^2 of sunlight irradiance, an average of 20°C (68°F) air temperature, and an average wind velocity of 1 m/s, with the back side of the solar panel fully open. The results of the STC and NOCT could be obtained from the technical specification sheet for each type of solar PV modules or from the manufacturers. This information is then used in solar PV system sizing calculations.

- Solar PV module degradation: The performance of a solar PV module decreases over time. The manufacturing processes, the quality of the materials used, even the assembling and the packaging of a module can impact the rate of this degradation. Climate and environmental effects are another factor. A regular maintenance and cleaning plan may result in a lower rate of degradation. However, the rate of degradation is mainly a function of the PV module's characteristics.

- Modules cost and efficiency: Assuming that maximizing the solar electricity generation for the lowest cost is a priority, then it would be best to consider the cost effectiveness of a solar module regardless of its technology and by scrutinizing its cost per rated output. However, the less expensive modules are often less efficient too and require larger areas to produce the same nominal power. Although some solar PV panels may be more expensive, it may also be more easily installed and thus less expensive overall. Generally speaking, solar PV panels may be the most expensive components of a solar PV system, but the costs of other components, installation, upgrades to existing power distribution network, cost of applicable permits, and cost of the maintenance and repairs should also be considered when estimating the overall cost of a solar PV project. Eventually, a life cycle cost analysis for the solar PV system—as a whole—would be required to determine the project payback and the return on investment.

- Certifications: There are internationally accepted standards for solar PV modules that are issued by the IEC. Additionally, there may be other standards accepted in a region. For instance, in the United States, Underwriters Laboratories Inc. issues the product safety testing certification. Underwriters Laboratories Inc. is a nationally recognized testing laboratory, and certification by a nationally recognized testing laboratory for solar PV modules is mandatory in the United States. In Canada, all solar PV modules must conform to Canadian Standards Association's (CSA) relevant standards. Similar standards regulate issues related to health, safety, and environmental requirements of such products in the European Union.

- Mounting systems: As mentioned earlier in this chapter, the mounting of solar modules on a structure is a must in order to provide the panels with the protection and the structural support they need. These systems are usually designed according to site specifications such as location, solar irradiance, available space, and cost. Depending on the application, the location, and the size of a project, these systems may be designed by a structural engineer whose designs will be used by a racking company to create the racking structure for the modules. The structural engineer would also need to consult the racking manufacturers for loading issues depending on each application and their specific needs.
- Sizing of a solar PV system: In general, solar PV modules are connected together and form arrays to meet various energy needs. The solar arrays are then connected to a power conversion system (PCS) that converts the DC generated by the solar PV arrays into AC. As previously described, there are two main applications for interconnecting DG systems. They are either grid-connected (grid-tied) systems or off-grid/islanded (stand-alone) systems. Both could also include battery energy storage backup systems. Applications that could function while connected to the grid, as well as detached from it, are called grid-interactive systems. A solar PV system should be sized and designed in such a way that meets the specific requirements of each application. For instance, in off-grid applications, in order to meet the load demands during lower solar availability, the solar PV arrays (and associated battery banks) must be carefully sized. In grid-connected applications, the existence of a bulk utility power eliminates the need to closely match the system size with the year-round electrical loads. However, there are other considerations that must be taken into account when designing a grid-tied application.

   In summary, the sizing of grid-connected PV systems can be approached in a number of ways depending on the project requirements. For instance, for an urban residential solar PV system, the objective may be offsetting the household's annual electricity consumption, reducing the family's carbon footprint by using alternative and renewable energy sources, or reshingling a south-facing roof with solar PV roofing tiles, as well as taking advantage of available unshaded roof area.

• Estimate the usage: It is always beneficial to determine the amount of energy a site (i.e., a residential, a commercial, an industrial, or an institutional building) consumes over a year. Then depending on the application (grid-tied or isolated from the grid) and what fraction of energy consumption is desired to be offset with a solar PV system, the usage can be determined. There are a number of ways that the usage can be estimated or calculated. One is to conduct a load study. For example, for a residential application, this load study could be completing a simple electric load work sheet. This can be used to list all the appliances and their power consumptions and calculate how much power they use each day. Additionally, the energy consumed by each household load—i.e., kitchen appliances—can also be measured using metering devices (watt-hour meters). These devices measure the energy used by loads plugged directly into them, as opposed to in-home energy use displays, which display the aggregate energy used by an entire household.

 For more complex projects such as large commercial or industrial applications, more comprehensive studies and measurements are required.

• Production modeling: The information collected from various stages of a project is used to estimate the energy production for a solar PV system. Production modeling helps designers compare the performance and the cost of different layouts and equipment. It is done to verify that a solar PV system is able to generate the power that is estimated and the financial returns and to help justify the investment. The modeling may be done by a professional to verify the design work, the commissioning, and the operation of the system. The PV potential (kWh/kW) is a simple estimate of how much AC electricity (in kilowatt-hours) on average a solar PV system is expected to generate over its lifetime. This only applies to typical grid-connected solar PV systems without battery storage and is calculated for per unit of PV system rated DC power (in kilowatts) at STCs.

For example, if the annual PV potential at a given location is 1000 kWh/kW, this indicates that for a system with a rated STC power of 4 kW, the annual electricity production should be approximately 1000 kWh/kW × 4 kW = 4000 kWh. There are a number of tools that may be used to assist with such calculations. For example, to evaluate the PV generation potential across Canada, Natural Resources Canada has developed a tool, called the *photovoltaic potential and solar resource maps of Canada*, which can help professionals estimate the solar PV electricity production for over 3500 Canadian municipalities and illustrate monthly and annual electricity generations per kilowatts of an installed solar PV system.

• Incentives: Government and utility incentives may exist for various applications. This should also be considered when exploring the pros and the cons of a solar PV system.

As pointed out previously, solar panels are one of the main components of a solar PV system. But how a specific technology is selected also depends on other factors as well. For instance the amount of energy that is needed, the site location and available space, the climate, whether the system is connected to the utility grid in an urban area or isolated (i.e., a remote island) or for a mobile site (i.e., military applications), the cost, and other project-specific requirements. The next sections describe some considerations required to be taken into account when designing a solar PV system.

• Design and construction: As discussed earlier in this chapter, the design stage of a project may include the selection of solar PV modules, the preparation and the submission of permit applications, the selection and ranking of contractors, the finalization of tender documents, etc. Some of these activities, such as obtaining permits and approvals from various authorities, may take a considerable amount of time and should be started earlier in a project timeline.

  • Designing a solar PV system: Assuming the successful completion of the preceding tasks, the design stages of a solar PV system starts with the corroboration of known constraints. For instance, the solar PV modules—in a fixed-tilt angle—have to be placed on a south-facing structure, with a tilt from the horizontal axis, roughly equal to the local latitude. A solar PV system may be required to either assist, offset, or completely eliminate the need for utility-supplied power. In that case, to determine the size of the system, certain parameters need to be considered, e.g., the energy consumption per day in kilowatt-hours averaged over 1 year, the number of peak sun hours per day, the ratio of STC power to real power, the efficiency of the inverter, the system losses, and the losses due to solar PV panel degradation. In a well-designed system, the overall system losses vary between 8% and 2%. Along with solar PV system sizing, the module layout needs to be specified. Certain layouts may allow for a more efficient use of space. Other considerations may include snow clearing, presence of other components, such as heating, ventilating, and air conditioning units, on a roof, and compliance with fire safety codes and ease of installation.

- BOS selection and considerations: BOS normally refers to the other components of a solar PV system other than the solar PV panels. Along with the sizing of the solar PV array, the size of the required electrical components, such as power conditioning systems, inverters, conductors, disconnect means, and circuit breakers, will have to be determined to maximize the performance of the system. Other considerations may include space requirements, expansion of the system in the future, and use of harsh weather-rated components.

- Inverter: Where required, the DC power generated by a solar PV plant is controverted into AC. This is done by a solid-state electronic device called an inverter. The AC power from the inverter is then suitable for interconnecting with the utility grid or servicing local AC loads. Some inverters use techniques such as maximum power point tracking that enables them to maximize the power output of a solar PV plant. No single inverter suits all applications. For instance, inverters in a grid-tied mode include the anti-islanding mechanism and must automatically shut down and disconnect from the utility grid in case of loss of grid power or when it deviates from the spec. These types of inverters periodically test the grid, and if conditions were restored in compliance with the spec for an uninterrupted period, then the equipment would resynchronize and connect back to the grid. A number of standards exist to ensure a higher level of safety and quality of performance of inverters. In terms of conforming to the standards, these requirements depend on the location of the project and the specific type of inverter used in a project. In Europe, inverters must be Conformité Européene compliant, whereas in the United States all grid-tied systems that use inverters and charge controllers must pass the UL 1741 test standards and have the applicable labels. In Canada, these inverters must conform and be certified to CSA 22.2 No. 107.1 standard.

- Project permits and approvals: As mentioned, solar PV installations have to be compliant with a wide variety of national, provincial, and municipal codes and standards. Such standards cover a wide range of parameters including safety, security, and environmental concerns.

- Power quality/grid code compliance: As mentioned, grid-connected PV systems are connected to the utility company at the PCC or the point of delivery. To ensure safe interactions between customer-owned assets and utility-owned cogeneration assets, interconnection codes need to be adhered to. Whether a distributed generator intends to sell the power back to the utility, synchronize with the utility, or temporarily transfer load to/from a standby generation to/from a utility, there are specific requirements that need to be met.

The power quality and grid code requirements vary depending on the location and the country. As such, it would be difficult to provide universal guidelines that could govern such interactions. In Canada, utilities assist in determining the most appropriate interconnection process, depending on the site location and the proposed power output of the generator. Each utility conducts their own set of investigation and review to ensure that the proposed customer-owned generator is able to be connected to the utility network and to assess its impact on their systems and assets.

The utility's interconnection review is a detailed evaluation of the impact of a proposed project on the reliability of the utility grid. The impact review may include the estimated cost for equipment, engineering, procurement, and construction work that may be required to support the IPP's assets.

Upon the successful completion of the review process, an interconnection agreement may be concluded between the utility and the IPP, which identifies each party's roles and responsibilities. For instance, the IPP may be required to install code-compliant equipment (e.g., electrical, safety, building), while the utility agrees to purchase the electricity from the IPP at predefined rates.

- National and local electrical codes: The designers for solar PV projects should familiarize themselves with electrical codes. All line diagrams must be created in accordance with standards as specified in national and local electrical codes. All calculations, such as evaluation of open circuit voltages, short circuit analysis, and the like, should also be conducted in full compliance with all nationally, provisionally, and municipally imposed codes and standards.
- Installation of solar PV systems: Solar PV modules should be installed by qualified installers with adequate solar installation experience, in full compliance with the applicable codes. Given the tight tolerances of such modules, and their sensitivity to improper storage, transportation, unpacking and installation, significant personal injury and equipment damage could result from inadequate care and mishandling.

4.1.3 System Testing and Commissioning

The objective of the site-acceptance testing (SAT) process is to review, verify, and document that the project design and the construction meet project requirements and to develop a set of baseline test results for comparison in future testing to identify equipment degradation. Commissioning activities ensure a fully functional system that is installed to applicable codes and to acceptable industry practices and standards. It verifies that the system has been proven to meet all the design criteria, functional specifications, and operational requirements and consistently operates at acceptable efficiencies and with the intended performance under expected conditions.

4.1.4 Inspection and Maintenance Plan

In general, solar PV plants have low maintenance and servicing requirements. However, a suitable maintenance plan is essential to optimize the energy production and maximize the life of the system. Inspection and maintenance plans should be designed considering all equipment installed to form a solar PV system.

Some of the abovementioned concepts could be further elaborated within the context of a case study. Here, we will review BCIT's Energy OASIS project as the underlying application for what has been discussed so far.

4.1.5 Case Study: BCIT's Energy OASIS Project

Energy OASIS is a grid-interactive system, consisting of a number of subsystems: a 250 kW solar PV parking canopy system, a 500 kWh battery energy storage system (BESS), BOS equipment—including a 280 kW inverter—and loads. The purpose of the OASIS solar PV system is to locally generate power, provide energy to the BESS and/ or the BCIT internal power distribution network, and also support microgrid loads. This section describes the steps taken in various stages for the design, the installation, and the commissioning of OASIS solar PV system.

- OASIS feasibility study: Real estate and weight was a concern (which often is with solar panels). Concerns with the weight of the installations disqualified the initial choice of rooftop areas of most BCIT buildings, which (due to their age) could not accommodate such additional weights without significant investments in structural reinforcements. The choice was then focused on the real estate available on the campus in terms of walkways and parking lots. Nevertheless, since the real estate across the campus was mostly at a premium, and given their surface area requirement, monocrystalline panels appeared to be the best option to use. Further studies showed that c-Si were the most suitable technology to employ in the prevalent environment and the geographical conditions of the lower mainland of British Columbia.

Furthermore, given the shading concerns with tall buildings and vegetation around most of the parking spaces on the campus, the largest parking lot with relatively fewer buildings and vegetation was chosen as the site of the parking canopy installation.

Moreover, the lifespan of a c-Si cell is claimed to be about 25 years, making them a long-term investment. However, these panels were extremely fragile. It meant that a rigid mounting system was needed; as such, several design options for the superstructure were investigated[5,6]: (1) pre-engineered carport-style installations, (2) free standing, column-supported installations on individual footings, and (3) moment-frame installations oriented either north-south, east-west, or with a horizontal slope. A geotechnical assessment for the proposed location was carried out. The information resulting from this assessment was later used in the detailed design of the superstructure for the solar canopies. The solar PV site had to be located in close proximity to the electrical distribution substation, the PCS, and the battery storage system to reduce voltage drops and costs of installation. The superstructure system included a five-year service life.

- Initial planning: The PV array subsystem was initially planned to be a 290 kW DC system. The preliminary design included 968 solar PV modules to achieve a 290 kW DC power-generation capacity. Further reviews were conducted to finalize the design of this system. Several initial layouts for the PV subsystem were designed, among them solar canopies, solar trees, etc. Initial cost estimates showed that, given the geographical location of the installation, parking canopies were the most cost-effective option.
- Detailed design and specifications: As mentioned, carport structures were chosen as the most cost-effective option for this project. The design of such structures had to incorporate rainwater and runoff collection, as well as bird dropping

control. The carport system was chosen to be modular in structure and customizable to fit the target parking areas. The configurations of the module arrangement were optimized for the spatial cut out of the parking area, as well as for the local boundary conditions (such as ground conditions, wind loads, and snow loads). This enabled the design to achieve the project's cost target, while complying with all applicable structural requirements. Moreover, the choice for the foundation design was determined to be cast in place. The design calculations were provided by the technology providers. Sizing dimensions were met in every case in order to guarantee the structural safety of the carport. The reinforcement plans were also created according to structural regulations.

- Solar PV modules: The final design has 814 × 305 W modules, grouped in strings of 11, capable of generating approximately 250 kW DC. All other electrical components of the system were carefully selected and designed for this application. The PCS included bidirectional DC/DC converters—for the purpose of charging and discharging the BESS—a solar DC/DC converter, four-quadrant bidirectional grid-tied inverter, and all the required protection and control. There was also a large amount of electrical work such as trenching and cabling between the solar PV parking canopies and the PCS for data and power cabling and routing.

- Solar PV modules specification: Energy OASIS solar PV modules are designed and certified to be universally compliant with North American PV standards, as well as CSA standards. The monocrystalline silicon modules selected for this project have a linear output power of 305 W for 25 years. The degradation is expected to be less than 3% of their maximum power in first year. Less than 0.7% of the P_{max} per year degradation in subsequent years is expected. Their operating temperature is from –20°C to +45°C. Moreover, the PV modules consist of aluminum-framed glass/foil laminates with interconnected crystalline silicon solar cells, a junction box, and double-insulated wires terminated in touch safe specific PV DC connectors.

- Installation process: The mounting system for an OASIS solar PV system is a steel frame structure on a series of concrete (cast-in-place) foundations. The cast-in-place foundation is essentially made up of the base plate and the base pedestal. The base plate is laid below the frost line as per the supplier's mounting instructions. The base pedestal also serves as impact protection. The cast-in-place foundations were laid by BCIT and the consultant company. The dimension and the position of the anchors for the carports were provided by the supplier. The anchors were then thoroughly encased in concrete. Eventually, 814 of these solar PV modules were installed and structured as two solar PV canopies in one of BCIT Burnaby campus' parking areas. These two parking canopies, shown in Figure 4.2, cover approximately 120 car stalls in an area of 1664 m².

- SAT and system commissioning: Key functional tests were witnessed by either the electrical engineer of record, the consulting engineers, or the BCIT personnel. A test report was delivered to BCIT after the completion of the on-site tests. The purpose of the SAT for the solar PV system was to provide a guide for the commissioning of the system, up to the PCS, and to provide the format for tracking and recording results. The materials and the information resulting from the SAT process were also

Figure 4.2   Energy OASIS solar parking canopies.

included. A commissioning plan was specifically developed for the Energy OASIS PV array. The processes and the procedures outlined in the SAT document had been tailored to meet the scope of this project as it pertained to the solar PV array.

- Project approvals: The approvals and the permits secured by the OASIS project included—but were limited to—the city of Burnaby for the electrical installation and operation as well as the structural approval for the solar canopies. An agreement was also reached between BCIT and BC Hydro for the interconnection of the system to BC Hydro's distribution network, which stipulated OASIS to be responsible for the design and installation, the maintaining operation, and the maintenance of all equipment, station, and distribution line facilities from the PCC to the OASIS' generation facility. The OASIS also obtained all regulatory approvals, including environmental assessment approvals for the construction and operation of its facilities. OASIS submitted all specifications of its facilities and detailed plans to BC Hydro for review prior to receiving the permission to connect to BC Hydro.

  - Interconnection with utility: BC Hydro is the third largest electric utility in Canada, which serves customers in an area containing over 94% of British Columbia's population. As mentioned, being a grid-interactive system, OASIS is capable of operating in parallel with, as well as completely isolated from, BC Hydro. The interconnection of such a system with the utility is covered under BC Hydro's load displacement program and was required to meet the technical requirements of "35 KV and below Interconnections requirements for Power Generators."[7] These requirements aim to ensure safe isolation for maintenance, islanding, grid-tied operation, protection, fail safe, transient stability, and harmonics propagation. These requirements and the tests/analysis conducted to prove full compliance with these requirements were subsequently captured in an interconnection agreement document concluded by relevant stakeholders. This section provides an overview of the OASIS project, using a highly simplified single line diagram of the whole system as shown in Figure 4.3.[8]

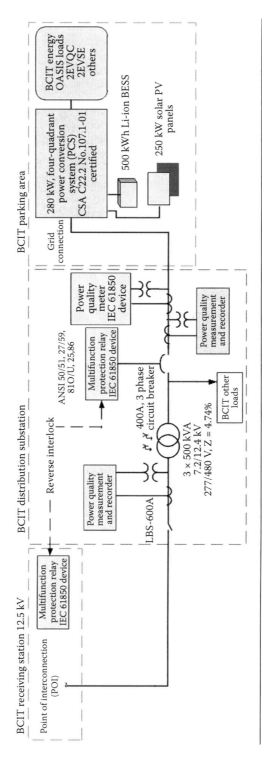

Figure 4.3   OASIS single-line diagram (SLD). (Courtesy of CIGRE 2014, Toronto, Ontario, Canada.)

As illustrated in Figure 4.3, Energy OASIS is connected to the BC Hydro system through a three-phase, four-quadrant, bidirectional inverter. The system is connected to one of BCIT's existing substations, which in turn is connected to the BC Hydro network. The PCC is one of BCIT's existing receiving stations. It is located on the campus and connects to a 12.5 kV BC Hydro overhead line. In order to meet BC Hydro's "35 KV and below Interconnections requirements for Power Generators," OASIS installed a grid-connected inverter compliant with CSA 22.2 No. 107.1 standard. The automatic synchronization to the grid is done by inverter control and protection system. Additionally, the secondary anti-islanding protection is also provided by this inverter. Moreover, OASIS upgraded one of BCIT's existing substations and installed a controllable breaker on its feeder. The operation of this breaker is controlled by a multifunctional protection relay, featuring up to 20 flexible protection functions. OASIS' passive islanding protection is provided by the power quality elements (over/under voltage and under/over frequency) within this multifunction protection relay. OASIS also designed and put in place a reverse interlock system with the feeder protection relay in the PCC. This system comprises both hardwired copper and IEC-61850 network generic object oriented substation event (GOOSE) messaging communication medium.

- Project completion: The final sign-off process of OASIS verified that OASIS' power generation facility was designed, constructed, and tested in accordance with the requirements stated in BC Hydro's requirements, in terms of being safe for BC Hydro employees and agents, for BC Hydro customers, and for the general public, at all times. OASIS met BC Hydro's operating, revenue metering, and protection requirements and was consistent with the required regulatory agencies and authorities' codes and standards, such as the British Columbia Utilities Commission and the Western Electricity Coordinating Council.
- Inspection and maintenance plan: Regular cleaning is recommended for the solar PV modules for the Energy OASIS project. The inspection of the BOS is also included in BCIT's overall annual electrical maintenance and service plan.

- Demonstration and knowledge dissemination: Since its inception, OASIS has been the focus of numerous demonstration and knowledge-transfer activities for various national and international research and educational institutes and universities. Several papers, educational materials, and professional practice seminars have been developed to address more advanced solar PV system designs. The system is an excellent case study for solar PV installations in British Columbia and can be used to support academic and professional courses, as well as a tool for public awareness and education of renewable energy technologies and their applications.

4.2 Wind Installations

Ancient civilizations have tapped the power of wind energy for a variety of different purposes, from powering their sailing vessels to grinding grains and pumping water for irrigation. Today, generating electricity from wind is one of the fastest growing methods of energy generation in the world. Wind turbines convert kinetic energy from moving air into electricity. The electricity so generated can be used, stored, or fed into the electricity grid. By the end of 2012, there were more than 225,000 wind turbines operating around the world in about 80 countries. Predictions indicate that the share of wind energy in total U.S. electricity generation may grow from 6% today to 20% by 2030.[9] Similar publicly available data indicate that as of December 31, 2014, Canada had over 5130 wind turbines operating on 225 wind farms for a total installed capacity of 9694 MW, compared with only 60 wind turbines, 8 wind farms and 27 MW in 1998.[10] The year 2015 was another remarkable year for wind energy in Canada. The country finished 2015 with over 11,000 MW of total installed capacity.

This section begins with a review of wind power technologies and applications. It explores the technical considerations involved in the selection and the integration of wind systems. Then a case study will be described: the vertical axis wind turbine at BCIT. The requirements and the specifications of that system will be reviewed. This includes the objectives, the design requirements, and the equipment selection considerations.

4.2.1 Technology Fundamentals

A typical wind turbine consists of blades, nacelle (generator and gear-box), tower, and base. The spinning blades are attached to the generator through a series of gears. Depending on the type of the generator, the electricity may be produced at a varying frequency, which must be corrected to 60 cycles/s before it could be used. The tower supports the structure of the turbine and may be made from tubular steel, concrete, or steel lattice. Depending on the type and the size of a turbine, the foundation or the base may be made of concrete reinforced with steel bars. A turbine may also include an anemometer, a brake, a controller, low- and high-speed shafts, a pitch system, a rotor, a wind vane, a yaw motor, and a drive.[11,12]

- Scale of wind power: Wind turbines are classified by their size or capacity, in other words by the amount of electricity they can produce: small turbines at less than 100 kW, medium turbines between 100 and 500 kW, large turbines from 500 kW to 5 MW. Small wind turbines could be used in both grid-connected and off-grid applications. However, they are usually used for homes, farms, and remote sites, where grid electricity is not available. Medium wind turbines are often used for microgrids or in hybrid systems together with diesel generators for remote community electrification. Large wind turbines are employed by utility companies or IPPs, to generate bulk energy at utility transmission level.[11]
- Types of wind turbines: The blades of a wind turbine are installed perpendicularly to the rotating axis and form a certain angle. Wind turbines exist in two basic varieties: horizontal axis wind turbines (HAWTs) and VAWTs. Depending on available wind resources, requiring low-speed or high-speed wind turbine, the number of the blades changes.

4.2.2 Planning a Wind Project

Site suitability, wind speed, tower type and height, and rotor diameter are only a few factors to name when planning a wind project.

- Site qualification: Numerous considerations have to be taken into account when selecting a site for a wind turbine (or a wind farm). The site must be suitable for steady wind flow. Wind consistency is an important consideration for the design of wind power systems. A suitable location is a site with fewer obstructions for wind flow. There are useful tools that could be used to assess the site suitability for wind projects. For example, Environment Canada's Wind Energy Atlas website includes a meteorological tool that could be used to qualify wind sites in Canada. In the United States, the National Renewable Energy Laboratory's Geospatial Data Science Team offers both a national wind resource assessment of the United States and high-resolution wind data. Moreover, the target location should contain no impediment to assembling and erecting wind towers.
- Approvals and permits: To mitigate the concerns associated with the development of wind turbines, including safety, audio noise, and land use, many jurisdictions across North America have developed codes and guidelines. For instance, turbines have to keep a minimum distance from built-up areas, residences, natural features, and infrastructure. Another concern is the interconnection of a wind project with the utility grid. Wind cogeneration systems may operate in parallel with the utility grid (grid-connected). For this purpose, utilities have specific requirements that aim to ensure safe isolation for maintenance, islanding, grid-tied operation, protection, fail safe, transient stability, and harmonics propagation.
- Economics of a wind project: Detailed feasibility studies are required to determine whether the wind resource in a certain area makes a wind system economical. By knowing the kilowatt-hours per year produced by a wind turbine and the local electricity costs per kilowatt-hours, the savings can be calculated. Designers also need to determine the electricity needs for any given site by looking at the monthly or the yearly electricity usage. Additionally, the costs of a turbine, tower, installation, permits and approvals required for this installation, maintenance and repair of the system should be taken into account. There may be other costs associated with specific projects. Many governments and utilities offer

incentive programs for renewables that positively affect the return on investment.
- Power of the wind and measuring electrical production: As discussed, many parameters impact the productivity of a wind turbine, measured as the amount of electricity in kilowatt-hours produced over the course of a year in a specific wind resource. The amount of electricity a wind turbine generates in a year is called annual energy production. The annual energy production is mainly based on the wind power available for a turbine to capture and convert to electricity, determined by the size of the rotors (blades and hub), the speed of wind at a specific height, the air density, and the temperature and turbulences. A simple formula often used to estimate the wind power in an area is

$$w = 1/2 \times \rho \times A \times v^3,$$

where w is the power, ρ is the air density, A is the rotor area, and v is the wind speed.

Another consideration is the efficiency of a wind turbine based on two factors: wind utilization ratio and generator efficiency. Publicly available data reveals that in the wind turbine industry, a ratio of 0.45 is a good number to consider for wind utilization ratio. For generator efficiency, it varies from 75% to 85%.

- Horizontal axis or vertical axis wind turbine: The choice between a HAWT and a VAWT is not often straightforward. Factors such as gear box, blade rotation space, noise, environmental impacts (such as effect on birds), power generation efficiency, power curve, starting wind speed, wind cut-off speed, rotating speed, failure rate, etc. have to be taken into account.

For instance, VAWTs do not require a gear box. This is one less mechanical part that needs to be considered in the inspection and maintenance plan. VAWT starts producing power in lower wind speeds compared to a HAWT. The ratio of the utilization of the wind power of a VAWT is higher than that of a HAWT. The structure of a VAWT is not as complicated as the one for HAWT. On the other hand, the technology of the HAWT is more mature.

4.2.3 Case Study: BCIT's Vertical Axis Wind Turbine

BCIT's smart microgrid includes a 5 kW wind turbine at BCIT's smart demonstration home shown in Figure 4.4.

The purpose of this project was to connect a VAWT to BCIT's net-zero home, to monitor the electrical generation of the wind turbine, and to integrate this generation data into BCIT's EMS. Of particular interest for the researchers were the integration issues of wind energy into BCIT's microgrid at grid-connected and off-grid scenarios.

- Site study: The geotechnical study analyzed the soil composition of the target location to determine its structural stability to accommodate the structure for the VAWT by conducting a subsurface investigation, which was needed to finalize the design and the construction of this new structure.
- Technical specifications: The turbine is designed to self-start with wind speeds of 2.1 m/s. The blades are mounted on a 50 ft custom-designed monopole that can be lowered, using a portable hydraulic power pack, for maintenance or training purposes. The turbine interfaces with a variable power high-frequency inverter developed specifically for the wind power market. The inverter enables wind turbine data to be captured, stored, and published to BCIT's custom-developed

Figure 4.4   BCIT's VAWT.

web-based EMS, providing users with integrated data communications, data collection, and analysis capability.

• Interconnection with the utility grid: Provisions are in place by the local utility company-BC Hydro for distribution-connected customers to connect a small energy source (less than 100 kW) to the utility's distribution system to offset their load and participate in the net metering program. It is not expected that VAWT exports power to the grid because of the size of the turbine (5 kW) and is considered to be a load displacement component only. As such, the technical interconnection requirements for connecting small generators to the distribution system apply. In that regard, the utility requires the inverter for this wind turbine to not only meet the applicable codes but also contain provisions to safely disconnect from the grid, if and when required. Moreover, the applicable anti-islanding code requires the inverter to cease energizing the distribution system within 0.1 s upon loss of the grid supply. This is critical for the safety of the electrical workers and the public. A wind turbine inverter—as a grid-dependent inverter—is designed to only energize when the grid supply is present and cannot operate in stand-alone (islanded) mode. Detailed interconnection requirements between the cogenerators and the grid will be discussed in the next section. Figure 4.5 depicts a highly simplified one-line diagram for this installation.

4.3 Power Conversion System

As discussed before, the battery energy storage and the solar PV mediums are predominantly direct current systems in nature. To interface such systems with the present electric utility grid, the energy must be converted to a standard AC and regulated through a conversion system. This requires a bidirectional conversion from AC to DC and DC to AC, performed by PCS.

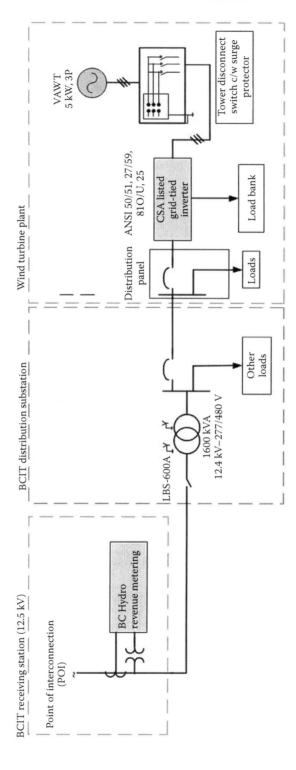

Figure 4.5 SLD for BCIT's VAWT.

4.3.1 Overview of Energy OASIS' Power Conversion System

The BESS and the solar PV subsystems are integrated through a high-efficiency PCS that converts between AC and DC to provide real and reactive power as well as a bidirectional energy flow to the grid and to the BESS.[13] The PCS for the Energy OASIS project consists of DC inputs for battery connections, DC input for solar PV connection, an integrated four-quadrant bidirectional inverter, which in turn provides isolated AC output for loads—through an integral isolation transformer—and a connection to the grid. The integrated bidirectional inverter complies with IEEE 519 and IEEE 1547 requirements including anti-islanding provisions.

The inverter within the PCS supports two modes of operation: grid-tied (operating in parallel with the utility grid) and islanded (stand-alone and isolated from the utility grid). It is also designed to support both the battery energy storage subsystem and the solar PV arrays with integrated maximum power point tracking scheme. This bidirectional inverter is specifically designed for grid-tied BESSs and solar interconnections. The PCS for Energy OASIS, shown in Figure 4.6, manages multiple distributed energy resources on the same distribution network including optimal dispatch and islanding.

4.3.2 Modes of Operations

The bidirectional inverter inside the PCS operates in two distinct modes: grid-tied and stand-alone modes. There are also a number of minor submodes in both grid-connected and stand-alone modes; for instance, PCS is capable of providing power from only batteries or solar PV system or both. In the grid-tied mode, the control is a real power command and a reactive power command, issued by Energy OASIS control system. The inverter can also take analog and digital power command inputs set by the user. In the stand-alone mode of operation, the inverter controls the voltage and the frequency. In the grid-tied mode—after a grid fault (voltage or frequency excursion)—the system will disconnect from the grid and switch over to the islanded mode, keeping the microgrid load powered with minimal transfer transient. Upon grid voltage restoration, the inverter synchronizes its output to match the grid voltage and the frequency prior to

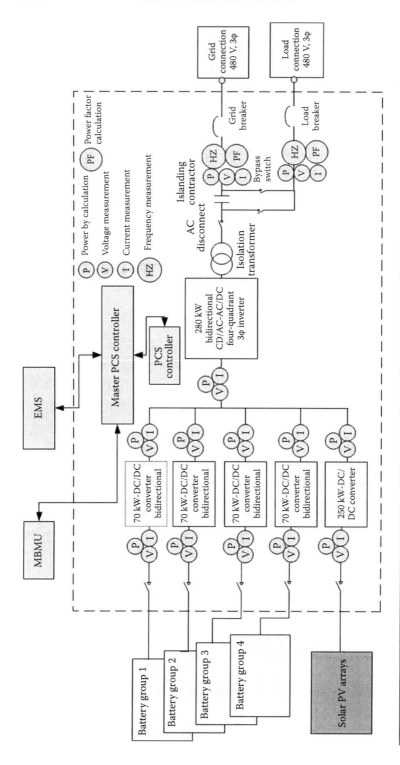

Figure 4.6   SLD for PCS. MBMU, master battery management unit.

transferring back to the grid. The inverter within the PCS can also transfer between grid and stand-alone operations as commanded at any time during the operation (intentional islanding). The control circuit uses advanced digital signal processing to operate, monitor, and protect the PCS.

4.3.3 System Operational Features

In the grid-connected mode, the inverter attempts to supply continuous power at rates up to 110% and down to 88% of the nominal line voltage. The system automatically synchronizes to the AC line. The conditions of line faults in the grid-connected mode are overvoltage, undervoltage, underfrequency, and overfrequency.

If any of these conditions occur beyond the allowed time, the unit is automatically disconnected from the line, and it enters into stand-alone operation. In the stand-alone mode, the inverter operates as an AC voltage-controlled voltage-source unit. The inverter adjusts the voltage and the frequency to the microgrid load per the set voltage and frequency adjustment command. The default output follows nominal system rating—i.e., 480 VAC at 60 Hz for Energy OASIS system. The set voltage and frequency adjustments would be applied on top of this. Voltage and frequency accuracies are within ±1% of rated. The conditions of line faults in the islanded/stand-alone mode are overvoltage, undervoltage, underfrequency, and overfrequency.

4.4 Applicable Standards

In Canada, all electrical and gas-powered products must be certified for their intended use. These products shall meet the safety and performance requirements of the codes and standards that they are certified to. This allows for consistency in manufacturing and installation practices.

With a growing number of DGs in smaller scales, such as residential and commercial solar PV systems, wind turbines, microhydrogenerators, fuel cell technologies, and combined heat and power units, there is a need for national guidelines and policies for connecting these systems to a public electricity grid. Chapter 8 summarizes the safety and power quality standards and related codes that Canadian provinces and territories have already employed, along with those in the international community that can serve as reference for Canada.

Similarly, most jurisdictions across the world have their own set of codes and standards that apply to a complete DG system. Requirements exist for equipment, protection, power quality, commissioning, testing, and operation and maintenance of DG systems that are connected to utility grids.

Nevertheless, and given the fact that protection, power quality, and grid code, equipment selection, testing and commissioning, operating and maintenance requirements vary depending on the location/country, it is not possible to provide guidelines that are universally applicable.

As discussed, DG systems are designed as either grid-connected or isolated from the grid. Grid-connected systems are connected to the utility company at the PCC or the point of delivery. A majority of the utilities offer interconnection services to connect IPP to their distribution network. There are specific requirements for DGs, which intend to sell power back to a utility, synchronize to the grid, or temporarily transfer load to/from a standby generation to/from a utility.

In Canada, utilities assist in determining the most appropriate interconnection process, depending on the site location and the proposed output power of the generator. Interconnection requests are reviewed by the utility to ensure that the proposed generator is safe to be interconnected with their network and to also assess the impact of the proposed generator on the utility's systems and facilities. This process would also enable DG owners to gain a better understanding of the risks and costs involved in interconnecting such a system with the larger grid.

Once all studies are completed, an interconnection agreement will be negotiated by both the utility and the DG plant. The agreement determines the rules and responsibilities of each party as well as the applicable standards and provisions that need to be in place in order for the DG power plant and the main grid to be safely interconnected. Details of the interconnection review process will be discussed in Chapter 8.

References

1. International Finance Corporation (IFC) (2015) *Utility-Scale Solar Power Plants*. Available at http://www.ifc.org/wps/wcm/connect/f05d3e 00498e0841bb6fbbe54d141794/IFC+Solar+Report_Web+_08+05 .pdf?MOD=AJPERES.
2. Natural Resources Canada (2016, March 7) *Photovoltaic Potential and Solar Resource Maps of Canada*. Available at http://pv.nrcan.gc.ca/.
3. Office of Energy Efficiency and Renewable Energy (EERE) (n.d.) Power Electronics Design, *Photovoltaic System Performance Basics*. Available at http://energy.gov/eere/energybasics/energy-basics. Penton, New York.
4. Electronic Design Library (2013) *Focus on: Alternative Energy*. Available at http://powerelectronics.com/site-files/powerelectronics.com/files/uploads /2013/08/AlternativeEnergy.pdf.
5. Read Jones Christoffersen Ltd (2012, November) *BCIT SMART Grid Lot 7 Solar Installation Feasibility Study*, RJC. Doc. No.: VAN.107081.0001, Read Jones Christoffersen Ltd, Vancouver.
6. Panasonic Eco Solutions Canada Inc. (PESCA) (2014, July) *Section 5E As built drawings: PV System as a Whole*. Technical Information document, PESCA, Mississauga, ON.
7. BC Hydro (2010, May) 35 KV and below interconnections requirements for power generators. Technical Documentation.
8. Minoo Shariat-Zadeh, Ali Palizban, Hassan Farhangi, and Calin Surdu (2014) *Analysis and Validation of Interconnection Requirements of a Large Renewable Energy Installation with the Utility Grid*. CIGRE, Bologna.
9. Global Wind Energy Council (2015) *Global Statistic*, p. 8. Available at http://www.gwec.net/global-figures/graphs/.
10. Natural Resources Canada (n.d.) *About Renewable Energy*. Available at http://www.nrcan.gc.ca/energy/renewable-electricity/7295#wind.
11. Canadian Wind Energy Association. *Small Wind Turbine Purchasing Guide*. Available at http://www.ontario-sea.org/Storage/39/3065_Small _Wind_Turbine_Purchasing_Guide_-_Off-grid,_Residential,_Farm _&_Small_Business_Applications.pdf. Canadian Wind Energy Association, Ottawa, ON.
12. Office of Energy Efficiency and Renewable Energy (n.d.) *Wind*. Available at http://energy.gov/eere/renewables/wind.
13. Dynapower Company. (2012) *280 kW/kVA Compact Power Conversion Inverter: 5-in-1*. System Specification Document: Rev. 05; 280 kW/ kVA Power Conversion Inverter, System Operation and Maintenance. PESCA, Mississauga, ON.

5

ELECTRICAL STORAGE SYSTEM

ERIC HAWTHORNE

Contents

This chapter explores the role of an electrical energy storage system (ESS) in a microgrid and the technical issues in the selection and integration of storage technology. The chapter begins with a brief overview of use cases for energy storage in a microgrid; how storage can be used when the microgrid is operating off-grid (islanded), and how it can be used when the microgrid is operating connected and in parallel with the larger power grid.

Next, broader technological requirements and trade-offs for energy storage will be discussed, by way of exploring several storage technology options. Then a case study will be described: the battery energy storage system (BESS) of the Energy Open Access to Sustainable Intermittent Sources (OASIS) microgrid at BCIT. The requirements and specifications of that system will be reviewed, including physical and safety considerations and electrical specifications. Microgrid storage control design and controls and monitoring integration will be discussed. The chapter will conclude with some lessons learned during the design, integration, and testing of the OASIS microgrid BESS.

A microgrid that incorporates intermittent renewable sources of generation, such as PV and wind, requires an energy storage system (ESS), to perform several interrelated functions in the microgrid power system.

- ESS when the microgrid is islanded (off-grid)
    - *Load matching (generation leveling and time-shifting):* Over the course of a day or several days, the ESS is used to time-shift the energy generated by intermittent renewables so that power is available to microgrid loads when the loads demand the power. For example, demand may peak in the morning and afternoon, while PV generation peaks at noon and wind generation peaks in the middle of the night. The ESS should be controlled to have storage capacity headroom at the right time so that it can be charged to full state of charge (SOC) with the excess PV or wind power.

Then the discharge of the ESS may match the evening and early morning peak demand. Consider a remote community off-grid microgrid seeking to minimize use of fossil fuel backup generator power. Leveling and time-shifting of local renewable generation is the key, since without it, renewable energy will often be wasted due to low demand, and polluting and costly backup generators will be needed for more energy and longer periods when demand exceeds renewable generation.

- *Optimally operating diesel generation alongside renewables:* If an off-grid microgrid has intermittent renewable generation such as solar PV but must rely on diesel generators when renewable generation is insufficient, then the renewable generation must be controlled whenever it is generating in parallel with the diesel generator(s). It is inefficient and damaging to operate diesel generators at low power compared with their rated electrical power output, and it is inefficient and damaging to start and stop them frequently. An ESS can be charge/discharge controlled so that it acts as a buffer to accept power from varying renewable generation while the generators are running so that the generators see a stable load that is in their high-power operating range.

- *Voltage and frequency control:* If a microgrid is islanded (off-grid) and is currently running a throttleable generator, then the generator has a controller that matches generator alternating current (AC) power output to varying load (net of varying renewable generation). The generator's controller monitors and counteracts frequency or voltage swings in the microgrid by varying fuel supply to the generator. But a key goal of a renewable-heavy microgrid is to reduce or eliminate the operating time of fossil fuel generators. When the controllable generator is not operating, then the ESS must be used as the source of power to rapidly match load increases or renewable generation drops and avoid voltage drop or, conversely, as the sink of power to rapidly match intermittent renewable generation increases or load cutoffs and avoid overvoltage conditions in the microgrid. Furthermore, any DC/AC inverter operating without an external frequency reference in the off-grid microgrid must be able to rely on the ESS as a flexible power source to support AC frequency/phase control.

- ESS when the microgrid is grid connected
  - *Optimizing power flow to and from the larger grid:* When a microgrid is operating parallel to (connected to) the larger power distribution grid, the ESS can be used to have the microgrid send power to the larger grid, or draw power from the larger grid, at times controlled by the microgrid energy management system (MEMS). The MEMS, using the ESS as its controllable energy reservoir, can send power from the microgrid to the grid whenever the price that the grid would pay for power is highest. Or if the price paid for generated power from a distributed energy resource (DER) (such as the renewable microgrid) is fixed but the grid operator has time-of-use tariffs or dynamic energy pricing, the MEMS can use the ESS to avoid drawing power from the larger grid into the microgrid when grid power is expensive. If neither of these pricing methods is applicable, there may still be demand charges for high rates of power consumption from the larger grid, and the MEMS, controlling the charging and discharging times of the microgrid ESS, can avoid demand charges by leveling the microgrid's consumption of power from the larger grid over the course of each day.

    In the case of BCIT's Energy OASIS microgrid, the microgrid as a whole acts as a dispatchable DER within the larger BCIT campus distribution grid, which is then connected to the utility grid. The microgrid can act at times, when it has surplus energy, as a load-displacement local generation source for the campus. In such a case, the MEMS can schedule microgrid ESS charging and discharging so that the microgrid performs demand peak shaving in the BCIT distribution grid, potentially reducing demand-charge costs for the institution and making the large-scale electricity customer a better citizen, with more level demand, on the larger grid.

In a broader and longer-term context, many smart microgrids connected to a larger smart grid could each use their local ESS to schedule their demand for power from the larger grid, and their contribution of DER power to the larger grid, in a manner influenced by price signals (or frequency variation, demand forecasts, or explicit power requests) from the larger smart grid. By doing so, a robust decentralized grid stabilization system could be created.

5.1 Technology Fundamentals

Energy storage technology is diverse and rapidly evolving, as large-scale penetration of intermittent renewable generation seems increasingly inevitable and as electrification of transport gains momentum. There are many criteria on which to evaluate storage technology. Some storage technologies may be more suited to large macrogrid-scale application. Some are highly site characteristic specific, with limited opportunities for general application in an arbitrarily located microgrid. Some technologies remain in the experimental phase and are not efficient or reliable or have enough cost reduction for routine application yet. A few technologies stand out as the conservative available choice for a microgrid at present, but there are important performance envelope distinctions between subvarieties of the leading candidate technologies.

This section will review a range of energy storage technologies, comparing and contrasting technical and economic aspects of the presently more realistic choices, then briefly mentioning a range of innovative storage technology alternatives and those more suited for larger grid-scale applications. The realistic energy storage choices will be compared in terms of attributes such as specific energy and energy density, specific power and power density, round-trip energy efficiency, cost, life span, safety, and performance in a range of temperatures.

Specific energy is the energy storage capacity per unit of mass of the storage system. *Energy density* is sometimes used in place of *specific energy*, but strictly speaking, *energy density* refers to energy storage per unit of volume.

Specific power is the maximum charging power or discharging power per unit of mass of the storage system. *Power density* is sometimes used in place of *specific power*, but strictly speaking, *power density* refers to charge/discharge power per unit of volume.

Round-trip energy efficiency refers to the percentage of the energy input to the storage system that can be retrieved from the storage system later. Compare the energy efficiencies of alternative storage systems carefully, since the efficiency rating may be given including AC/DC and DC/AC conversion inefficiencies or excluding those and considering only the core storage component (e.g., battery) charge and discharge round-trip energy efficiency. How energy efficiency should be compared depends on the application and which of AC or DC electrical power the application supplies to and requires from the storage system.

In a more detailed comparison between storage technologies, for selecting a particular project, *costs* should be compared in terms of total storage system cost, including controls, containment, siting and connection, safety certification, and environmental conditioning if required as well as the cost of the core storage component. Cost should be assessed with reference to the usable energy storage capacity or charge/discharge power requirement. Of course, cost to a microgrid over time must consider the life span of the storage system and/or its components, and its operating costs.

The *expected life span* of an ESS is often given in terms of number of full charge–discharge cycles to a recommended maximum depth of discharge, and in the case of electrochemical battery storage, it refers to the time at which the battery declines to 80%, 70%, or sometimes 60% of its original energy storage capacity or to the time at which the battery should be replaced for safety reasons.

Thermal performance refers to the range of ambient temperatures in which the core storage component can operate (or operate with reasonable storage capacity, efficiency, and power), and so thermal performance relates to the cost and complexity of the thermal monitoring/management system required or to the range of feasible locations on earth that the system could be used.

5.1.1 Microgrid-Suitable Energy Storage Technologies

A variety of electrochemical battery technologies are presently feasible for microgrid-scale energy storage applications.

- *Lithium-ion batteries*—These feature high specific energy (100–265 Wh/kg), high energy density (250–620 Wh/L), high power density (ability to charge and discharge rapidly, for example, at 1C or faster), and cycle lifetimes ranging from 2000 to 3000 cycles. One factor that makes them suitable for grid storage is their high round-trip charge/discharge efficiency (DC) of 80–92%. Lithium-ion battery systems are relatively expensive compared with, for example, lead-acid batteries, but the low cycle life (500–800 cycles at 50% depth of discharge) and low energy density and low charge/discharge efficiency at the high charging rate of lead-acid batteries make them less suitable for daily cycling microgrid applications. The thermal stability of lithium-ion batteries has improved with the advent of new hybrid cathode chemistries, but thermal management and safety concerns with lithium batteries require complex containment and fusing design, and a complex battery monitoring and charge and discharge control system.
- *Nickel–metal hydride batteries*—These have a wide temperature operating range (–30 to +65°C) and a fairly long cycle life (500–2000 cycles), but they have less specific energy (60–120 Wh/kg) and energy density (140–300 Wh/L) than lithium-ion batteries. Weighing against their use as grid storage is their relatively low charge/discharge efficiency of only 66%. They require less complex thermal management systems than lithium-ion batteries.
- *Nickel–iron batteries*—This energy storage technology has been used for over 100 years, powering early electric cars at the beginning of the twentieth century. The batteries have been used since then as electric streetcar and electric train batteries. This battery technology is being resurrected as a potential grid storage technology. The batteries have extremely long cycle life (some have operated for 30–50 years without loss of storage capacity), but they have very low specific energy

(25 Wh/kg) and energy density (30 Wh/L); they are also large and heavy and this can restrict siting possibilities. Their round-trip charge/discharge efficiency is 65–80%. Their specific power is only 100 W/kg, about a third of that of lithium-ion batteries.

Of these storage technologies, lithium-ion batteries may be the best overall choice for microgrid applications in temperate climates currently, due to their energy efficiency, high specific power and energy, and a maturing market of off-the-shelf Li-ion storage system solutions available commercially. For extreme hot or cold climates, nickel–metal hydride batteries may be the best choice, as less capital and operating energy need be spent on a cooling or heating system.

5.1.1.1 Pros and Cons of Different Lithium-Ion Battery Chemistries

LiMnO₂.   Among lithium-ion batteries, lithium manganese oxide batteries support fast charging and discharging (high specific power) and high thermal safety, but they have a high cost, a short life span, and a low specific energy.

LiCoO₂.   Lithium cobalt oxide batteries have high specific energy but low specific power, relatively high cost, and moderate thermal safety and life span.

Lithium–Nickel–Manganese–Cobalt Hybrid.   A hybrid cathode chemistry with a combination of nickel, manganese, and cobalt hits a sweet spot of high specific energy, moderate specific power, and good thermal safety and life span at moderate cost. Nickel–manganese–cobalt batteries are a good choice for moderately large intermittent renewable microgrids which can afford the thermal management and safety systems that are recommended by nickel–manganese–cobalt battery manufacturers.

LiFePO₄ or LiYFePO₄.   Lithium iron phosphate batteries have poor specific energy, but they have excellent specific power, thermal safety (low self-heating), and life span at a relatively low cost. The newer LiYFePO₄ chemistry adds yttrium doping to the cathode and boasts an even longer life span and a higher specific energy. For smaller-scale microgrids that cannot afford an expensive thermal isolation and cooling design and an elaborate fire-safety system but can stand a heavier battery system to get storage capacity, lithium iron phosphate batteries are a good choice.

5.1.2 Larger Grid-Scale Energy Storage Technologies

5.1.2.1 Pumped Hydro Storage Water is pumped uphill into a hydro-dam reservoir then released as needed. According to the Electric Power Research Institute, this is the most widely deployed grid storage technology, representing, as of March 2012, 99% of bulk storage capacity worldwide (21 GW in the United States and 38 GW in the European Union). It is suited to very large-scale storage projects, but it has limitations such as requiring vertical terrain and very specific siting, a high degree of environmental impact, dwindling available locations, and seasonal unusability (for grid excess power absorption) due to full reservoirs.

5.1.2.2 Sodium–Sulfur Batteries These molten-salt batteries have a high energy density (150 Wh/L) and a very long cycle life (2500–4500 cycles), and a charge/discharge efficiency of up to 89–92%, but they operate at 300–350°C and are highly corrosive. Because of the latter factors, sodium–sulfur batteries require considerable support infrastructure, including complex containment and high power heating systems, and are most suitable for large-scale grid storage applications. New lower-temperature sodium–sulfur battery technology is in the research and development (R&D) phase, capable of operating at only 100°C, and may become viable for microgrid-scale applications.

5.1.2.3 Molten-Salt Heat Storage A large molten-salt thermal mass can be combined with a thermal steam generation plant to store heat over almost an entire 24-hour day and substantially increase the capacity factor of a solar-concentrator solar-thermal plant.

5.1.3 Experimental Energy Storage Technologies

5.1.3.1 Redox Flow Batteries These comprise two tanks of electroactive liquids that generate electricity by transferring ions to each other through a membrane, similar to a fuel cell. However, the reaction is reversible on application of a potential, allowing recharging of the flow battery by reverse transfer of ions through the membrane. Advantages are longer cycle life than conventional batteries due to no solid–solid phase transitions, no need for cell equalization, ease of SOC determination, low maintenance, and tolerance to overcharge/overdischarge. Energy densities are comparatively low, and the systems tend to be complicated due to the need to store and pump liquids. Flow batteries are still largely in the R&D phase.

5.1.3.2 Hybrid Ultracapacitor and Battery Systems   These can ramp up their rate of charge or discharge faster than battery-only storage, so they can be employed for "bumpless" grid or microgrid stabilization in the face of outage and restoration of power sources or routes. They require complex control, have lower energy density and specific energy than conventional batteries, and are currently significantly more expensive than batteries alone.

5.1.3.3 Compressed Hydrogen Storage with Electrolysis and Proton Exchange Membrane Fuel Cells   This could be used at a large centralized facility for regional grid storage—for example, time-shifting and capacity factor increase of wind energy. Compressed hydrogen storage has relatively low round-trip energy efficiency (20–45% AC to AC efficiency) but has potentially very large scalability at a low incremental cost.

5.1.3.4 Underground Pumped Hydro Storage   With two water-filled caverns at different heights, this operates on the same principle as hydro-dam pumped storage, but it can be deployed in level-terrain regions. Creating large caverns underground means high capital construction costs.

5.1.3.5 Compressed Air Energy Storage   This technology is being tested in several varieties: sealed underground caverns, lake-side underwater air balloons, and advanced adiabatic compressed air energy storage (CAES), which extracts and stores the heat of compression and reapplies it during decompression. As of 2011 there were several hundred megawatts of CAES deployed worldwide. Adiabatic CAES R&D projects are aiming for a round-trip energy efficiency of about 70%.

5.1.3.6 Gravity Energy Storage This involves heavy railcars with electric motors/generators moving up and down a long gradual slope. This would be very site specific and large scale.

5.1.3.7 Undersea Evacuated Sphere Energy Storage A proposal to colocate large undersea concrete spheres with offshore wind farms. To store surplus wind energy, seawater is pumped out of the spheres, creating a vacuum. Energy is generated later by allowing seawater, under ocean pressure, to refill the spheres, with a turbine in the refilling pipe.

5.2 OASIS Storage System

The Energy OASIS grid-interactive microgrid at BCIT includes a 500 kWh BESS that uses lithium–nickel–manganese–cobalt batteries and is housed in three quarters of a standard 40-foot shipping container. The remainder of the shipping container houses the control systems and power distribution equipment for the microgrid.

Only 360 kWh of energy storage is utilized; the top 10% and bottom 18% of the full depth of discharge of the batteries are unused, to conserve cycle life span.

The BESS includes battery management units (BMUs). Each BMU monitors the state of its batteries, voltage, current, and temperature and uses battery-switching modules (power electronics) to allocate charge and discharge current so as to balance the voltage of all battery modules of a battery group. The BESS, via the power conversion system (PCS), is given an overall charging power or discharging power command from the energy management system (EMS) of the microgrid and makes a best-effort attempt to meet the request. A number of control integration challenges between the BESS, PCS, and EMS presented themselves in the microgrid project, and these will be described in subsequent sections of this chapter.

5.2.1 Planning Considerations

Lithium-ion batteries were chosen partly because a reasonably sized and reasonable weight battery container would provide sufficient energy storage capacity to store several hours of the 250 kW PV array's power output and would provide high enough discharge power (at a sustainable 0.5C) to fast-charge two electric vehicles simultaneously while supporting other microgrid loads. Another factor was that lithium-ion batteries are now a proven technology: according to the U.S. DOE Global Energy Storage Database, 192 MW of lithium-ion grid-scale storage projects have been commissioned as of August 2014. Lithium-ion batteries were considered low risk and cost effective for the required performance, compared certainly with technologies such as compressed hydrogen, flow batteries, or sodium–sulfur batteries. Lead-acid batteries were ruled out due to low cycle life, energy density, and charging rate.

Planning was required to determine where the energy storage could be located on campus. It needed to be close to both the PV array and the microgrid loads to minimize cable runs. It needed to be separated from occupied buildings on campus for fire safety. And the site had to be evaluated from a ground loading and seismic perspective, given the weight and size of the system.

5.2.2 Design Considerations

After the battery system technology was chosen and it was sized to meet the microgrid power and energy requirements, other design elements were considered. The battery manufacturer and the contractor for the battery container worked together to design the arrangement of the batteries and wiring and ancillary systems such as heating, ventilation, and air conditioning systems. The battery manufacturer arrived at a design that featured four independently operable 70 kW battery rack groups in parallel, each with 70 1.8 kWh battery modules containing cylindrical lithium-ion cells.

Each rack group (cabinet) contains power wiring, control-and-monitoring wiring and electronics, cooling fans, and a BMU and battery-switching module. Each rack group will provide up to 125 A at 550–725 V. A master BMU control server also resides in the battery room. It sends BESS monitoring and status data to the microgrid EMS and receives commands from the EMS, and coordinates the four rack-group BMUs to achieve the desired charging or discharging power.

Figure 5.1 depicts the BESS container, with four battery groups, the master BMU, and the separate room housing microgrid control

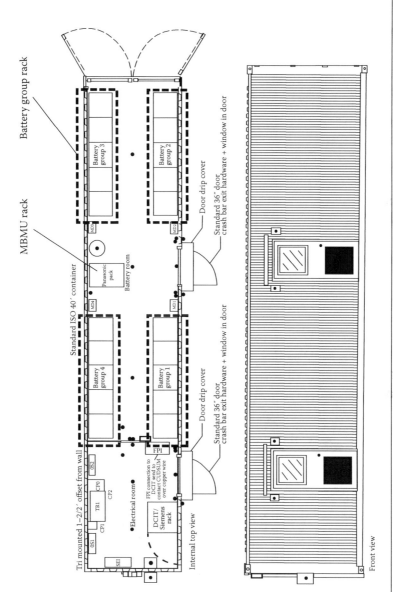

Figure 5.1 BESS container. (From Panasonic Eco Solutions Canada Inc., *BESS Instruction Manual*, PESCA, Ontario, Canada, 2014. With permission.)

and electrical distribution equipment. Figure 5.2 is an interior view showing the battery group racks in the container's battery room.

The electrical integration design for the BESS in the microgrid was to interface the four battery rack groups, via a DC/DC converter each, to a 1000 V DC bus residing within the PCS. The PV array of the microgrid was also attached to the same DC bus via another maximum power point tracker DC/DC converter. PV output could then be sent to the batteries without DC/AC and AC/DC inversion. The DC bus feeds a four-quadrant bidirectional inverter to convert the DC to AC to serve microgrid loads. The inverter can also be used to feed excess PV (or BESS-stored PV) to the grid, or to accept power from the grid, according to the microgrid EMS's energy cost optimizing power flow plan.

The block diagram in Figure 5.3 shows the BESS components and their electrical and control interconnections with the PCS and energy management system.

5.2.2.1 Evolution of the Design   The initial design for the BESS and its electrical and control integration evolved during the microgrid project over a series of three design summit meetings and a system integration

Figure 5.2   BESS container's interior.

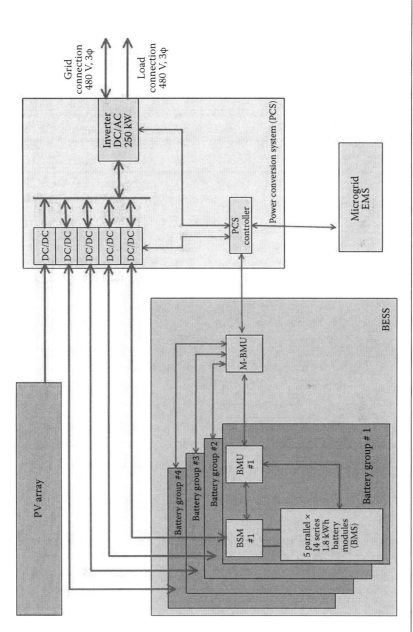

Figure 5.3 BESS components and interconnections. (From Panasonic Eco Solutions Canada Inc., *BESS Instruction Manual*, PESCA, Ontario, Canada, 2014. With permission.)

summit meeting, all involving the battery system manufacturer, the PCS supplier, the battery container integrating company, the EMS provider, and the BCIT project engineering team. Given that the companies were based in Asia, Europe, eastern Canada, the eastern United States and the site was in western Canada, substantial additional design negotiation was conducted via the Internet and teleconference and the opportunity for face-to-face codesign with multiple parties present was limited. This decentralized system design and component development environment proved to be a challenge, since the individual components; BESS, PCS, and EMS, could not be described as off the shelf or plug and play, and substantial detailed design coordination was required to make these components operate compatibly with each other's capabilities, limits, and design assumptions.

Here, as an illustration that may inform future large-scale microgrid BESS integration projects, is a catalog of BESS design changes that occurred during the project and had to be coordinated across the multinational team:

- In the earliest design iteration, consideration was given to housing the PCS in the shipping container along with the lithium-ion batteries. A fire in a similarly designed system in Hawaii, where the fire propagated from the PCS to the lithium batteries, resulting in total system loss, led to a design for the OASIS system where the PCS was placed in a separate National Electrical Manufacturers Association standard-compliant enclosure external to and slightly separated from the battery container. Another reason for this design shift was to avoid the combined heating effect of a large inverter system coresident with the lithium batteries.

- The next design iteration therefore had an entire 40-foot shipping container available for the BESS battery system. A decision was made to use a substantial portion of the 40-foot shipping container (one-fourth of its length) as a separate OASIS system control and electrical distribution room, leaving less room for the lithium batteries. That decision was motivated by the decision to give the entire OASIS system black-start (and true grid failure) operating capability, and for that, OASIS would need all of its control computers (including its EMS), and its essential communications equipment such as network switches, housed in the container and powerable by the islandable OASIS microgrid. This necessitated a change in the battery rack design to fit into a smaller footprint and was one reason the number of BMUs was reduced from 19 to 4 and battery modules were changed to vertical orientation within racks.

- The battery modules were initially specified to be horizontal, stacked vertically in standard racks, with each rack having only a rack-top exhaust fan for cooling. This was changed to a vertical orientation of each battery module, with a cooling fan per module, to increase air cooling, while allowing compact packing of battery modules into racks.

- As a further consequence of battery arrangement changes for size and cooling and the reduction of BMUs, the series-parallel arrangement of the battery modules was altered and more power-monitoring and control boards had to be added to the racks.

- These changes necessitated custom-designed racks, as depicted in Figure 5.4, and a cost increase in battery rack design and manufacturing.

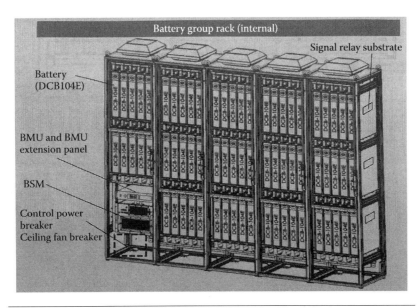

Figure 5.4 BESS rack assembly. (From Panasonic Eco Solutions Canada Inc., *BESS Instruction Manual*, PESCA, Ontario, Canada, 2014. With permission.)

- It was uncertain until late in the project whether active fire suppression was required, leading to delays in container customization design, heating, ventilation, and air conditioning design, and container delivery.
- The control and monitoring (digital communication) interface of the BESS became much more complex in the final design than as originally specified in the OASIS system design document that had been developed from the design summits. In the system design document, the interface was specified to have two control set points (SetBatteryChargeDischargeRate, SetBatterySystemMode) and four monitoring measurement and status points (MaxUsableCharge, RemainingUsableCharge, BatteryNetPowerOut, BatterySystemMode).
- The design intention was that a single or small set of fault status points would complete the control and monitoring interface. In the final design, the BESS control and monitoring interface, as seen by the EMS, included 17 control set points and 142 monitoring measurement and status points. The consequences of this change to the microgrid development project and to the microgrid's operability will be explored later in this chapter.

5.2.3 Installation Process

As Figure 5.5 illustrates, the battery (and microgrid controls) container was assembled, with wiring, power distribution switchgear and panels, empty control computer racks, and empty battery racks, off-site at the container integrator's facility. Off-site testing included "ringing out" (connectivity testing) all electrical connections. Then the container was trucked to the microgrid site, crane-lifted into place, secured, and populated with battery modules and control computers. It would have been too heavy to ship or lift with the batteries preinstalled. Then the container's power and control lines were connected to underground cables which had been laid. All told, the BESS container off-site assembly, siting, and connection took 3 or 4 months.

5.2.4 Special Considerations

Because the BESS was to operate on a campus, campus facilities management insisted on Canadian Standards Association certification of

Figure 5.5 BESS installation process.

the BESS. Since the battery components did not have this certification, a system-specific Canadian Standards Association inspection of the assemblies of parts in the BESS container was done. Integration of the BESS fire detection system with the campus life-safety system, and inspection and certification of the fire alarm system to pertinent standards, was also required. The battery racks required seismic design (bracing) and certification of seismic design by a structural engineer.

5.2.5 Testing and Commissioning

A subset of the batteries and BMUs were shipped to the PCS manufacturer's site in the eastern United States for integration testing. A brief monitoring and control "ping" test was conducted at that time over the Internet with the EMS, which was being developed in Germany.

After installation at the microgrid site, the battery supplier and PCS supplier began commissioning and testing BESS discharging as controlled by the PCS and BMUs, using a 480 V three-phase load bank and a very long extension cord for mains power for controls, because the power feeder line from the substation to the microgrid site was not complete. Commissioning was completed a month later after the feeder was landed, tested, and connected to the PCS. This commissioning and on-site acceptance test verified the physical assembly, wiring assembly and connectivity, and BESS operation under a range of control inputs in both islanded and grid-connected operation.

Finally, there was an integration test with the EMS and a brief microgrid use-case testing period, during which the integrated BESS, PCS, and EMS were taken by the development team through several typical operating scenarios (varying PV power levels, loads, grid interaction), to verify that the integration met grid-interactive microgrid operating objectives.

5.3 Storage Control

Control of BESS battery charging and discharging was achieved in the OASIS microgrid by a collaboration of different control and monitoring systems acting in concert and at different timescales and granularities.

At the top of the control tree, acting at the slowest timescales, the microgrid EMS planned the BESS charge or discharge power level for each 15-minute interval for several upcoming days, seeking to minimize virtual energy costs in the operation of the microgrid.

If the microgrid was grid tied, the EMS then actually controlled BESS charging and discharging, via a Modbus-communicated set point passed through the PCS. The EMS adjusted its BESS power set point once per minute, to correct for measured deviations from expected PV power or load demand.

The PCS distributed the EMS power request equally among the four parallel battery groups. The PCS was also specified to curtail the EMS's power request if battery-group SOCs were low or high, deliberately making the BESS underperform on the EMS's power request in a controlled manner. As described in Section 5.5, there was some confusion on microgrid component responsibility for such curtailment.

The PCS enacted its battery group power targets by adjusting the current control on the PCS's four digitally controlled DC/DC converters.

The battery-switching modules within each BESS rack group distributed the current among the 70 battery modules under BMU control while the BMU listened for digitally signaled voltage, current, or temperature limit or fault alarms from the individual battery modules and stood ready to stop the BESS operation should any fault be signaled.

When the microgrid was islanded, the PCS did not receive a battery power request from the EMS; instead it took over BESS charge/discharge control, employing a fast (subcycle) digital current-control loop acting on the PV and battery group DC/DC controllers to ensure that $p(\text{PV}) + p(\text{BESS}) = p(\text{Load})$ at all times, preventing voltage or frequency swings.

The complexity of this multicontroller tree of control acting at several timescales with different microgrid operation modes and different objectives and limits at each layer of the tree led to significant integration issues during the development of the microgrid.

5.4 Storage Integration

As a case study, the following issues arose during the control integration of the BESS into the OASIS microgrid. The project eventually overcame the critical integration problems, but delays in dealing with them led to a high technical risk persisting throughout the project.

There was a tendency of the BESS and PCS suppliers to present as interface to the microgrid EMS their equipment's off-the-shelf digital interface, or a slight variant of it, rather than to add a control and monitoring interface compliant with the interface specification in the microgrid design document.

Faced with this, the EMS supplier was requested to effectively ensure early in the project that BESS control and monitoring interfaces would be compatible with the EMS. Upon receiving elaborate off-the-shelf BESS control and monitoring interface specifications, the EMS supplier implicitly agreed, by lack of review, but requested (after roughly 6 months of project time had elapsed) significant late-project changes to the manner that the EMS and PCS would operate the BESS.

Apart from the elaborate nature of the BESS interface, which the EMS had no scope to deal with, there was a control philosophy divergence. The BESS and PCS suppliers presented an interface allowing the EMS to control inverter output power to/from grid and loads, leaving the PCS to manage the combination of PV and BESS power, but requiring the EMS to issue mode-change commands altering the priority of PV and BESS power use. After many discussions, the EMS supplier requested that the EMS directly control the BESS charge and discharge power only, as the original microgrid design document had stated. A redesign of PCS control logic was required, leaving some unplanned artifacts in PCS operation of the batteries.

Additional integration problems and some project consequences and recommendations arising out of such control integration problems are elaborated in the next section.

5.5 Lessons Learned

In the process of designing, integrating, and testing the BESS in the BCIT Energy OASIS microgrid context, lessons were learned. A few have to do with project process and ensuring good system engineering practice. Others have to do with the desirable characteristics of a BESS designed for microgrid integration. And, finally, some have to do with control integration from the perspective of how an EMS should control a BESS in an urban microgrid, depending on the use cases of the microgrid and the larger grid's electricity pricing policy.

Regarding the microgrid development project process, several major gaps in BESS control logic persisted until late in the integration and system testing phases of the project and some are still being resolved in an extended microgrid commissioning period.

- When the BESS design change was made to four independent parallel groups of batteries, the battery supplier assumed that the EMS supplier would take care of SOC balancing between those groups, whereas the EMS supplier assumed the validity of the original interface specification of the BESS which had them receive a single SOC estimate for the whole BESS and provide a single charge/discharge rate request.

- Appropriate lithium-ion battery charge control logic: Specifically, charge current ramping down at high battery SOC was improperly implemented in the BESS/PCS combination. Charge control is being achieved by the PCS repeatedly hitting voltage protection limits, pausing, then reattempting full current. Overvoltage faults in the PCS DC bus or DC/DC converters at high battery SOC are not uncommon. The poor charge control is due to persistent misunderstandings as to which of the battery supplier, the PCS supplier, or the EMS supplier was to be responsible for charging current regulation. Battery monitoring data including real-time battery-voltage-aware charging-current limits were provided by the battery supplier to the PCS and are also readable by the EMS. The PCS supplier believed it was the EMS's job to set charging current for each of the four battery groups based on these dynamic limit values, but the EMS supplier justifiably thought this was in the purview of the battery system supplier working with the PCS supplier.

    The order-of-magnitude increase in BESS control-and-monitoring interface complexity from initial system design document to delivered equipment required extensive negotiation over control logic responsibility between the battery and PCS supplier and the EMS supplier, in the last quarter of the project, and left significant control logic gaps as neither party wished to increase their subsystem's scope. The EMS supplier eventually added programming to fill several of the gaps, for example, controlling the process of battery capacity learning cycling of the battery system, but this was not implemented until the last month of the project.

These control responsibility misunderstandings provide the lesson that key aspects of systems engineering practice or standards must be maintained in an enforceable way throughout the microgrid project and not just during the initial requirements and specification phase. This is particularly true in a higher-power, larger microgrid project in which each complex power system component (such as a large BESS in a shipping container) is not a fixed-specification unit at the beginning of the project but has its design and implementation evolving during the project. With complex and evolving digitally controlled power equipment components, there is a vast room for component interaction incompatibility, and Murphy's law applies in this respect.

Systems engineering practices essential for microgrid development:

- A systems engineer's role with authority backed by project financial structure: It is important that some party to the project be explicitly responsible for maintaining design adherence and that the project have a performance-payment structure, and an engineering changes contingency fund, which grants effective authority to the system engineer when they call for design adherence or when they make a decision on a key technical change during the project.
- Firm, agreed, nonextendable component control interface specifications: Most importantly, control and monitoring interface specifications between major complex power system components, such as the BESS, the PCS, and the EMS, must be finalized early in the project; explicit formal, signed agreement on these specifications between parties must be reached; and consequences ensuring correction must ensue for any lack of adherence to the interface specification by either party's delivered equipment. It is important to distinguish between a piece of equipment's off-the-shelf control interface (factory specification document) and the agreed control and monitoring interface *for use between* components in the particular

microgrid system. The latter microgrid-system-level interface must be explicitly agreed between the different interacting-component suppliers, as supervised by the system engineer, and that fully agreed interface may very well be a small subset of the off-the-shelf interface specifications of a component or may include higher-level logical commands and computed or summarized monitoring values.

For any control and monitoring aspects that the agreed intercomponent interface specification does not cover, it is exclusively the responsibility of the developer/supplier of the individual component to design and implement that component to self-manage (self-monitor, self-control) in those extra degrees of freedom. Adding, or revealing after interface agreement, extra "levers of control" for another component's use, compared with the agreed "interface-in-this-system" specification, is counterproductive, because it places a late-in-project burden on equipment B's engineering team to learn the complexities of component A's operation and adapt equipment B to control component A's complexities at the last moment. The formally agreed interface specification constitutes both the minimum and, importantly, *the maximum* interface that the component can present to components it interacts with in the microgrid system.

There was a tendency on the part of component suppliers in the OASIS microgrid project to rely only on the adherence of each power system component to a particular digital communications standard and to believe that control and monitoring integration would therefore be simple. Digital communication standards, such as Modbus, or even IEC 61850, are too open ended to ensure component communications compatibility. Furthermore, these standards generally standardize communication aspects only at layers below the application semantics level, and so adherence to the standard does not ensure a meaningful or correct system control conversation. IEC 61850 is an improvement in this regard in that it attempts to standardize the signal names for various application-level concepts, but IEC 61850 is further ahead in standardization and adoption in the power protection domain than in the DER or battery storage monitoring and control domain, and the BESS and PCS available to the OASIS project did not have IEC 61850 interfaces. Regardless of protocol standard, however, there will still be ambiguities in monitoring and control interaction logic and control responsibility distribution. System-specific interface specifications between major microgrid power components must be created that are suitable for the conjunction of the particular power and control components and are tailored for joint achievement of the particular use cases of the individual microgrid.

• Midproject command-and-control integration tests: If a microgrid has digital monitoring and control interfaces between major power equipment components such as the BESS and the EMS, then the project process should include a midproject control and monitoring interaction test, using the Internet if equipment cannot be colocated in time for such tests. Such a test could use the actual component on each end, if feasible midproject, or could use a software stub (emulation) of the component. The entire set of interfaces should be exercised, ideally with equipment live in test harnesses. This will identify not only communication misconfigurations and value misinterpretations but also gaps in control logic that neither component is handling.

In the OASIS project, such tests were scheduled, but some component suppliers were reluctant to participate, and only minimal ping tests were able to be conducted in some cases, or tests of three or four control/monitoring points of a 100+ point interface. Unanticipated communication protocol interpretation incompatibilities were revealed by this testing in time to be fixed before final system integration. However, the full command and control communication and logic tests could not be performed until the last 3 weeks of the project, when the BESS and EMS were installed and powered up on site and had been individually commissioned. A complex and detailed interaction test was performed for the first time at that late date, requiring many adjustments to the control programming of "finalized" delivered equipment. The BESS supplier and the PCS supplier did not even then agree that such a test was required, relying on standards compliance of their interface, and on their equipment's "factory spec" interface, but not accounting for remaining interpretation differences or incompatibilities in actual versus assumed behavior of commands and components. An end result of this complex last-minute control interaction testing was the lack of time for microgrid system use-case testing in the project. Only a week of such testing was conducted with a subset of the component suppliers present, at the very end of the funded project period, with no time remaining for corrections of whole-system-level microgrid operational problems. Midstream detailed verification of the interactions of complex monitoring and control interfaces, such as the BESS–PCS–EMS interfaces, would have reduced the technical risk in the last quarter of the project substantially and would have led to a system more robustly able to perform all of its joint-equipment-operating use cases.

A smart microgrid is the *software*-controlled orchestration of computer-*software*-controlled smart power components. As such,

- The interface specification standards (an "interface" is a fixed set of remote-procedure signatures);
- The interface adherence enforcement on interface client and provider (system will not compile or link); and
- The interface stub testing (prior to full component implementation) conventions

that the software engineering industry employs to manage software subsystem interaction complexity are newly required in the power industry as it designs and assembles smart microgrids.

This leads to a description of some characteristics that the next-generation (or current) BESS component should have to enable its integration into a variety of microgrid applications.

- A lithium-ion BESS should be a self-managing "black box," with an inbuilt charge and discharge controller, a BMS with capability to balance voltage across all of its battery cells, and, to identify "spent" cells or modules, with a simple, fully specified (digital) monitoring and control interface. The interface should be expressed in a modern control and data communication protocol, such as DER/storage-domain IEC 61850, or RESTful web services (that is, an Internet of Things application program interface).

- Recommended "smart BESS" interface: A smart BESS should have a digital monitoring interface that provides the external system using it with information on present-time dischargeable energy (SOC expressed as usable kilowatt-hours), on total dischargeable energy capacity when at maximum routinely operable SOC, on the maximum presently allowed charging and discharging power, on the present-time measured charging or discharging power, and any warning, fault, or failure conditions. An extended interface could even provide an EMS with the data points of a dynamically computed charge–discharge power limit curve "box" for the battery system.

  The BESS control interface should be restricted to setting the charge/discharge power request, starting/stopping the BESS, if necessary setting it to be in a secondary operating mode, such as "capacity learning cycle" or "dormant—maintain 50% SOC," and perhaps setting a number of one-time-set and remembered operating configuration options. The BESS should override (limit) the charge/discharge power request whenever it exceeds the allowable charge/discharge rate.

  In other words, the BESS interface should speak the simple and high-level language of the EMS/microgrid controller that is going to orchestrate its functioning alongside generation and loads in the microgrid and should not burden that external controller with battery operating details.

- Tailoring BESS control to microgrid use cases: As experience was gained with how the OASIS microgrid EMS operates the BESS, several lessons were learned about the need to tailor control the BESS to grid-interactive microgrid use cases or operating goals.

  It was found that the energy cost optimization of the EMS was routinely storing PV to the point of full batteries at every opportunity, when the microgrid was grid connected, so that the system could delay the need to buy power from the grid in the evening. But since there was no peak pricing in the larger grid and since in any case the local distribution grid demand peak is at 2 P.M., this storing surplus PV was not useful. The PV power should have been "sold" back to the grid at the same time it was generated, leaving the batteries to sit at a more lifetime-prolonging 50–80% SOC. An EMS energy cost model should include a "tax" on BESS battery charging and discharging and/or a small cost for deviation from optimal SOC (40–50% SOC for lithium-ion batteries), and/or an accurate model of the energy loss of, for example, 4% on charging and 4% on discharging. Any of these small additional battery-use cost factors could prevent EMS optimization from unnecessary cycling and unnecessary full-charge maintenance of the lithium battery system while allowing the batteries to be topped up and cycled for more pressing reasons such as the opportunity to earn significant money selling power during designated peaks or the need to prepare for a long intentional islanding period.

The EMS was also found to be firming PV output to the grid to the level based on the PV power forecast. The EMS was adjusting the BESS every minute (including cycling from charging to discharging) to compensate for sometimes very significant fluctuations in PV. In this particular small microgrid grid interconnection, there was no power supply quality contractual reason to be firming the PV output to grid, so this constituted overcycling of the batteries. This "firming" control also applied in reverse. If microgrid loads were less than forecast or PV generation was higher than forecast, the BESS would be used unnecessarily, with charge/discharge rate adjusted on a minute-by-minute basis, to absorb the excess available solar power, rather than send it to the grid, which would have been a perfectly acceptable place for fluctuating excess generation to go in this small DER case.

Start with a careful review of what the grid-interconnected microgrid's power consumption and generation behavior with respect to the larger grid must be and what, if any, freedom it has to be variable. Then ensure by careful design review and by testing that EMS operation of the BESS batteries is done only for valid reasons while grid connected or generator

parallel and is not done for reasons that turn out to be artifacts of the EMS's control methodology.

In summary of experience from Energy OASIS BESS integration
into an urban microgrid, once EMS goal-directed digital control of
BESS battery charging and discharging replaces the traditional
method of letting battery voltage and load impedance determine
the flow of current to and from the energy storage system, high-
level monitoring-and-control logic design and integration becomes
key. Careful control interaction design is required between BESS,
PCS, and EMS, careful requirements specification of the operating
philosophy of the BESS in the particular microgrid application is
needed, early control integration testing is needed, and full use-case
testing of the BESS in the integrated microgrid in various generation
states and operating modes is needed, with time and funding reserved
sufficient to correct control logic gaps or unanticipated unstable or
BESS-life-span-reducing operating regimes. Electrical integration of
a BESS is based on a century of electrical engineering practice and
standards. Control integration of a digitally controlled BESS is a new
terrain that requires a carefully managed process of microgrid-specific
innovation and verification.

ENERGY MANAGEMENT SYSTEM

JANET SO

Contents

As discussed in Chapter 3, the British Columbia Institute of Technology (BCIT) smart microgrid includes an energy management system (EMS) stream. With the campus microgrid evolving over the years, its EMS had been under continuous iterative development. New data-monitoring tools were added as new components were installed. Various smart grid functionalities such as demand response (DR) and load control were implemented to study the impact and feasibility of different strategies.

One of the latest additions to the BCIT smart microgrid is Energy Open Access to Sustainable Intermittent Sources (OASIS). This system can act as a microgrid on its own since it is capable of operating in islanded mode while isolated from the grid. With a PV installation, a battery storage system, a power conversion system (PCS), a connection to the grid, and multiple electrical loads, Energy OASIS provided an opportunity for the development of a sophisticated EMS that would be capable of balancing the energy between the different components within the system.

6.1 Energy Management System Objectives

Energy management system is a broad term that describes the computer-aided tools that facilitate intelligence in a smart microgrid. The components in a smart microgrid, whether energy sources or electrical loads, either have built-in communication interfaces or are connected to devices with such interface (e.g., a smart meter). They are capable of providing data measurements regarding their state and accepting control commands to alter that state. As a central piece to a microgrid, the EMS connects to every component through these interfaces and performs three main functions: monitoring, optimization, and control.

Monitoring allows the EMS to aggregate data measurements across all components and have an overview of power flow within the microgrid. Equipped with the knowledge of the amount of generation from renewable energy resources, as well as the energy coming from conventional means (such as the grid) and energy consumption from all the electrical loads, the EMS can optimize the performance of the microgrid according to preset operational objectives. These objectives include, but are not limited to, minimizing energy cost, maximizing use of renewable energy resources, maintaining critical loads, and maximizing system lifetime. Optimization often involves a planning process that gathers generation and load forecast information to predict the future energy state of the microgrid. It takes into account the possible upcoming energy requirements of the system and does not solely rely on real-time information from monitoring in making its control decisions. The result of optimization is executed through issuing commands to the controllable components of the microgrid. With monitoring, optimization, and control functionalities, an EMS is capable of the following:

- Enabling the integration of renewable energy resources with conventional generation
- Enabling the integration of energy storage units such as battery and thermal systems
- Optimizing the dispatch of distributed energy resources (DERs) to reduce the total cost of energy
- Monitoring the system's electrical interchange and performing real-time corrections

- Managing different load types (e.g., fixed, controllable, interruptible, and reserve load)
- Providing monitoring and control tools for operators via user interfaces (UIs)

As a smart microgrid, Energy OASIS comprises a photovoltaic installation, a battery storage system, a PCS, several electric vehicle (EV) chargers (both DC fast chargers and level 2 chargers), and a connection to the local BCIT grid. The Energy OASIS EMS helps integrate all these components together. The main interface for monitoring exists between the PCS and the EMS, where the PCS provides data measurements for PV and batteries such as solar generation and state of charge (SOC). EV charging loads and the grid's point of interconnection are also monitored through a number of smart meters connected to these components. Through monitoring, the EMS has an understanding of how much energy is available from each energy source and how much energy is being consumed by each electrical load. Additionally, weather and load forecast as well as a grid constraint schedule (further explained in Section 6.2) is supplied to the EMS. The weather forecast, containing multiday temperature and solar irradiance data, is converted into solar generation forecast. Load forecast shows the amount of expected EV charging and the corresponding power requirement. All of this information is inputted into an optimization process that employs linear programming algorithms to produce a multiday energy-balancing plan.

Figure 6.1 shows the balance between energy sources (PV, battery discharging, grid import) and loads (EV charging, battery charging, grid export) in the first 24 hours of a sample energy plan. The y axis represents the power sources (above the x axis) and power consumption (below the x axis) in a 15-minutes interval. Due to the frequently changing nature of this microgrid, optimization is recalculated every 15 minutes, unlike planning for a larger system where once-a-day calculations may suffice. With an energy plan, the EMS is able to make high-level control decisions in how to operate Energy OASIS such as when to charge or discharge the battery storage (diagonal line pattern above or below the x axis), when to export or import power to or from the grid (dotted pattern above or below the x axis), and when to curtail the EV charging loads (horizontal line pattern). For example, during

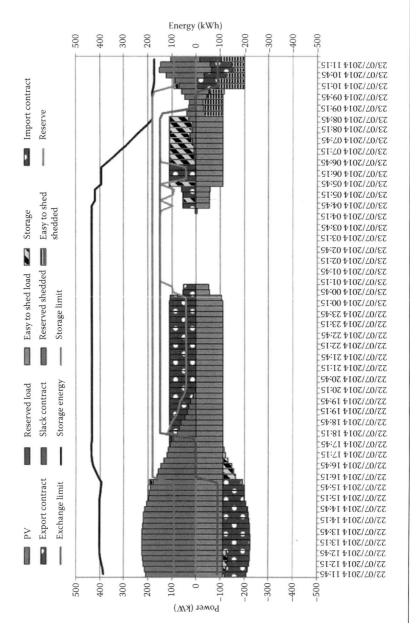

Figure 6.1   Balance of energy sources. (Courtesy of Siemens, Munich, Germany.)

periods of high PV generation, excess energy is stored into the batteries, whereas batteries are discharged to supplement low PV generation to fulfill loads. Control commands (battery set point, EV charger control) are issued accordingly through interfaces provided by controllable components. However, energy plans based solely on forecast will eventually deviate from real-time conditions of the microgrid. Therefore, the Energy OASIS EMS makes minute-to-minute adjustments to its control commands to account for the difference between forecast and monitored data values.

6.2 Energy Management System Applications

The control decisions made by the Energy OASIS EMS need to reflect the operational purpose set by system operators. The two main operating modes of Energy OASIS are grid-connected and islanded. Islanded operating mode can be further categorized as intentional islanding (planned) and unintentional islanding (unplanned). The EMS contains different logic and optimization strategies, which are used to derive its energy plans when the system is operating in different modes.

In the grid-connected situation, the local BCIT distribution grid is factored into the planning and optimization process. Power can be imported from the grid, and excess generation can be exported to the grid. A grid limit (constraint) schedule is inputted into the EMS to indicate the maximum amount of power that can be imported from the grid (as a negative limit) or the minimum amount of power that must be exported to grid (as a positive limit) at any given time of the day. Having such limit as an input to the energy planning process enables the EMS to facilitate the reduction in the peak demand of the local grid through the scheduled use of renewable resources and energy storage systems. Figure 6.2 shows a typical profile of weekly power demand of a portion of BCIT campus loads supplied by one feeder. The demand is near 3 MW (dark and light gray) during peak hours. Through the EMS, minimum export requirement can be set during those peak hours (light gray) to lower the overall consumption from the utility grid. If solar generation does not produce enough energy to meet the export requirement, the battery storage system can be discharged to supplement it. In this case, the batteries can be recharged during nonpeak times (horizontal line pattern) when power

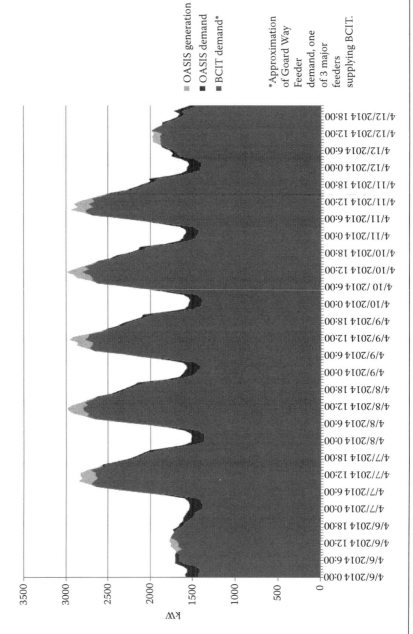

Figure 6.2 BCIT campus weekly load profile.

is allowed to be imported from the local grid by the grid limit. This use case of the EMS can be applied to cases in which utility pricing tariffs (time-of-use pricing or demand peak pricing) exist. The system can reduce the electricity bill by scheduling the use of renewable sources when energy cost is high and recharging from the grid during low energy cost periods.

With variable and sometimes unpredictable power coming from the renewable energy source in Energy OASIS, combined with the occasional need to meet peak demand reduction objective, the EMS must perform DR load management on the EV charging station to lower the energy needs in the microgrid. Two tiers of loads exist in Energy OASIS in the forms of reserved charging load and nonreserved charging load. This is used to demonstrate the EMS ability to prioritize and curtail loads based on their priority. Load curtailment allows the EMS to respond to generation and demand changes, which can occur frequently in a microgrid. It is also crucial that the EMS understands the priorities of the load such that less critical loads (nonreserved charging) are shed before more critical ones (reserved charging) have to be shed. This allows the most important loads to be protected in the event of power failure or outages (unintentional islanding) by ensuring the availability of energy for such loads.

While the role of the EMS in islanded mode operation is mostly managing loads, it is also responsible for several other planning and control tasks unique to this mode. The EMS enables system operators to schedule intentional islanding periods through an operator portal. When the EMS receives a request for an intentional islanding period, it evaluates the feasibility of entering into such mode by examining the available energy for that period and prepares for it by charging the batteries if necessary. At the requested time, the EMS opens or closes the appropriate contactors and circuit breakers to disconnect Energy OASIS from the grid. This process also triggers automatically when the loss of grid is detected during unintentional islanding. At the end of an intentional islanding period or if the EMS recognizes that the system is no longer able to support all its loads, the EMS reconnects the microgrid back to the grid. For unintentional islanding, the return of grid needs to be detected before reconnection occurs. These control capabilities of the EMS allow the microgrid to be easily switchable between operating in grid-connected and islanded modes.

The operation of a smart microgrid, in both the grid-connected and islanded modes, produces a large amount of useful data. Probed by the monitoring function of the EMS, these data readings are processed and presented to various types of users of the system via portals and other UIs. In Energy OASIS, system operators can view the real-time state of the system presented by a customized human–machine interface (HMI). They are also able to quickly respond to issues and problems that may arise within the microgrid with the help of e-mail notification of alarms and faults sent by the EMS. Additionally, the data collected are archived in the EMS. Historical data related to different components can be extracted to perform analysis on generation amount, consumption trend, and system deficiencies, etc. This can lead to changes and improvements that help advance the microgrid.

6.3 Planning and Design

Early in the design stage of Energy OASIS, high-level project objectives were defined. The key planning considerations for the Energy OASIS EMS had to ensure that it delivered those objectives in the most cost-effective and scalable manner. In other words, the monitoring, optimization, and control functions of EMS were designed to do the following:

- Integrate PV panels and energy storage by charging batteries when PV panels are generating power
- Mitigate the impacts of EV charging by discharging batteries based on EV charging station demand
- Manage multiple DERs on the same distribution network including optimal dispatch and islanding

The EMS was therefore designed to be capable of integrating with other Energy OASIS components. This included considerations of the characteristics of those components (renewable resource or controllable load) and how they should behave in different operational situations. To perform monitoring and control on those components, the EMS was equipped with the means to communicate with them via established protocols with clearly defined interfaces.

For Energy OASIS as a whole, the EMS performs energy optimization in both the grid-connected and islanded modes and makes decisions on how energy should flow in the microgrid. What should the solar generation be used for? In what situation should the grid be used for import or export? When should the EV charging loads be curtailed? How should the battery storage be used? The ideal design had to address those questions and establish strategies for the different ways in which the system could be operated. Once that was determined, it painted a clear picture of what inputs were needed for the optimization process and what control decisions should result from it.

While the optimization process would determine the amount of energy available for EV charging, the EMS had to decide on how individual chargers were controlled to ensure that they consumed only what was allocated to them. This decision depended on the control interface that was provided by the EV chargers. Many attributes had to be taken into account, such as whether or not the input power could be adjusted and, if yes, under what conditions or whether the chargers could be stopped prematurely. Moreover, the negative impact on EV drivers using the charger had to be taken into consideration and minimized when making these control choices.

Another important part of the Energy OASIS EMS was its UI for different users of the system. System operators needed to be able to view the monitored values, such as PV generation, load consumption, and battery SOC. They also needed to be able to run the system in various modes to demonstrate different optimization strategies. Lastly, they needed to be alerted to any nonnominal operation of the system's equipment or power levels in a manner that would allow them to respond quickly. Another group of users for the system was the EV drivers who would be interacting with the EV chargers. Since load management played a prominent role in the operation of Energy OASIS, load curtailment was regarded as a possibility that needed to be properly communicated to the EV drivers. Additionally, to demonstrate the ability to manage different priority of loads, a reservation system was planned as part of the EMS for EV drivers to reserve their charging session as a higher priority load than nonreserved ones.

After these EMS capabilities had been defined, several subcomponents were designed and implemented to fulfill the tasks necessary to achieve them. They are shown in Figure 6.3. The PCS, EV chargers, and the battery system are included to illustrate the communication path between them and the EMS used for monitoring and control.

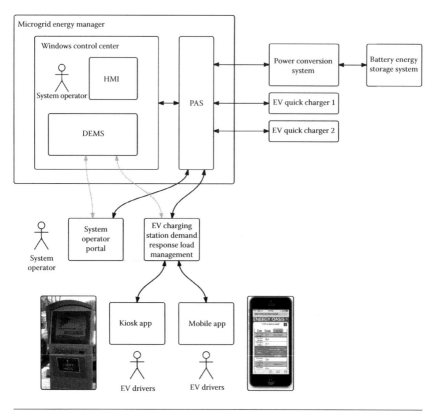

Figure 6.3 EMS integration with OASIS assets.

6.3.1 Microgrid Energy Manager

The OASIS EMS was built using components of a microgrid energy manager (MEM), an off-the-shelf commercially available product. It contained a suite of software modules that enabled microgrid energy optimization, collectively referred to as the decentralized energy management system (DEMS). MEM also included an HMI, which provided visualization of monitored data values and statuses of each Energy OASIS component and allowed supervisory control inputs from system operator for a wide variety of functions, such as starting up the system and enabling or disabling a particular component. Monitoring and communications were handled by the power automation system.

Despite being a readily available product, MEM was not a plug-and-play tool. It had to be customized by the design team, to meet the operational needs of Energy OASIS. DEMS performs the primary task of the EMS, which is energy optimization and planning. Figure 6.4 illustrates

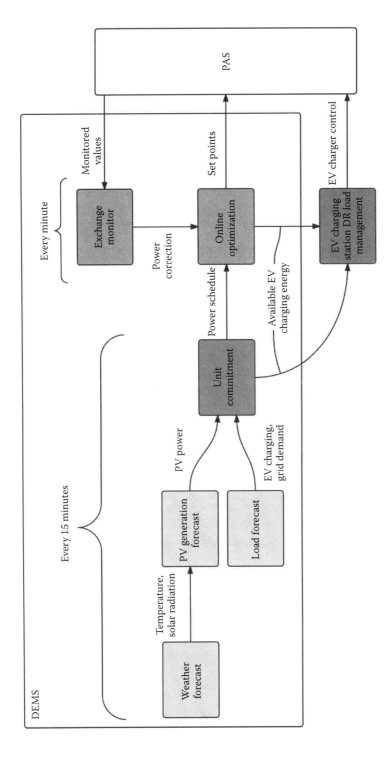

Figure 6.4 EMS energy optimization process.

the basic process for energy optimization (as discussed in Section 6.1). To recap, it takes weather forecast, load forecast, and grid constraints schedule as input. Along with real-time monitored values for current battery SOC and solar generation, DEMS would then attempt to produce a 3-day lookahead balanced energy schedule for the microgrid. Based on this schedule, control commands are issued by MEM to direct the power flow within Energy OASIS.

One of the components controlled by the MEM is the battery storage system. The initial design of battery control by MEM involved issuing a set point based on the result of DEMS planning. A negative value would indicate battery charging, and a positive value would indicate battery discharging. However, the design team opted for an alternative design. The MEM would control the inverter output power in the PCS and also choose from a number of PCS operating submodes, which combine the use of battery storage system and PV in various ways. This approach unnecessarily complicated the MEM's role in the control of the battery storage, as it put the burden of calculating the PCS output power on the high-level system. In the final design, the single battery set-point specification was restored and the PCS was made responsible for calculating inverter output power.

The calculation of battery set points, along with control decisions for EV charging, is now the outcome of the optimization process. To configure this process, components of Energy OASIS are modeled in the DEMS, which involves defining the PV panels, battery storage, EV charging loads, and grid power limit as DEMS units (such as generation unit, battery unit, controllable load unit). These units are represented by their characteristics, together with appropriate cost values assigned to each. For example, the storage system is represented by a battery unit, which has parameters such as maximum capacity and usable capacity (as constraints). Cost values are crucial in the execution of the optimization algorithm as they are used to determine the priority of energy sources and loads. The end goal of the algorithm is to minimize cost. Therefore, an energy source with a lower cost assigned will be used before a higher-cost one. On the contrary, a higher-cost load will be curtailed after a lower-cost one. Based on the project objectives, the design team created a DEMS model capable of generating optimization plans that perform the following:

- Maximize the use of PV generation
- Store excess PV generation in battery storage for future use
- Curtail lower-priority loads before higher-priority or critical loads
- Adheres to battery storage minimum SOC constraints
- Respects grid interchange power flow limits (import/export limit)
- Ensures energy availability for intentional (planned) islanding period

The cost model that enables the above is defined as follows:

1. Energy sources in increasing cost order
   a. PV generation
   b. Grid import below grid power input limit set by system operator
   c. Battery discharge
   d. Grid import above grid power input limit set by system operator
2. Energy loads in increasing opportunity-cost-if-missed order
   a. Grid export above grid power-out minimum constraint set by system operator
   b. Battery charge
   c. EV charging load without reservation
   d. EV charging load with reservation
   e. Grid export below grid power-out minimum constraint set by system operator

As a unit modeled in the DEMS optimization process, the battery storage system includes configuration for the minimum SOC. However, to ensure the availability of an "energy reserve" as preparation for unintentional islanding, two levels of battery minimum SOC constraints are defined. Otherwise, DEMS plan can result in situations where very little or no energy is available during power failure as energy level is close to, or already at the minimum, effectively disabling the battery storage system with no discharging allowed.

The inclusion of a secondary limit enables grid-connected operation of the system to use battery storage up to an upper soft limit value, and islanded (intentional and unintentional) operation to use battery storage up to a lower hard limit value. The buffer between soft and hard limits is currently set to be 20% (approximately 90 kWh), but it can be adjusted in the MEM UI. Once the two battery limits were implemented in the model, it was noticed that the DEMS never plans to use the buffer battery storage during intentional islanding requests even when renewable energy resource was not enough for loads. This was due to the fact that the DEMS logic required the battery SOC to return to the soft limit level immediately after islanding mode ended, which was impossible as the battery generally did not act as a load (charge) when there was low generation in islanding mode. A design change in the optimization algorithm was implemented to add a charging period of 1 hour after islanding mode ended to allow batteries to return to soft limit level SOC via grid power or PV generation.

With the model created, forecast values are required as inputs to the DEMS energy optimization process. One such forecast is weather data. The design team researched and assessed a number of sources for this data. An Internet-based weather service was identified as a candidate, capable of providing hourly forecast, including sky cover values, from present time to up to 10 days in the future. Additionally, a weather station located in the BCIT campus near the site of the PV panels is used to provide an array of current weather data, most notably a solar insolation value. An early attempt was made to integrate these sources into the MEM and use them in the DEMS. However, the design team was concerned that such solutions were often found to be unreliable in the long term. After researching into a number of more reliable sources, BCIT chose a research quality data feed from University of British Columbia, which provided solar irradiance and temperature values at 15-minute granularity for a 3-day period in comma-separated values (CSV) format at a fixed path on a hypertext transfer protocol server. The BCIT technical team developed an application to import these data on a daily basis, reformat these into a separate file, and place the file onto a fileshare (file transfer protocol [FTP]) for the MEM to integrate into the DEMS model. The load forecast and grid limit schedule, generated internally within other components of the EMS, were provided to the MEM via the same method.

Another vital EMS design decision was related to the frequency of the DEMS energy optimization process. Originally, the design team intended it to be run once a day, which was the typical use of the DEMS. The time required to run the optimization algorithm was thought to be long (around half an hour), which prompted the design team to discourage more frequent execution of this process. However, this was found to be impractical because Energy OASIS was essentially a microgrid system where parameters tend to change often. A once-a-day plan could not account for the real-time changes that occur within a microgrid on a minute-by-minute basis, including the fluctuation of PV generation, the unpredictability of load (humans are in the loop and can start or stop significant loads, such as EV charging, at times different from those predicted), and battery storage SOC variation from prediction. After some testing of the DEMS model representing the microgrid, it was realized that the optimization calculations did not take more than several minutes, perhaps due to the smaller scale of Energy OASIS. Therefore, the DEMS planning frequency was changed to every 15 minutes, which better accommodate the rapid changing nature of the microgrid and improved the control decisions by the EMS.

Through an iterative design process, the DEMS energy plans generated for various operational scenarios were examined to ensure that the control decisions were logical and followed project objectives. An issue was discovered regarding the curtailment of EV charging loads. The DEMS plan balances energy in 15-minute intervals as illustrated by the columns in Figure 6.1. In the initial version of DEMS planning, DEMS would often arbitrarily choose which several 15-minute future time slots in which to curtail EV charging, in case the entire multiday lookahead plan showed insufficient available cheap energy to meet all load demand. Often this resulted in the current-time 15-minute interval curtailing car charging.

Given that cars showing up are discrete unlikely events and that the DEMS actually has free choice of which 15-minute interval to curtail, it turned out to be better to give the DEMS a slight time-based cost factor to prefer curtailing loads later into its future plan than at the present time interval, should it have the freedom to choose.

The general principle is that the plan for the near-term future is based on more certain information than the plan for the later future, so a better plan to handle the deferred curtailment may be computable closer to that time.

Subjectively, this reduced the number of negatively perceived "charging unavailable or slow" messages for EV drivers. The process treats every quarter-hour interval equally. When there is not enough energy in the system to fulfill loads over a duration that spans multiple 15-minute intervals, the plan would arbitrarily select the intervals where energy for load is curtailed. For example, if there is only enough energy for 1 hour of EV charging in the next 5 hours, the plan might curtail EV charging in the first 4 hours and fulfill the charging load in the fifth hour. However, in a real-life situation, it is much more ideal to curtail loads in the future than in the immediate hour. As it has been pointed out previously, microgrid parameters change frequently. It is unlikely that the energy state of the system is the same as the current plan had forecasted when it reaches a time slot later in the future. Fulfilling immediate loads, rather than curtailing them based on arbitrary selection, is more optimal. To remedy this arbitrary selection, the DEMS model was adjusted such that EV charging load has a small decrease in the cost of curtailment over time. Curtailment of lower-curtailment-cost loads is more desirable in optimization, allowing the present time charging loads to be supported. However, the decreased cost of curtailing EV charging load must remain more costly than the price earned by exporting to the grid. Otherwise, loads will be curtailed in favor of grid export.

Apart from the complex task of energy optimization, the MEM also interfaces with other components of the system, directly or indirectly through other components (such as the PCS) via established industrial communication protocols (such as IEC 61850 or Modbus). The actual signals exchanged between them are largely defined through a collaborative process, managed by the EMS design team. These signals included values to monitor (e.g., component voltage, current, power) and commands to issue (e.g., set points, start, enable). Moreover, signals that required processing by the MEM (e.g., calculated values, splitting register bits) were identified and implemented. This is further expanded on in Section 6.4.

One special group of signals that the MEM monitors was the alarm and fault status of Energy OASIS components. However, there were an overwhelming number of individual alarms or fault signals available from individual components. A subset of the alarms and faults was selected for high-level monitoring, while related alarms or faults were grouped at the component level (e.g., all battery storage alarm). Alarm and faults monitored by MEM were meant to make the system operators aware of the existence of potential problems. Upon detecting such alarms, the operators would be expected to further investigate the issue. Therefore, detailed alarms and faults would not be required.

6.3.2 System Operator Portal

The system operator portal allows users to set and switch the operating mode of the system. It provides an overview of the system state and also communicates the alarms or faults monitored by the MEM to operators. As a high-level UI, accessibility and ease of use was a major consideration during the design. The portal required an interface with the MEM to acquire system state values (such as energy, power readings) as well as to send commands (e.g., set overall modes).

In the initial design, the system operator portal would simply allow an operator to select or change the overall Energy OASIS system operating mode in real time (e.g., choose one operating mode from a group of mode buttons) with immediate effect. For example, the operator would change the system immediately from a "taking power from grid" mode to a "no-grid-impact" mode or a "send power to grid" mode. Similarly, intentional islanding and return from islanding was to be initiated in this same immediate button-press manner. This design was changed to allow the operator to create and, in a second step, enact a schedule (up to 3 days forward-looking) of changes in Energy OASIS system operating mode. The system operator portal UI allowed the operator to visually draw the operating mode schedule on a timeline chart and then activate the altered operating mode schedule. The operator could also load predefined schedule templates of typical operating mode change patterns and then enact a schedule based on the template.

Originally, the overall OASIS system operating modes, to be commanded by the system operator portal and implemented by the MEM, were conceived as follows:

- EV charging from solar and stored solar only (grid-connected but not using grid power)
- Peak shaving campus load (sending battery power back to grid during demand peaks)
- Islanded operation
- Maximize asset lifetime value (grid-connected but minimal or no use of batteries)

However, in the interest of reducing system complexity, the operating modes were further simplified to

1. Islanded
2. Grid-connected

in conjunction with

3. High EV charging frequency
4. Low EV charging frequency

This led to an Energy OASIS control system design impasse, in that the new proposed modes allowed no way of explicitly demonstrating energy management configurations that could control the microgrid's impact on the grid. Nevertheless, such energy management configurations had already been defined in, or strongly implied by, the project objectives. In other words, the project objectives required the system operator to command the use of grid (import, export, not used) by selecting from these operating modes.

The impasse was eventually resolved when the BCIT team developed a new control interface, in which the system operator portal could send the MEM a mode schedule (command/set-point time series) that consisted of time periods of a special set-point value meaning intentional islanding, interspersed with grid-connected time periods where a varying grid limit was specified for the MEM in the schedule. The meaning of the grid limit (in negative value) was that the MEM should optimize the microgrid's energy use, or storage, and control the batteries such that Energy OASIS as a whole did not draw more power from the grid than the grid limit specified. The grid limit in the mode schedule could also take on positive values, which required that Energy OASIS send at least the specified level of power back to the grid. Effectively, a schedule of the single grid limit values, supplemented by a distinguished code value meaning "switch to islanded" (intentional islanding), would tell MEM to control the microgrid so that at prespecified times of the upcoming day Energy OASIS as a whole was one of the following:

- Grid-neutral (grid connected but using no grid power)
- Grid-supporting (sending power back to the grid)
- Grid-supported (able to draw a limited amount of power from the grid)
- Islanded
- Using unlimited grid power and minimizing battery use

These five situations, if grid-supporting and grid-supported were used in opposition to local grid demand peaks, were equivalent to the original four operating modes contemplated for the system but constituting a simpler control input to MEM.

The system operator portal was implemented as a web application that provided a 7-day chart, including 3 days of past values, present-day real-time values, and 3 days of future forecast. An example of such screen is shown in Figure 6.5. The system state values shown in the figure include PV generation, battery SOC, battery charge or discharge rate, grid interchange rate, and load consumption rate. The portal provides a minimalistic mouse-interactive interface for system operators to create the grid limit schedule. The interface allows simple dragging and clicking of polygons to indicate maximum grid import or minimum grid export value. Planned islanding can also be scheduled by dragging the polygon to the top of the chart. Additionally, the interface has a list of predefined schedules that can be utilized for various weather situations.

The grid limit schedule including islanding is converted from UI elements to a CSV-formatted file. The file contains a time stamp in local time zone and power limit pair with positive values indicating export to grid limit and negative values indicating import from grid limit. The time resolution of the data is 1 minute, and the length of data is at least 3 days. This file is imported by the MEM via a fileshare and is used in its energy optimization process.

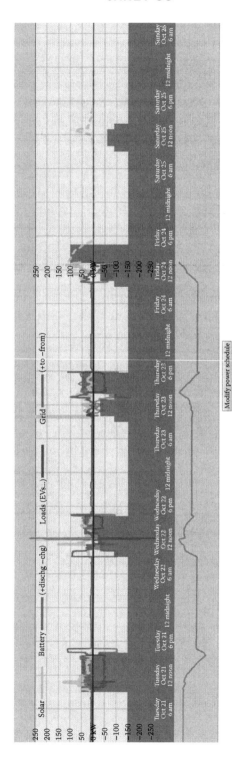

Figure 6.5 OASIS system energy schedule for grid power target and island mode.

6.3.3 Electric Vehicle Charging Station Demand Response System

The EV charging station DR system allows the EMS to interface with various types of EV chargers or supply equipment and coordinate the use of EV chargers by drivers in a manner supportable by OASIS energy available for EV charging. As the DEMS plan treats EV charging as a single load unit, the EV charging station DR system performs load management on individual chargers. Similar to the system operator portal, the DR system needs to interface with the MEM to acquire energy availability information for both real-time and longer-term periods, to send load forecasts, and to issue control commands (e.g., starting and stopping EV chargers).

Early designs of load forecast generated by the DR system considered EV charging reservations only and current in-progress charging sessions as loads. Using such forecast, the DEMS model would neglect to account for any upcoming EV charging sessions that were not from reservation, resulting in little or no energy allocated for EV charging when no reservations existed. To mitigate this, load forecast included two load types—a higher-priority reserved charging load and a lower-priority nonreserved charging load, where lower priority was always curtailed before high priority. For the lower-priority load category, an estimation of potential upcoming EV charges, made based on the time of day, was included in addition to nonreserved in-progress charges. This ensured that, should there be available energy within the system, the DEMS model would allocate some of it for EV charges that were not from reservations. The estimation of potential load is expected to improve as EV charging usage data are collected once the station is opened for public use.

With potential EV charges determined by estimation, data from EV charging reservations and current in-progress charging sessions were required to generate a complete load forecast, which was essentially a time series of power needs by the loads. The BCIT technical team designed and implemented a mobile-focused reservation web application and another web interface for an outdoor kiosk equipped with a touch screen and a keyboard located at the EV charging station (Figure 6.6) that EV drivers could interact with. Both applications were designed to be thematically similar in terms of look and feel and share the same account system where EV drivers would be asked to

Figure 6.6   EV drivers' kiosk.

register with their vehicle model and battery age information. This was used to determine the rate of power consumption of a vehicle during charge. For each reservation, a typical fast charging session from 30% battery SOC to 80% was converted into power consumption for the load forecast. However, when EV drivers would arrive at the station to start a charging session, with reservation made or not, the kiosk system would request the current EV SOC and their desired SOC to generate more accurate power need data for the load forecast.

The design of both UIs went through incremental changes by the BCIT team's web design specialist. These included graphical improvements, changes in color choices, and addition of audio or visual cues to enhance usability. Usability tests were also conducted with actual EV drivers, which resulted in significant additional refinements to the EV driver UI, mainly in the improvement of user attention guidance design elements and the increasing of the size of user input fields and control buttons to a kiosk-app-suitable size rather than a personal computer web-app-suitable size. Fewer and much larger elements on screen were a key to improved usability. Additionally, to assist EV drivers on their decision on charging needs at the Energy OASIS chargers, PlugShare, a database of EV charger locations, was integrated into the kiosk application during development. This enabled EV drivers to visualize available EV chargers on a map. Similar capabilities were also developed using comparable data from other sites, such as here.com.

With load forecast, the MEM is able to perform energy optimization planning that determines the amount of energy available for EV chargers. The EV charging station DR system acquires this energy availability information from the MEM to determine load management strategy. If there is enough energy for charging, the DR system is tasked only with enabling the charger and starting the charge when EV driver shows up. However, if curtailment is required, an algorithm is used to determine what actions need to be taken which can be a combination of the following:

- Reducing the power draw of an individual EV charger (from the maximum 50 kW)
- Stopping an in-progress EV charging session prior to reaching the driver-indicated desired SOC
- Disallowing charging on an individual EV charger

The strategy generated by the algorithm adheres to the available energy constraint given by the MEM while minimizing negative impact on EV drivers. This algorithm is run every minute to ensure that the control of the EV chargers is updated as new charging information or energy constraint becomes available. The overall EV charging station DR process is illustrated in Figure 6.7.

6.3.4 Communication Interfaces

Data communication between EMS components is shown by the arrows in Figure 6.3. With the system operator portal and the EV charging station DR system both being developed by BCIT and run on the same piece of hardware, their interface protocol with the MEM

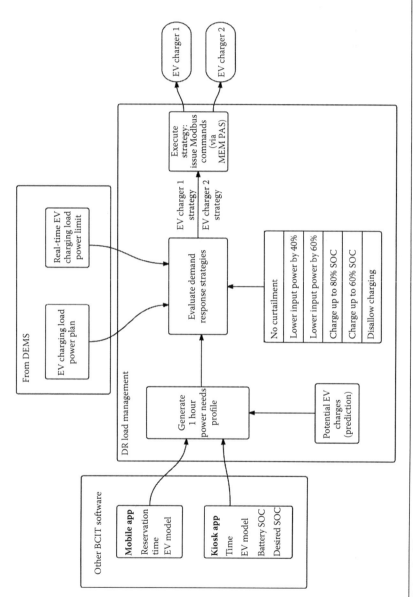

Figure 6.7 EV charging DR.

can be shared. Initially, BCIT proposed a RESTful web service interface for data and commands exchange with MEM. However, the decision was made to use a combination of Modbus protocol and a fileshare (a store-and-forward FTP fileshare with polling for updated files) instead because the MEM can more readily integrate with these methods of communication. The Modbus protocol is used for obtaining various real-time measurement readings and alarms status from the MEM as well as issuing commands pertaining to EV charging and DEMS replanning to MEM (dark arrows). FTP fileshare will be used for transmitting longer-term data such as multiday forecasts and power availability plans (light arrows).

As both the system operator portal and the EV charging station DR system require Modbus communications with MEM, a gateway program was developed as a protocol adapter to abstract out the communication protocol implementation needed for each process. The original design of the Modbus gateway creates a new transmission-control protocol connection to the MEM per request. The process involves opening a connection, making a request, reading the response, and closing the connection. However, during communication testing between the MEM and the Modbus gateway, it was found that the MEM's Modbus protocol communication component does not allow multiple connections from the same Modbus master. An additional function to maintain an open connection for identical Internet protocol addresses was added. The first request to the MEM will open a new connection, which remains opened. A subsequent request utilizes the existing connection to make a request and read response. In the event that the connection is lost due to communication errors, a mechanism reestablishes the transmission-control protocol connection before continuing with new requests.

6.4 Energy Management System Integration

As discussed in the previous section and illustrated by Figure 6.3, the integration between the EMS and other Energy OASIS components is handled by the MEM, which is configured to interface with the PCS, the EV chargers, and several smart meters connected to loads and the grid's point of interconnection.

Communication between the MEM and the PCS is established via the Modbus protocol with the MEM as the master and the PCS as the slave. Over 100 signals are read or written between the MEM and the PCS in implementing the PCS remote interface Modbus register map, provided by the power system designer. These signals include (but are not limited to) the following:

- Alive monitoring
- Cooling system readings
- Status (running/stopped), alarm and fault readings for overall system, inverter, battery DC/DC converters, and PV DC/DC converter
- System readings—voltage, current, power readings for grid and loads, etc.
- Converters readings—voltage, current, power, etc.
- Control settings—start/stop system, enable/disable converters, etc.

The battery storage system is integrated with the EMS through the PCS interface with the following signals read or written from the same Modbus protocol implementation:

- Control settings—start/stop, charge/discharge set points
- Battery capacity learning
- Status, alarm, and fault readings
- Overall and individual battery group SOC, state of health readings
- Voltage, current, charge and discharge limits

Communication between the MEM and EV fast chargers is also established via the Modbus protocol with the MEM as the master and the EV chargers as the slave. Approximately 40 signals are read or written between MEM and each EV charger including the following:

- Status, alarm, and fault readings
- CHAdeMO (EV charging protocol)-related readings
- Charger input power set point
- Enable/disable, abort commands

Lastly, communication between the MEM and the smart meters is established via the IEC 61850 protocol and is integrated by importing their configuration file. The primary signals monitored from the meters include instantaneous power and total energy readings.

An important step in integration is to ensure that all components work together as a whole. This means that the functions of the EMS on its own, and together with those of other Energy OASIS components it is connected to, need to be verified and validated through testing. First, the factory acceptance test of the MEM occurred approximately midproject with the partners and the BCIT technical teams present. During this period, the MEM HMI UI screens were reviewed and the DEMS energy-balancing plans in various use case scenarios were tested. Additionally, communication interfaces, internal between the EMS components and external with the Energy OASIS components, were examined through a ping test and protocol connection. Once the connections were established and verified, requests were made for a subset of signals defined for each interface and responses were validated to conclude a fully functional interface. At the end of the factory acceptance test period, a list of open points was produced, which was addressed internally by the technical partner and reexamined during the site acceptance test (SAT). This list included points related to MEM HMI adjustments, additional signal list implementation, and DEMS refinements.

A 4-week commissioning and SAT period occurred on site with all the technical partners and the BCIT team present. During this time, all Energy OASIS components were physically installed on site at BCIT. For the EMS, a standard 19-inch server rack, which housed all the hardware and software components (except reservation application) it comprised, was installed in the control center next to the battery storage room. This location was selected such that the server rack could be electrically connected within the islandable portion of the system to ensure that supervisory controls would continue to be powered by the system in the event of unintentional islanding (e.g., power outage). A separate server was used for the reservation application as a security measure since it was accessible via public domain. Firewalls, a virtual private network, and router configuration would then permit only a single narrow communication channel between the external reservation app server and the

EV charging station DR system operating on the server in the control center.

After installation, SAT occurred where a comprehensive list of topics were tested and verified. First, hardware equipment and the MEM software were verified to be operational with confirmation of valid software licenses. Full communication and signal testing between the MEM and the PCS, the MEM and the EV chargers, and the MEM and the BCIT EMS components was performed. The MEM HMI screens were reviewed, and the functional elements (e.g., button presses) were verified. The complete DEMS energy optimization workflow was tested which included the following:

- File data transmission to and from the MEM via fileshare FTP
- Automated (15-minute cycle), manual (HMI button press), and remote (command issued by the BCIT EMS software) DEMS planning process
- Examination of the DEMS energy-balancing plan generated for various operating modes—grid-supported, grid-supporting, grid-neutral, planned islanding

With the EMS and other components of Energy OASIS tested and validated individually on site, a list of system functional and solution use cases was performed toward the end of commissioning period. This major step was necessary to demonstrate Energy OASIS capabilities to meet the project objectives, in which the EMS plays a vital role. A test plan was developed prior to this period and includes the following test cases:

- Storage and later use of PV for EV quick charging with no impact on the grid
- Support loads
  - Support loads during power outage
  - Support loads until unable during power outage
- Intentional islanding
  - Intentional islanding—EV charging using BESS storage
  - Intentional islanding until unable to continue
- Optimal dispatch of energy in a microgrid
- Fault handling at the system level

The conditions for each test scenario were created, manually if necessary, for example, limiting PV generation during a particular period in both forecast and real-time values or opening a breaker to mimic power outage. The DEMS plans were examined to verify their logic and the planned flow of energy was as intended by the test case. After the DEMS plans were verified, the test case scenarios were allowed to run. The BCIT technical team observed the behavior of the system and recorded various monitored values. These were compared with the expected results of the test plan to ensure that the system demonstrated the project objectives. Since the EMS was the central controller of Energy OASIS, passing these tests was vital in showing a successful integration. (See Chapter 9 for details on Testing.)

6.5 Lessons Learned

In the design, implementation, integration, and testing stages of the Energy OASIS EMS, numerous challenges, some unforeseen, were met. Overall, it was difficult to do iterative development in a mixed hardware equipment and software project (e.g., time consuming, expensive), especially when the partner teams were spread out geographically. Hardware equipment was required to be commissioned before software testing and iterative refinement could occur. Development of the EMS in parallel with hardware components based on agreed-upon but not finalized interfaces with minimal integration testing throughout the project was problematic. Control and monitoring interface specification of how the MEM should interact with the other system components changed substantially during project execution due to changes in the design team and late discovery of constraints from off-the-shelf control components. Additionally, the control interfaces, the energy model, and the cost model were not finalized until very late in project execution, which resulted in a time crunch in the implementation of the MEM. All these led to time reduction in system level testing with the EMS during the commissioning phase. What was needed was more frequent testing between components that interact with one another, over the Internet if necessary, during the development cycle. Interface requirements needed to be firmly defined and adhered to strictly by both the provider of the interface and the party using it.

In terms of the energy optimization and control functionality, the MEM has certain deficiencies and could hardly be a perfect fit for Energy OASIS. Moreover, the key objective of the DEMS was to manage energy exchange between the microgrid and the local distribution grid (point of interconnection). This differed from Energy OASIS' objective, which was not to curtail PV if generation was higher than grid limit target, rather to firm PV if generation was low. Often, the grid limit from the system operator portal was interpreted as a hard limit instead of upper or lower bounds in the DEMS, causing the constant change in battery set point when PV was fluctuating. Moreover, the DEMS energy optimization and load control period of 15 minutes were both too long, when compared with PV fluctuation, which occurred every few seconds. The DEMS was also inherently unable to deal with significant load changes, which within the context of a microgrid could happen instantaneously. This lead to set-point oscillation and unstable control. One-minute power correction cycles alternate the charging and discharging of battery rapidly, which would not be ideal for battery longevity. Many of these control decisions made by the MEM resulted in overutilization of the battery system. One potential solution to this was to add in a cost in the DEMS model for the use of battery system that was separate from the cost of power related to battery charging and discharging. The command to charge or discharge regardless of the power set point would increase the price of that control decision. This one-time usage cost would discourage cycles between charging and discharging of battery due to fluctuation of PV. It was easy to view the optimization of a microgrid just as the control of power flows between its components when in fact many other characteristics such as usage frequency, efficiency, and conversion loss should be under consideration as well.

As discussed, potential EV charging load was regarded as lower-priority load in the load forecast at all times. This caused the DEMS to create an energy-balancing schedule that was often unachievable as that load was rarely realized. The adjustment made by the DEM regarding the excess energy allocated for load was to charge the batteries. Again, this contributed to the overutilization of batteries, but it was potentially fixable with the addition of usage cost. Furthermore, the lack of existing EV charging power consumption data made the EV charging station DR load management algorithm inaccurate. Iterative adjustments were required as charging information was obtained while the system was being commissioned and tested, but seasonal weather changes also affected EV battery and charging performance. Additional ongoing refinement for this portion of the DR system is necessary. However, even with accurate charging data, there was difficulty in evaluating load management strategies in terms of negative impact on users without having actual EV drivers' inputs or extensive use case testing. This highlights the importance of the inclusion of users (EV drivers) in design process.

As Energy OASIS has been running for more than a year, some challenges were discovered with its daily operation via the EMS. During the planning stage, some alarms were misinterpreted as vital in healthy operation of the system and were included in the high-level system operator notification system. As a result, the system operator was flooded with potentially insignificant alarm e-mails. One particular type of alarm was an alert related to close-to-full battery SOC. As mentioned earlier, this occurs frequently due to the nature of control by the EMS. These routine alarm e-mails may potentially suffocate important alarms or faults, which could delay corrective action by an operator and possibly harm the system.

Lastly, the operation of Energy OASIS through the MEM HMI, shown in Figure 6.8, is complex and requires specialized training to operate or troubleshoot. Additional operation automation and UI simplification would be needed to enable wide-scale deployment of microgrid EV charging station (similar to gas stations).

It can be said that the EMS is not complete even after being integrated into Energy OASIS, especially when relatively new technologies, such as the EV fast chargers, are involved. As ongoing operational data become available, it may show unexpected behaviors resulting from the way the system is controlled by the EMS. It is important to capture these data and analyze these to understand the reasoning behind those behaviors. From that, refinements can be made to the EMS to improve its decision-making processes in the control of the smart microgrid.

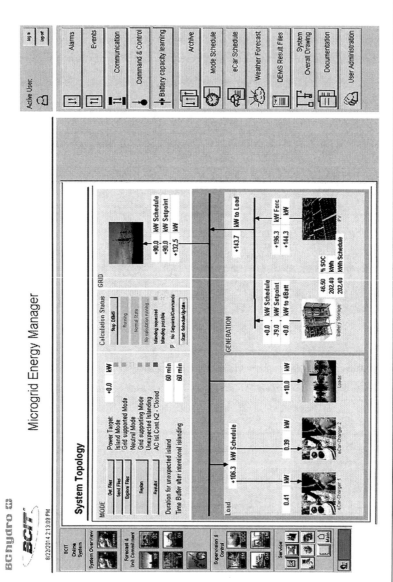

Figure 6.8   Energy OASIS EMS HMI. (Courtesy of Siemens, Munich, Germany.)

7

MICROGRID COMMUNICATION AND CONTROL

HASSAN FARHANGI
AND KELLY CARMICHAEL

Contents

Communication technologies and data management play an important role in smart microgrids. These technologies help to place a layer of intelligence over a microgrid's infrastructure, thereby allowing command and control applications to operate and engage with the microgrid's assets. In fact, the convergence of communication technology and IT with a power system is what makes a microgrid smart or intelligent, enabling a host of fundamental applications to emerge.

It is interesting to note that although the foundation of smart microgrids is built upon a lateral integration of its fundamental assets, its smartness and intelligence will be built upon the vertical integration of the upper layer applications with the lower layer components. For instance, a critical capability, such as demand response, may not be feasible without a tight integration between a variety of middleware, field assets, and termination devices placed in various management layers, which provide inputs as well as get influenced by the real-time load status of the system.

7.1 Command and Control Strategies

As discussed earlier, what distinguishes a smart microgrid from a conventional microgrid is the pervasiveness of real-time monitoring and command and control across the nodes of the system. That requires relevant microgrid nodes to have the capability of generating real-time data and communicating those with other nodes across the system. Such data would be required to enable control and planning applications, such as energy management system (EMS), to have access to and apply appropriate controls, to the relevant nodes of the system, regardless of where these nodes are or what their functions may be. In other words, monitoring and control within a smart microgrid system has to be an end-to-end exercise and encompassing (preferably) all nodes of the network.

That requirement calls for command and control strategies, capable of dealing with microgrid events through localized intelligence. In other words, individual components, such as power conversion system (PCS), batteries, etc., may have their own dedicated management and control intelligence, interfacing with higher level control systems and applications (such as EMS) to receive set points and inform them of their status and events. That distributed command and control approach relaxes the performance requirements of upper-layer control functions because those only need to be informed of the occurrence of the events and the local actions taken to attend to them. This essentially frees the upper-layer control applications from the need to assume the task of time-sensitive and critical control, prescribing and/or implementing remedies for local subsystem issues. For instance, the EMS would only be required to deal with overall energy planning and system management issues and would leave time-sensitive and event-driven command and control to local intelligences built into individual subsystems and components. By default, this notion points to the need for the constituent components of the microgrid system to have the inherent ability to generate, receive, process, and analyze real-time data and make informed decisions and/or attend to their preassigned tasks based on the set of local and global attributes available to them.

In other words, the smartness of a microgrid is thus determined by the level of closed-loop intelligence, which allows the desired level of automation, energy management, and protection to be built into the system. This definition is further extended to encompass the scaled-down subsets of a microgrid, such as a building, a home, or even an electric car as a nanogrid. Regardless of such differentiations, the basic characteristics of microgrids are their ability to implement the desired smart grid capabilities and functions in a well-controlled environment, minimizing the risks associated with the level of maturity, or lack thereof of the required technologies used in realizing the planned smart grid capabilities and functionalities.

7.2 Microgrid System Requirements

As discussed earlier, smart microgrid communication systems need to enable end-to-end connectivity and data-exchange capability between different nodes in the system. In that regard, attributes such as security, access, bandwidth, and latency requirements of the prevailing functions and applications, such as EMS and demand response, will determine the performance requirements of communication systems. That means that the design of the communication system for a microgrid has to allow individual components to use a variety of wired and wireless communication technologies.

Nevertheless, regardless of the chosen technology, an optimum communication system should be able to deal with massive bursts of data (on polled or event basis) that the components may be expected to receive or transmit. Such information may considerably vary in size and latency requirements. They may include consumption data (with end-to-end latencies in the order of tens of seconds), all the way to other types of time-sensitive information, such as alarms, sample values, or over-the-air firmware upgrades, which may require bursts of 1 Mbps with end-to-end latencies in the order of a few milliseconds. In other words, these technologies will have to meet certain bandwidth, security, and latency requirements, and as such, they will be optimal to carry certain throughput and meet certain latency targets.

7.3 Microgrid Application Requirements

At the heart of a smart microgrid is the need for a timely exchange of information and commands, which requires a robust communication network technology and its associated protocols. The network must connect smart digital systems across the microgrid area with varying data requirements from high-bandwidth and low-latency applications to low-bandwidth and latency-insensitive applications with the ability to deal with missing data.

It goes without saying that there is no perfect network medium that could be regarded as a silver bullet for building a smart microgrid network, capable of satisfying all stakeholders' requirements. A complete network could be designed using fiber optic cables, but the installation in a wide area becomes prohibitively expensive or impossible. Alternatively, one may design a network using wireless technologies such as WiMAX, ZigBee, or Wi-Fi, but some applications will not work well with the higher latency and the dropped data packets when there is interference or congestion in the radiofrequency spectrum. Other mediums are only suitable for shorter distances such as CAT5 Ethernet, which has a 100 m maximum distance between switches. It quickly becomes apparent that a hybrid system of different network technologies are required to best solve the networking challenges for a smart microgrid.

Traditional IT networks have time synchronization services today that will keep devices time synchronized down to the second, but some of the applications in a power system require much higher-quality time sources than is provided in a traditional IT network. Where a traditional IT network may only need to have accuracy down to the second, some power applications such as synchrophasor measurements need to be accurate better than 1 ms to compare waveforms at different points in the smart microgrid. To achieve such a high degree of precision, a global positioning system (GPS) clock is used as the primary source for time synchronization in a power system network. To avoid the cost of having many GPS clocks in a single network, the IEEE 1588 protocol was developed to enable high-precision time synchronization over a network.

The network is also complicated by the need for bringing live data from remote sensors and meters into the back-office systems and supervisory control and data acquisition systems, potentially allowing intruders into the systems that did not normally allow external data communications. Several layers of firewalls are required to ensure the proper isolation between the field area networks and the back-office systems.

A primary attribute of any microgrid is having local generation, and if we are using renewable generation sources, then we will need to have good forecast and models of when the renewables will be online, how much power will be available, and how much energy will be produced over several timescales. Having this data is essential for optimization systems to make feasible plans for when the microgrid should export energy, import energy, store energy, and manage consumption. We have local weather stations that give real-time data on wind speed and solar irradiance, but the forecasting data are downloaded from the Internet. For this reason, we need to have our microgrid network connected to the Internet and have additional firewalls to protect the system from intruders.

On the other side of the energy generation forecasts are the load forecasts. This is typically a combination of historical consumption data and possibly a future-looking forecast using data that can give approximations of how much energy is needed, such as to support the electric car reservation system. Moreover, in some cases, the same renewable generation data may be used to calculate how much energy would be available to serve microgrid loads.

Furthermore, distributed protection functions require a network to transfer state information that requires very low latency to do protection. Normally, the requirement for protection is to respond within 3 ms. The two networking mediums that are suitable for this level of protection are Ethernet over copper and Ethernet over fiber optic; the wireless technologies have much higher latency and thus would not provide adequate protection.

In a microgrid, the inverters and the converters are in control of making the energy flow, and those inverters need a network to connect with the higher-level controller to command the inverter and the converters. The speeds at which these commands get to the inverter are not required to be as fast as the protection functions. The changes to the settings for the inverter and the converters may happen at a frequency of less than 1 time/s and may happen at lower frequencies of 1 time/min. Wireless options would be suitable for such a connection, but Ethernet over copper is a suitable choice if the distances between the systems that command the inverter are within a 100 m distance reach of the Ethernet over copper.

The battery storage system needs to communicate with the battery charge controller, which is normally part of the inverter and converters. The battery storage system needs to let the battery charge controller know the limits for charging and discharging the battery, as the battery approaches its full charge status, it can no longer accept a full speed charge. Similarly, when the battery gets close to being fully discharged, it is no longer able to supply the same amount of current. The network requirements for this are similar to the other data that are sent to the inverters and could be done via wireless or wired connections.

As discussed earlier, the EMS is the central component in a smart microgrid, which needs to communicate with many components. It needs to get the renewable forecasts, as well as the load forecasts, to plan when and where to use the energy. The system also needs to see near real-time consumption data to make decisions when the plan does not match the actual consumption or generation. With the amount of data sources it needs to communicate with, it is advisable that the system uses a wired network solution.

Smart loads are fundamental components of a smart microgrid, allowing the EMS to command them to use less or more energy. As such, these smart loads need to receive commands from the EMS to control their energy consumption. They generally do not need high-speed low-latency communications. This means wireless communications would be an acceptable method to communicate with these devices. In a home environment, this could be on Wi-Fi or ZigBee. In a campus environment, this could be done over WiMAX.

In an environment where the loads are not controllable via digital signals, controllable relays can be installed to disconnect the loads. Sometimes, it would be critical to reduce the microgrid loads to maintain the smart microgrid stability in the present or ensure its viability in the near future. The networking to the controllable relays can be wirelessly done. However, to ensure that the target loads get turned off, when needed, it may be advisable to use a hardwired solution for this if it can be done easily.

7.4 Campus Communication Networks

The British Columbia Institute of Technology (BCIT) has deployed several communication networks for smart grid research. Each network is tasked with providing relevant services for specific functions. And given the fact that each function may have its own specific requirements, the technologies are chosen on the basis of their ability to optimally and reliably provide the required service. As shown in Figure 7.1,[1] these communication networks have been deployed to test the reliability, the

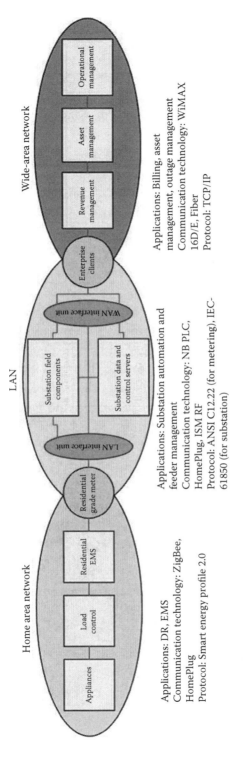

Figure 7.1 BCIT/BC Hydro smart microgrid hybrid network. DR; demand response; NB; narrow band; ISM; industrial scientific medical. (From H. Farhangi, Smart grid and ICT's role in its evolution. In *Green Communications: Theoretical Fundamentals, Algorithms, and Applications,* edited by J. Wu, S. Rangan, and H. Zhang. Boca Raton, FL: CRC Press, 2012.)

performance, and the suitability of the technology, as they would fit into different portions of a smart microgrid.

As shown in Figure 7.2, a ZigBee mesh network was deployed in the campus residence buildings, an area of the campus that has a dense population with many Wi-Fi devices. The Wi-Fi system utilizes the same radiofrequency spectrum as the ZigBee network. This mesh network is being used to transport meter data from smart meters for the residence buildings back to the AMI system. ZigBee networks are being utilized in a smart grid primarily as the home area network. In a smart home of the future, the ZigBee network may be used by the major appliances in the home to participate in demand response programs. This would typically include controlling the thermostat for heating/cooling, controlling the delay timer for the dishwasher, restricting when the freezer decides to go through a defrost cycle, limiting the energy used by the clothes dryer and the range, while not impacting the homeowners' ability to live a normal life.

WiMAX is a longer-range networking technology that has also been deployed at BCIT; it is designed to be much more robust than a traditional Wi-Fi network, where encoding and encryption settings make it more secure and reliable. The encoding adds additional resilience to bit level transmission errors and is able to correct those errors without requiring the higher-level transmission control protocol/Internet protocol to retransmit packets. The bandwidth can

Figure 7.2 BCIT residences ZigBee network.

be allocated to separate streams to ensure the quality of service for critical applications. As shown in Figure 7.3, BCIT's 5.8 GHz network has been configured to connect all the substations across the campus to the AMI network and test new substation communication standards including IEC 61850 across a wide-area network.

The primary long-range communication is Ethernet over fiber optic cables. The bandwidth available on a fiber optic cable is almost unlimited, with the ability to use multiple light frequencies to share the same fiber optic strand. Fiber has the best latency of any of the technologies used and is most suitable for critical protection functions that are latency sensitive. Nevertheless, and as stipulated in Figure 7.4, WiMAX has the potential to be configured as a hot redundant communication system in support of the campus' fiber network. This is not the case at the moment in BCIT's microgrid system. However, the idea would be interesting to pursue in the future.

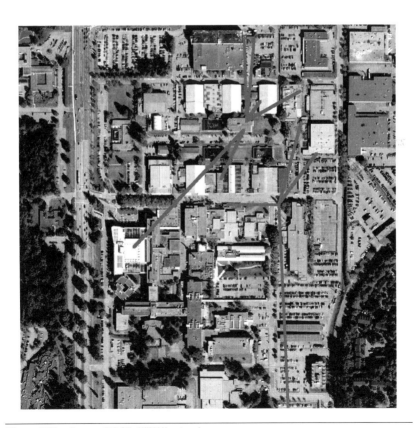

Figure 7.3   Campus 5.8 GHz WiMAX network.

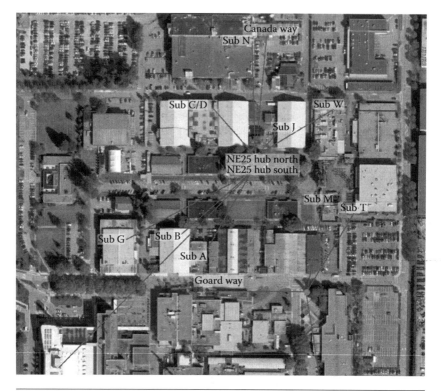

Figure 7.4 BCIT/BC Hydro smart microgrid network domains.

In summary, a hybrid communication system is required for BCIT smart microgrid applications. These applications include the following:

- High-resolution time services
- Substation automation
- Protection and control
- Energy management
- Energy generation forecasting
- Energy demand forecasting
- Real-time monitoring

The high-resolution time service on the BCIT smart microgrid utilizes a GPS timeserver that acts as a local timeserver for all Windows computers on the network, and our network switches support IEEE 1588 time (precision time protocol [PTP]). This is suitable for our hardwired connections. PTP does not work over wireless links, as the

latency and the jitter are not reliable to determine the delay of transmission. The network switches have specific requirements to make
PTP work. They need to understand the exact delay for each interface, enabling them to adjust the time delay information inside the
packets. That means standard fiber small form-factor pluggable modules cannot be utilized; hardwired modules that have specific delay
times are used only.

BCIT microgrid's substation automation networking utilizes either
Ethernet over fiber or Ethernet over copper depending on the equipment's interface options. The networking is unique as it utilizes IEC
61850 generic object oriented substation event (GOOSE), which runs
over Ethernet layer 2 and does not use transmission control protocol/
Internet protocol. It instead uses its own frame type and unacknowl-
edged transmission. The protocol deals with packet loss by retrans-
mitting values on a regular basis. The data being transmitted are more
like a radio than a point-to-point communication system. The trans-
mitter defines the broadcast address it will send to, and any equipment that wants to receive the information is programmed to listen
for those broadcast messages. In this scenario, it makes no sense for
a receiver to acknowledge that it received the packet. When there is
a critical issue, like a voltage goes out of range, the relay will immediately transmit the new data instead of waiting for its regular scheduled transmission and then will proceed through a series of back-off
retransmissions until the delay between the packets is back to its normal retransmission time. Since these data are not within an Internet
protocol frame, the data cannot be easily routed beyond the local layer
2 network.

Protection functions need high speed and low latency for proper
operation. For that reason, the equipment that is participating in protection functions is connected via Ethernet over fiber or Ethernet over
copper. In the case of the relays that reside in our receiving stations,
required to trip on voltage or frequency issues from the BC Hydro grid,
a 48 V normally high hardwire connection has been implemented to
act as the failsafe solution to disconnect Open Access to Sustainable
Intermittent Sources (OASIS) when the protection equipment trips.
We also have an IEC 61850 GOOSE message that will be sent from
our receiving station. What is interesting is that experiments have
shown that this trip signal has been recorded as arriving 17 ms faster

than the hardwire trip signal. The GOOSE message has been configured as not failsafe, which means the fiber optic connection could be unplugged, and it will not cause the OASIS system to isolate itself. Once there is more confidence in this technology, we would like to see this configuration changed to make the fiber optic connection set as failsafe.

The control aspects have different networking needs, depending on how critical the control messages are to having a stable system. The more interconnections a component has, the less desirable it is to use wireless connectivity to it, but other individual components may be deemed less critical and thus more suitable for wireless communications.

The EMS is one of those components that need a very reliable communication path. It must communicate with many components, using several protocols, some of which are very bursty in nature such as IEC 61850 GOOSE, which could saturate a wireless connection for short periods.

Solar irradiance forecasts are downloaded for the OASIS system from the University of British Columbia on a daily basis; a three-day forecast is used in conjunction with the models for the solar panels installed at BCIT to produce an energy generation forecast.

The primary load for the OASIS system is currently a cluster of EV-charging stations. There are two sources of forecast data that are used for generating the load forecast for electric vehicle (EV) charging. The primary source is using historical EV-charging data, and the secondary source of data is from an EV-charging reservation system.

Moreover, there are electrical meters installed at several locations in the OASIS network to monitor energy, power, harmonics, and other valuable data about the smart microgrid. Real-time data from these meters are utilized in the EMS to ensure the existing plan matches with reality.

Finally, and as pointed out earlier, the reliability and the performance of the communication networks are some of the most critical factors that determine the reliability, the functionality, and the performance of a smart microgrid system. As discussed before, the smartness or the intelligence of a microgrid is a function of the degree of integration between the upper layer command and control systems and the microgrids' assets and components. This degree of integration is determined by the reliability and the performance of each and all

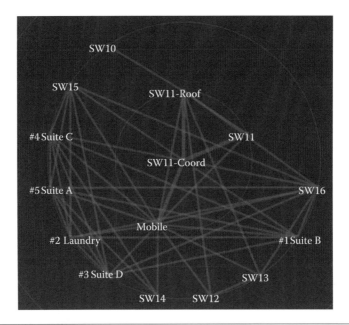

Figure 7.5   BCIT/BC Hydro smart microgrid communication map.

communication links that need to be established between different actors in energy transactions within a microgrid. In other words, for each transaction to succeed, the actors have to be guaranteed a reliable connection with optimum performance to their target components. Ideally, this may mean the following:

1. More than one communication medium
2. More than one communication protocol
3. More than one path between the communicating parties

That may be an acceptable proposition for a lot of mission critical applications. However, in our campus microgrid application, we could not justify implementing 1 and 2. Nevertheless, the design team managed to realize 3. This is shown in Figure 7.5.

Reference

1. Hassan Farhangi (2012) Smart grid and ICT's role in its evolution. *Green Communications: Theoretical Fundamentals, Algorithms, and Applications*, edited by Jinsong Wu, Sundeep Rangan, and Honggang Zhang. Boca Raton, FL: CRC Press.

8

INTERCONNECTION

ALI PALIZBAN

Contents

As discussed earlier, grid-tied microgrids can operate in both grid-connected (grid-tied) or islanded modes.[1] Microgrids are usually connected to the low-voltage side of the power distribution system of the main power grid. When islanded, the microgrid acts as an autonomous power system, in which the frequency and voltage has to be tightly controlled, while the system is held stable and reliable for load variations under different operating conditions. Similarly, when the microgrid is connected to the grid, it should not adversely impact the operation of the main power system and its interconnected distribution system.

Connecting and disconnecting a microgrid to the utility grid creates technical challenges for both the utility grid and the microgrid itself.[2] Some of these challenges are related to safe operation, power quality, reliability, and stability for both sides. Before interconnecting a power-generating plant such as a microgrid to the main grid, the plant needs to demonstrate that its operation will not adversely impact the reliability, the stability, the safe operation, and the maintenance of the interconnecting networks. Such an interconnection needs to meet applicable interconnection standards, such as IEEE 1547,[3] Canadian Electric Code, as well as jurisdictional requirements set by the utility grid operator for reliable operation and safety. Usually, these requirements are clearly stated in a project interconnection requirements (PIR) document issued by the power system operator of the utility grid.

8.1 Screening Studies

Utilities usually devise procedures that prescribe how microgrids should be interconnected with the utility's main grid.[4] These procedures require the following studies to be performed by applicants, which seek the permission to interconnect with the grid. Depending on the size of the microgrid, its generating capacity, and the loads, some of the analysis explained herein may not be necessary and can be waived by the permitting utility. The other critical factor is the actual location of the point of interconnection or point of common coupling (PCC). If this point is situated at a weak point of the distribution grid, then the impact of the interconnection may be significant and a more detailed analysis may be required.[5]

1. Initial scoping study: The initial scoping study is used to review the interconnection requests and scope of interconnection, documentation requirements, interconnection procedures, and process. There may be initial meetings between the microgrid applicant and the interconnecting utility grid representative to start the screening process.

2. Interconnection feasibility study: The interconnection feasibility study is used to determine the point at which the microgrid distributed generations (DGs) will be connected to the utility grid and where the PCC is and also to determine if there are obvious challenges and obstacles for interconnection and if the capacity (rating) of the grid interconnecting equipment such as transformers, breakers, cables, and buses allows for microgrid interconnection. This may require the installation of new equipment and/or the upgrading of existing ones.

3. Interconnection impact study: The interconnection impact study is used to determine the impact of the microgrid operation on the interconnecting distribution network. This is to make sure that the reliability, safety, and power quality of the distribution grid is not adversely impacted by the operation of the microgrid. The study usually includes the following separate studies:

   a. Equipment rating analysis: The equipment rating analysis study identifies if the utility's existing equipment has the required capacity to handle the microgrid's generation and loads at full capacity.

   b. Distribution power flow and voltage drop analysis: The distribution power flow and voltage drop analysis simulation study looks at the power flow of the interconnected distribution system as well as the microgrid itself. The study includes the microgrid operation in grid-tied and islanding modes. Different scenarios with variations of loads and power flow to or from the microgrid to the distribution network are studied. Worst-case scenarios at full load or full generating power should also be included in the study. This study should identify issues related to the voltage drop at different buses, equipment overload, issues with flow of active and reactive powers, and power factor at each node of the system.

4. Power quality study: The operation of DGs, especially DC/AC inverters, creates harmonics that propagate to the interconnected distribution system. A power quality study includes the following subsets:

   a. Harmonics study

      After the microgrid is designed and its components are specified, a simulation study is required to identify the level of harmonics that will be injected into the distribution system by the DGs and the nonlinear loads they serve, such as electric car charging stations. If the simulation predicts harmonics generation above the acceptable level set by the utility grid, then mitigation strategies would have to be proposed to reduce the level of generated harmonics.

b. Flicker study

As a sharp and sudden voltage variation, flicker is regarded as a problem in microgrids. Microgrids could experience voltage flickers when large loads are switched on or off or when the microgrid disconnects or connects to the grid. Simulation studies should be performed to make sure that the flicker frequency and duration does not exceed the acceptable limits.

c. Voltage stability study

The voltage stability study can be done together with the power flow study to make sure that the voltage at different buses of the system remains within the acceptable range. Also, the power factor at each node should be predicted to ensure that the microgrid does not drop very low. Modern inverters may be equipped with means of voltage and reactive power optimization (volt var optimization [VVO]). If this capability is used, then the voltage stability of the nearby distribution system including the capacitors banks and the tap-changing transformer close to the microgrid must be studied to make sure that the inverters, the capacitor banks, and the tap-changing devices do not oscillate together causing voltage fluctuation.

5. Protection and coordination study: When a microgrid is connected to an existing distribution system, it changes the short-circuit behavior of the network in its vicinity. Consequently, a detailed short-circuit analysis and a coordination study is needed to determine the short-circuit levels of affected buses and cables and the rating of the current-interrupting devices, such as beakers and fuses and to make sure correct coordination exists between them. Also, the settings of the protection

relays must be revaluated to ascertain that faults do not adversely impact the reliability of the microgrid as well as the distribution system.

6. Grounding and bonding analysis: The interconnection of the DGs may significantly impact the ground fault current levels. As such, a detailed analysis of the impact of an interconnected microgrid on the grounding and the bonding of the neighboring equipment might be necessary.

7. Stability analysis: The interconnection between a microgrid and the main grid cannot be allowed to noticeably affect the frequency of the grid. However, in islanding mode, the frequency and voltage of the islanded network is controlled by the microgrid DGs, and it may significantly vary. Nevertheless, despite the fact that the microgrid is not connected to the main grid, its loads require the same frequency and voltage stability as the main grid loads. In fact, the voltage and the frequency of such loads should not vary more than what is specified in codes and standards.

The final stage of the interconnection screening process is called *facility study*. The outcome of this study includes detailed project execution plan; detailed design for infrastructure, facility, and equipment upgrades; list of material; and required skilled labor. This study also estimates the cost of equipment, engineering, construction, installation, and tasks specified by the other screening studies. For example, Figure 8.1 shows interconnection application flowchart for the State of California.[6]

After the system is designed, analyses and tests are needed to prove full compliance with PIR. The results are then captured in an interconnection agreement between the utility and the applicant.

In this section, the impact of connecting a microgrid to the distribution network is explained and then interconnection requirements, test, and commissioning procedures to measure the impact are discussed, and finally the methods to minimize the adverse impact of microgrid interconnections are explained. A case study and an example are also included for readers to better understand the process.

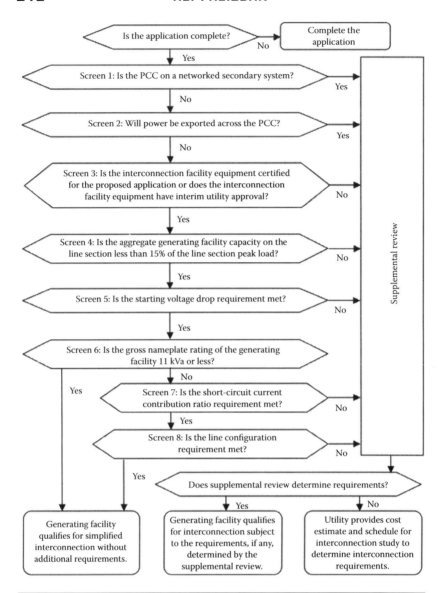

Figure 8.1 Interconnection application review workflow for the state of California. (From Overdomain, LLC Endecon Engineering Reflective Energies, *California Interconnection Guidebook: A Guide to Interconnecting Customer-owned Electric Generation Equipment to the Electric Utility Distribution System Using California's Electric Rule 21*, California Energy Commission, Sacramento, CA, (2003). With permission.)

8.2 Microgrid Elements

Figure 8.2 shows a block diagram of a typical microgrid, consisting of the following main elements:

a. Operation, control, and energy management system
b. Data communication network
c. PCC
d. Microgrid loads
e. Power plants
f. Islanding breaker
g. Synchronizing mechanism

Item a was discussed in Chapter 6 of this book, while item b was covered in Chapter 7. What follows is the discussions on items c through g.

8.2.1 Point of Common Coupling

PCC is defined as the point where the microgrid is connected to the main utility grid. Circuit breaker (CB) 3 in Figure 8.2 represents the PCC. CB3 is also called the islanding breaker. When this breaker opens, the microgrid is disconnected from the main grid, enabling it to operate as an autonomous power system.

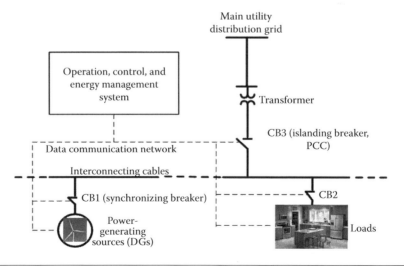

Figure 8.2 Single-line diagram (SLD) of a simplified microgrid.

8.2.2 Microgrid Loads

Figure 8.2 represents microgrid loads in a single cluster. In reality, different types of loads are connected to the microgrid network at different locations. Critical loads such as emergency lighting can also be connected to the microgrid network. The advantage of this arrangement is that if the main grid is down, the critical loads can be supplied by the microgrid sources. In case of a microgrid power limitation in islanding mode, a microgrid load management and control system is programmed to shed noncritical loads and keep supplying power to the critical loads.

8.2.3 Power Plants

Microgrids may generally include different types of energy sources, such as wind, solar, small steam, or hydroturbines. For simplicity though, Figure 8.2 lumps all such sources together and represents the microgrid's power plant as a single source connected to the network through a synchronizing breaker. There might also be an energy storage system connected to the microgrid network via an inverter. The power plant on the diagram represents all such sources. Renewable sources of energy, such as wind and solar, are often intermittent. To mitigate such intermittencies, energy storage system care is often used within microgrid networks to compensate for generation variation. The energy storage system can inject power (discharge its batteries) into the main grid or absorb power (charge) from the grid. Regardless of the type of power source, a microgrid requires a synchronizing breaker to be able to synchronize itself with the grid. CB1 represents a synchronizing breaker in the block diagram. The function of this breaker will be explained later in this section.

As discussed earlier, power-generating sources in a microgrid could include solar plants or wind installations. Due to their specific technologies, each source may have its own requirements for interconnection to the grid.

For instance, solar energy consists of arrays of solar panels that are connected to a single-phase or three-phase inverter. The output of solar panels is a DC voltage, which needs to be passed through a DC/AC inverter prior to its use in the microgrid network.

Figure 8.3 shows a solar energy source. The solar panels convert the sun's energy into a DC voltage, which in turn is converted to AC at 60 Hz frequency at a voltage equal to the grid voltage by the inverter. There is a control system in the inverter to control the voltage, the frequency, and the power to or from the main grid. The maximum power point tracking control system maximizes sun energy conversion by controlling the current (I_{pv}) out of the solar panels. This is needed because the sun's energy changes during the day due to the sun's radiation angle, clouds, and shading due to the surrounding environment. The maximum power point tracking controls the panels' output currents based on their voltages, such that the maximum power of the sun is converted to DC power at any point of time.

Since the sun energy is intermittent during the day and not available at night, a battery energy storage device may also be integrated into the system to be able to better control the flow of the energy in and out of the whole system. Based on the design, the storage system can be connected to the DC bus if the inverter is a bidirectional inverter.

Figure 8.4 depicts a wind energy installation. Wind energy is converted to electric energy by wind turbines. Wind turbines may produce from a few watts to several megawatts of power. Two main technologies are used to convert wind energy to electric power. These technologies are briefly explained here.

The wind turbine in Figure 8.4 comprises a permanent magnet asynchronous generator, which generates a variable frequency voltage, and therefore it could directly be connected to the grid. The generated AC voltage is converted to DC voltage by an AC/DC converter. The

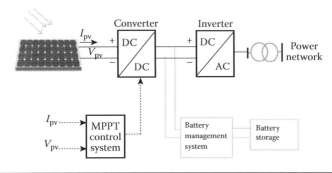

Figure 8.3 Solar energy conversion system.

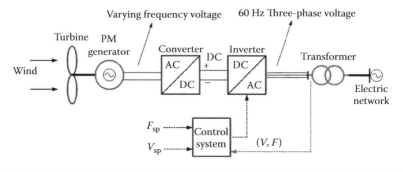

Figure 8.4 Wind turbine power generator with an inverter. PM, permanent magnet.

DC voltage is converted to 60 Hz AC voltage compatible with the voltage and the frequency of the grid. The inverter is controlled by a synchronization mechanism that regulates the inverter output voltage and frequency in full synchronization with the grid.

Larger wind turbines use a doubly fed induction generator (DFIG) with an inverter to connect to the grid.[7] Figure 8.5 shows the block diagram of a large wind turbine power generation systems. In the DFIG configuration, the wind turbine's rotor is coupled with a DFIG rotor via

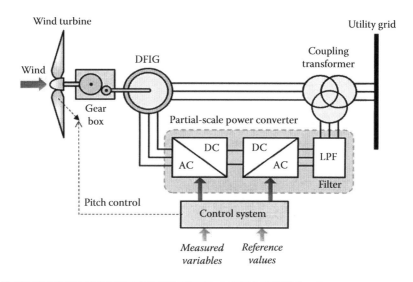

Figure 8.5 DFIG wind turbine with control and PCS. LPF, low pass filter. (Modified from Marcelo Gustavo Molina and Juan Gimenez Alvarez, *Technical Regulations, Potential Estimation and Siting Assessment,* http://www.intechopen.com/books/wind-farm-technical-regulations-potential-estimation -and-itingassessment/technical-and-regulatory-exigencies-for-grid-connection-of-wind-generation. Intechopen, Rijeka, Croatia, 2011. With permission.)

a gearbox. The pitch control system allows wind turbine blade angles to be optimally controlled for a wide range of wind speeds. That means that the rotor speed is not fixed, and it varies with the wind speed.

In synchronous generators, the rotor speed should be kept at a sonorous speed to be able to synchronize the generator to the grid. But with DFIG, it is possible to control the stator voltage and frequency by controlling the rotor excitation (field) current and frequency and synchronize the DFIG stator. In spite of the rotor speed variation, the stator voltage of DFIG can be controlled to 60 Hz and to a level equal to the grid voltage and then synchronize the stator with the grid similar to a normal synchronous generator. The following formula show how this is achieved. F_{Rotor} is the frequency of the excitation (field) current of the rotor. Depending on the rotor speed (N_{Rotor}), the frequency of excitation current is determined and an AC variable frequency current with frequency equal to the F_{Rotor} is supplied to the field of the DIFG. This is achieved by controlling the AC/DC and DC/AC circuits as shown in Figure 8.5.

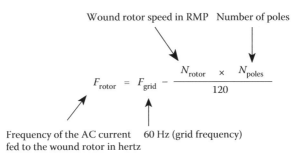

The DC/AC inverter is a normal bidirectional inverter, and it is also synchronized and connected to the grid. Therefore, this kind of wind turbine requires a two-point connection to the grid. The AC/DC converter works as a variable frequency drive. Larger wind turbines use this technology to synchronize to the grid. The main advantage of this technology is its ability to capture the maximum wind power. Its disadvantages are the complex power electronics circuitry and the control system.

8.2.4 Islanding Breaker

Inverters can be divided in two different categories in terms of their islanding capability. Some can work totally isolated from the grid, meaning they can regulate the voltage and the frequency of their associated power sources. And some would require the grid's signal to be able to make that happen. In a microgrid, both types of inverter could be used. A microgrid that requires having an islanding capability has to use the former, while those that do not need to have such capability can use the latter. In the former case, which is in an islandable microgrid, a mechanism would be required to detach the microgrid from the main grid. CB1 in Figure 8.6 shows an islanding breaker. This breaker is opened when the microgrid needs to operate in islanding mode. This is called intentional islanding. CB3 is controlled either manually by an operator or by a microgrid controller system. It can be closed when CB1 is open enabling the microgrid's power plant to be synchronized to the grid by CB1. CB1 is usually incorporated into the inverter control circuitry and controlled by the inverter. Power plants with synchronous generators or DFIG also need a synchronizing breaker such as CB1.

Unintentional islanding (also known as unplanned islanding) may happen as a result of a protection function. In general, this will happen when both entities on either sides of the PCC fail to keep the integrity and/or the safety of their services. In that case, protection systems on either side of the PCC may force the CB3 to trip. For example, one may consider situations in which the main grid is tripped due to a fault in the main grid's distribution system or for utility-initiated

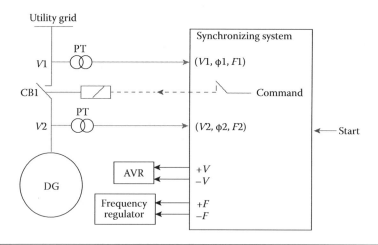

Figure 8.6   DG synchronization with grid. AVR, automatic voltage regulator.

Table 8.1   IEEE 1547.2 Synchronization Parameter Limits for Synchronous Interconnection

AGGREGATE RATING OF DR UNITS (kVA)	FREQUENCY DIFFERENCE (Δf, Hz)	VOLTAGE DIFFERENCE (ΔV, %)	PHASE ANGLE DIFFERENCE ($\Delta \Phi$, °)
0–500	0.3	10	20
>500–1500	0.2	5	15
>1500–10,000	0.1	3	10

Source: IEEE Standards Association, IEEE Std 1547.2-2008:IEEE Application Guide for IEEE Std 1547(TM), IEEE Standard for Interconnecting Distributed Resources with Electric Power Systems. IEEE, Piscataway, NJ, 2008. With permission.

maintenance work. In that case, the islanding breaker must be opened to avoid feeding the fault forward or prevent the microgrid from feeding its power back to the main grid, thus allowing utility maintenance workers the safety they need to work on their side of the network.

8.2.5 Synchronizing Mechanism

Circuit breaker CB1 in Figure 8.6 is a synchronizing breaker. The synchronizing system (relay) measures and compares service parameters (i.e., voltage, frequency, and phase angle) from both sides of the breaker. If the values are within the specified range as recommended by the IEEE 1547.2 standard,[8] then CB1 is closed by the synchronization relay. If, however, the differences are outside the specified range, then the relay sends command signals to the DG control system to bring the voltage and the frequency of the DG closer to the grid voltage and frequency.

The values recommended by IEEE 1547.2 for differences in service parameters are given in Table 8.1.

These recommendations also provide the maximum limits for manual synchronization, which rarely happens. Repeated synchronizations using such limits may shorten the CB1's life and may cause damage to the DG. For regular synchronization, a synchronizing relay or a synchroscope should be used. With current synchronization relays, together with proper DG control system, it is possible to close the breaker at a point where the difference between both sides is almost zero.

8.3 Microgrid Impacts

Despite many benefits and advantages that microgrids have to offer, they have the potential to create power quality and harmonic issues for their interconnecting main grid. That is generally due to the fact that most DGs are connected to the grid via a power electronics inverter. Inverters are nonlinear switching devices that tend to generate harmonics. If proper filters are not incorporated in the inverter, these harmonics will find their way into the main grid. Newer multilevel inverters create fewer harmonics and may be a better option to be used for power conversion in microgrids.[9]

The installation of a delta-wye, a delta-zigzag, or a wye-zigzag provides an effective means of preventing triplen (3rd, 9th, 15th, etc.) harmonics from passing to the load side of the transformer. The other odd harmonics should be cancelled using proper filtering techniques.

The recommended level of harmonics generated by a microgrid is given in IEEE 1547.2[8] and IEEE 519-1992[10] standards. Tables 8.2 and 8.3 show the IEEE recommended acceptable current and voltage harmonics levels generated by a source.

Table 8.2 Current Harmonics Limit in a Microgrid

	MAXIMUM HARMONIC CURRENT DISTORTION IN PERCENT OF I_L					
	INDIVIDUAL HARMONIC ORDER (ODD HARMONICS)					
I_{SC}/I_L	<11	$11 \leq H < 17$	$17 \leq H < 23$	$23 \leq H < 35$	$35 \leq H$	TDD
<20[a]	4.0	2.0	1.5	0.6	0.3	5.0
20 < 50	7.0	3.5	2.5	1.0	0.5	8.0
50 < 100	10.0	4.5	4.0	1.5	0.7	12.0
100 < 1000	12.0	5.5	5.0	2.0	1.0	15.0
>1000	15.0	7.0	6.0	2.5	1.4	20.0

Source: IEEE Standards Association, IEEE Std 519-1992: IEEE Recommended Practices and Requirements for Harmonic Control in Electrical Power Systems. IEEE, Piscataway, NJ, 2008; Marcelo Gustavo Molina1 and Juan Manuel Gimenez Alvarez, California Interconnection Guidebook: A Guide to Interconnecting Customer-owned Electric Generation Equipment to the Electric Utility Distribution System Using California's Electric Rule 21, Intechopen, Rijeka, Croatia, 2011. With permission.

Note: Even harmonics are limited to 25% of the odd harmonic limits above. Current distortions that result in a DC offset, e.g., half-wave converters, are not allowed. TDD, total demand distortion.

[a] All power generation equipment is limited to these values of current distortion, regardless of actual I_{sc}/I_L, where actual I_{sc} is the maximum short-circuit at PCC and I_L is the maximum demand load current (fundamental frequency component) at PCC.

Table 8.3 Voltage Harmonics Limits

BUS VOLTAGE AT PCC	INDIVIDUAL VOLTAGE DISTORTION (%)	TOTAL VOLTAGE DISTORTION THD (%)
69 kV and below	3.0	5.0

Source: IEEE Standards Association, IEEE Std 519-1992: IEEE Recommended Practices and Requirements for Harmonic Control in Electrical Power Systems. IEEE, Piscataway, NJ, 2008; Marcelo Gustavo Molina1 and Juan Manuel Gimenez Alvarez, California Interconnection Guidebook: A Guide to Interconnecting Customer-owned Electric Generation Equipment to the Electric Utility Distribution System Using California's Electric Rule 21, Intechopen, Rijeka, Croatia, 2011. With permission.

Note: THD, total harmonic distortion.

8.3.1 Voltage Regulation

Voltage variation and flicker is also important in microgrids. Flicker is a sudden change of voltage magnitude that may cause lights to flicker. Voltage variations and flicker could damage motors and home appliances if these happen too often or if the absolute value is too high. Flicker is common in grids that have large amounts of intermittent energy resources, such as solar and wind. In islanding mode, this could prove to be more damaging since the main grid that acts as a slack generator is disconnected. To minimize flickers, fast-responding energy storage systems, parallel to intermittent DGs, are necessary to work as a slack source to dampen voltage variations.

A DG unit can operate in parallel with the grid without causing a voltage fluctuation at the PCC, if its output is within ±5% of the prevailing voltage level of the grid at the PCC and meets the flicker requirements.[8]

The flicker limit for distribution systems including microgrids is also given in IEEE 141-1993 standard as shown in Figure 8.7. The figure shows acceptable voltage flicker limits most utilities use as their baseline. There is a visibility curve (the lower curve) beyond which the flicker is observable. The upper curve is the limit where the flicker is intolerable and objectionable. At 10 per hour, people begin to detect incandescent lamp flicker for voltage fluctuations larger than 1% and begin to object when the magnitude exceeds 3%.

The voltage sag is also an issue in microgrids especially in islanding, when large loads could be switched on. Prolonged voltage sags could damage the loads connected to the microgrids. Voltage sags are due to a large motor starting or a short circuit. Proper motor starting

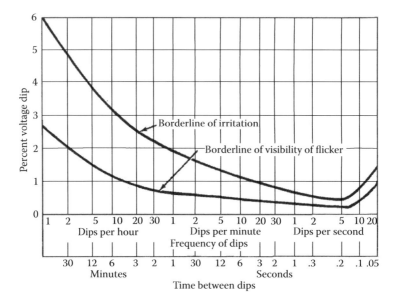

Figure 8.7 Flicker limit in distribution systems: IEEE STD 141. (From IEEE Standards Association, IEEE Std 1547.2-2008:IEEE Application Guide for IEEE Std 1547(TM), IEEE Standard for Interconnecting Distributed Resources with Electric Power Systems. IEEE, Piscataway, NJ, 2008. With permission.)

procedures such as soft starter should be used if the microgrid feeds large motors. Fast charging stations may also cause prolonged voltage deeps if they draw large currents for fast charging.[11]

At a steady-state operation, the voltage limits at the PCC, where the grid is connected with a microgrid, are specified in ANSI C84.1 Range A.[8]

8.3.2 Direct Current Injection

The injection of DC from DGs such as inverters into the power network causes the displacement of the AC voltage peak value and results in power transform cores to saturate faster. For this reason, the standard requires that the DGs' DC injection should not exceed 0.5% of the full rated output current at the point of interconnection.[8] Usually, larger inverters are connected to the network via an isolating connected transformer. The isolating transformer blocks the DGs DC injection as well as prevents triplen harmonics from propagating through the distribution network.

8.3.3 Power Factor

Some utilities require a power factor at the PCC to be maintained within 0.9 lagging or leading.[5] Moreover, most modern inverters coupled with an energy storage system have the capability of operating in four (P, Q) quadrants, where P indicates the active power and Q denotes the reactive power. Figure 8.8 shows a four-quadrant inverter's operating zones. It is seen that the inverter can inject (discharge) or absorb (charge) a certain amount of active and reactive power to the distribution system. This functionality can be utilized to control the voltage and the power factor at the PCC or use the inverter as a volt var optimization device.

8.3.4 Protection

A microgrid's connection with the main grid's distribution system may adversely affect the protection settings of utility assets in the vicinity of the PCC.[12] A new coordination study is necessary for the interconnected system around PCC. In legacy distribution systems, faults are fed by the utility source only. In such cases there are well-developed techniques to coordinate protection equipment, such as breakers and fuses, for distribution systems. In a microgrid connected to the main grid, a fault can be fed from both the utility and microgrid sources. Figure 8.9 shows fault current contributions from a microgrid DG

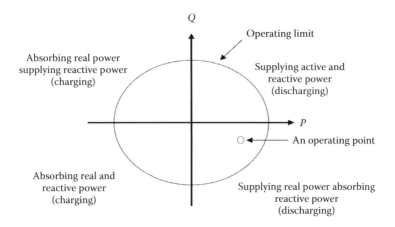

Figure 8.8 Operating range of a modern four-quadrant inverter.

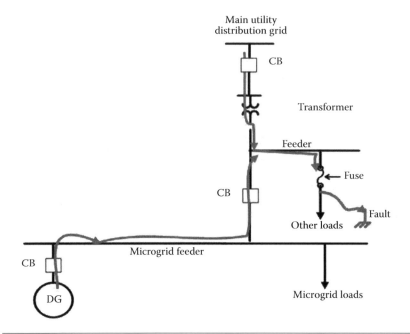

Figure 8.9   Fault contributions of DG to the short-circuit fault.

and from the utility grid. All DGs will contribute to the fault. The figure shows that the short-circuit level of the feeder is changed due to the microgrid connection. The microgrid fault current contributions may alter the short-circuit levels to the point where a fuse–breaker miscoordination could occur. This could affect the reliability and the safety of the distribution system. Therefore, it is necessary to make a new coordination study to consider the contribution of the DGs to the fault currents and coordinate the fuse and breakers accordingly.

Also, the feeders and cables' capacity may need to be upgraded after the microgrid is commissioned.

The protection limit setting and the normal operating range of microgrids at the PCC are usually defined by the local utility. For example, BC Hydro's technical requirements for connecting DGs with less than 100 kW to the BC Hydro grid is explained in a detailed document called distributed generation technical interconnection requirements (DGTIR)-100.[5] The document also specifies applicable Canadian electric codes for interconnecting DGs. Similarly, the California Energy Commission has issued a guideline for interconnecting electric-generating equipment to the grid. Table 8.4 shows a

Table 8.4   Summary Table of Trip Settings and Operating Requirements

	RANGE		MAX TRIP TIME[a]	
VOLTAGE AT PCC[b]	VOLTS: 120 V BASE	%	CYCLES	SECONDS
Fast under	$V_{POC} < 60$	<50%	10	0.167
Under	$60 \leq V_{POC} < 106$	50–88%	120	2.0
Normal	$106 \leq V_{POC} \leq 132$	88–110%	Normal Operation	
Over	$132 < V_{POC} < 165$	110–137%	120/30[c]	2.0/0.5[c]
Fast over	$V_{POC} > 165$	>137%	6	0.1

	RANGE		MAX TRIP TIME[a]	
FREQUENCY[b]	Hz: 60 Hz BASE	%	CYCLES	SECONDS
Under	<59.3	99.2%	10	0.167
Normal	59.3–60.5	98.8–100.8	Normal Operation	
Over	>60.5	100.8	10	0.167
Flicker	Generating facility should not cause the voltage at the PCC to exceed the limits defined by the maximum borderline of irritation curve in IEEE STD 519-1992.			
Harmonics[b]	Generating facility harmonic distortion shall be in compliance with IEEE STD 519-1992. Exception: shall be evaluated using the same criteria as for the loads at that site.			
Power factor	Between 0.9 leading and lagging. Operation outside this range may be acceptable for power factor correction purposes or if otherwise allowed by utility.			
DC injection	≤0.5% of generating facility rated output current			

Source: *California Interconnection Guidebook: A Guide to Interconnecting Customer-owned Electric Generation Equipment to the Electric Utility Distribution System Using California's Electric Rule 21,* California Energy Commission, Sacramento, CA, 2003. With permission.

[a] Maximum trip time is the maximum allowable time between the onset of the abnormal condition and the Generating Facility ceasing to energize the distribution system.

[b] PCC means point of common coupling; it is a defined term in Rule 21. For generating facilities ≤ 11 kVA, set points may be fixed. For generating facilities > 11 kVA, set points and trip times shall be field adjustable, and different voltage set points and trip times may be negotiated with the utility.

[c] Trip times are for generating facilities ≤ 11/>11 kVA.

summary of the protection setting and the normal operating range of a microgrid at the point of interconnection for the state of California.[6]

8.3.5 Overvoltage Switching Transient

Microgrids with a large generating capacity may inject unacceptable overvoltage transients into the distribution grid when switching on and off DGs, or connecting/disconnecting large microgrid loads, or due to a ground fault. High overvoltage transients may damage the equipment connected to the grid. Especially when a microgrid is connected to the main grid via transformers, where one or both sides of them are isolated from the ground, severe overvoltage transients may happen. For larger microgrids, an overvoltage transient study is needed to make sure that the overvoltage transient beyond the acceptable limit does not happen on the microgrid network and on the distribution grid.[13]

8.3.6 Voltage and Frequency Stability

The control of the voltage and frequency of a microgrid in islanding mode is an important task of the microgrid control system. The control system should be able to keep the voltage and the frequency within the acceptable limits in spite of microgrid load variations. Because the system is disconnected from the grid (weak system), any small variation of load may cause a fluctuation of the voltage and the frequency of the DGs, and the DGs may start to oscillate with each other and go out of synchronism easily.[14]

8.3.7 Antiislanding Protection

Antiislanding protection is a safety and protection requirement for microgrids. Antiislanding protection ensures that an interconnected microgrid stops injecting power into a powered-down main grid within a short period (0.1 s) by activating the microgrid's islanding breaker. This ensures safety for the electrical workers working on the disconnected distribution system as well as the public.[5] DGs and inverters should have built-in protection circuitry to detect antiislanding situations and act accordingly.

8.4 OASIS Case Study

The Open Access to Sustainable Intermittent Sources (OASIS) microgrid is located on the British Columbia Institute of Technology (BCIT) main campus in Burnaby. It incorporates two parking canopies covering 120 car stalls in an area of 1664 m². The project consists of arrays of solar photovoltaic (PV) panels and Li-ion battery energy storage system (BESS) connected to one of BCIT's existing substations through a 208 kW bidirectional three-phase DC/AC inverter, which in turn is connected to the BC Hydro network. The PCC is the existing BCIT receiving station—located on the campus, which connects to a 12.5 kV BC Hydro overhead line.[15]

BCIT's Burnaby campus receives power from three main receiving stations. One is a 12.5 kV overhead feeder that supplies the North campus receiving station. The area served by the North receiving station contains a peak load of 2.12 MW and the full load capacity of 9.2 MVA. The distribution to the designated buildings (loads) is through 11 substations in the North campus area.

As discussed, the OASIS microgrid is a grid-interactive system—which includes an energy storage system—and is capable of operating in parallel with a utility as well as operating completely isolated from BC Hydro's grid and in stand-alone (islanding) mode. Therefore, the OASIS microgrid requires having access to the available power on the utility feeder. The interconnection of such a system with the utility grid is critical. To obtain the permit to interconnect with BC Hydro, the OASIS microgrid had to implement the process discussed earlier and conduct all the required studies and reviews.

Given the fact that BCIT's power consumption at the point of interconnection was much higher than OASIS' generating capacity, the OASIS microgrid fell under BC Hydro's load displacement program and was required to meet the technical requirements of "35 KV and Below Interconnection Requirements for Power Generators." These requirements aim to ensure the safe isolation for maintenance, islanding, grid-tied operation, protection, fail safe, transient stability, and harmonics propagation. These requirements and the tests/analysis conducted to prove full compliance with these requirements were then captured in an interconnection agreement document concluded by relevant stakeholders. This section provides an overview of the OASIS project, referring to a highly simplified SLD of the whole system included in Chapter 4 (Figure 4.3).

8.4.1 *General Requirements*

The OASIS microgrid needed to meet the requirements stated in BC Hydro's DGTIR document "35 kV and Below Interconnection

Requirements for Power Generators." This document outlines project responsibilities, general requirements (such as the physical location of the PCC, safety, synchronization, safe isolation), and certifications that are required to certify that OASIS' power generation facility was designed, constructed, and tested in accordance with BC Hydro's DGTIR spec. This document also outlines and describes the performance requirements for power quality (switching overvoltage transients) and voltage and current harmonics. Additionally, the impacts of harmonic injections from the OASIS microgrid bidirectional, four-quadrant, CSA C22.2 No. 107.1-01-certified DC\AC inverter and electric vehicle charging stations were required to be explored through a harmonic distortion analysis.

8.4.2 Protection

The OASIS microgrid provided protections with adequate sensitivity to detect and clear all electrical faults on its premises coordinated with other BCIT and BC Hydro protection systems. The OASIS microgrid installed a controllable CB on its feeder, associated with a multifunction protection relay. The overcurrent protections were required to protect the OASIS feeder in scenarios where the current flow in the OASIS feeder exceeded the protection preset value and were achieved by implementing an instantaneous and time-overcurrent protection (ANSI 50/51).

To meet the service entrance protection requirements, the OASIS microgrid utilized the under/overvoltage (ANSI 27/59) and under/overfrequency (ANSI 81) within its protection relay. During abnormal operating situations or a fault on the BC Hydro system, OASIS may experience voltage deviations. Through the implementation of timed undervoltage tripping (ANSI 27) and overvoltage (ANSI 59) tripping, OASIS would be able to protect its equipment. For safety, a preventative and corrective interlock system was implemented. As such, the multifunction protection relay on the OASIS feeder was interlocked with the BCIT feeder protection relay in the upstream receiving station. OASIS would disconnect and stop supplying power to the BCIT/BC Hydro distribution lines—in case the receiving station feeder protection relay was activated. Additionally, the OASIS inverter was equipped with an antiislanding protection mechanism to disconnect OASIS in case the BC Hydro/BCIT networks were disconnected from the main distribution network.

Moreover, the CB would trip if any of the phases was lost or there was loss of power to the protection relay. By implementing these measures, OASIS' generation facility was able to detect the loss of phase and power and isolate itself from the distribution system.

The automatic synchronization to the grid was done by the inverter control and protection system. Moreover, OASIS' equipment was rated to carry and interrupt the fault levels that would be or will be available at OASIS' generation location.

A protection coordination study analysis was conducted to assist with identifying the service entrance protections. Subsequently, it was identified that the main relay in the upstream receiving station did not meet the required standard for the clearing time and would not clear a fault more than 0.4 s before the BC Hydro substation breaker opens. While these relays do technically coordinate, BC Hydro required the relay to clear faults faster. To implement the recommended settings, a complete site-wide coordination study was required for the BCIT campus distribution network before any adjustments were made to the main entrance relay at the PCC.

OASIS was also required to operate its generation facility in such a way that the voltage levels on the BC Hydro distribution system would stay within their acceptable range. OASIS utilized the necessary functions to trip its feeder CB when the voltage was outside the predetermined limits. OASIS' generation facility was also required to cease to energize the BC Hydro system within the clearing times as indicated in BC Hydro's DGTIR document for 35 kV and above systems. As for the under/overfrequency trip settings and timings, BC Hydro determined those limits on a case-by-case basis. These functionalities were implemented and utilized in the multifunction protection relay installed at the OASIS feeder.

For safe isolation, the applicable standards required the inverters to cease energizing the distribution system within 0.1 s upon loss of the BC Hydro supply, as specified in BC Hydro's DGTIR document. The DG system would stay deenergized until the grid was returned to its normal state. This functionality was provided by the CSA-certified bidirectional inverter in PCS.

8.4.3 Control and Telecommunications Requirements

As described in BC hydro's DGTIR interconnected at 35 kV and below, the monitoring and control of generators that connect to the BC Hydro distribution system was required only for projects that were 1 MVA or higher in size. Although there were no specific requirements for this plant, however, as part of the research and demonstration aspect of the project, OASIS installed power quality measurement meters and recorders at its feeder (480 V), at the high voltage (12.5 kV) side of the step-up wye–wye transformer in BCIT's distribution substation, and also in the power conversion system on both AC and DC connections.

The data gathered from these metering and recording devices were visualized and made available to the system operators through human–machine interface (HMI) for the substation automation system as well as for the EMS.

8.4.4 Project Interconnection Requirements

The DGTIR for connecting to BC Hydro at 35 kV and below only identified the minimum technical requirements a distributed generation system must meet and outlined the expected system conditions that DG facilities could encounter while connected to BC Hydro's system. When required, more site- and project-specific studies and requirements for additional protection and control equipment would be stated in the PIR. In OASIS' case, this document was jointly prepared by BCIT and BC Hydro. BC Hydro needed to make sure that the addition of the OASIS microgrid did not negatively impact the safety of BC Hydro personnel or the general public or the reliability and the power quality for customers already connected to the feeder that the power generator was connected to. To ensure that the OASIS project—as an interconnection customer—would meet these requirements, OASIS was required to submit to BC Hydro a series of documents as described in the PIR and included the following: OASIS facility construction issues of the overall one-line diagrams, protection, control, data communication, three-line AC diagrams, site plan(s) of OASIS microgrid, private line (complete with major pieces of equipment, location of PCC, and a piece of BC Hydro feeder), substation (with all major buildings and pieces of equipment, property fence, main gates, and access road), interconnection protection settings (magnitudes and timings), interconnection protection coordination study (from the interconnection customer protection to the BC Hydro feeder protection), DC system (batteries, chargers, DC supplies), power distribution and alarm schematics, manufacturer's technical specifications (or data sheets) of the generator unit, inverter, entrance CB and interconnection protection relay, interconnection verification and inspection (i.e., commissioning tests) plan for review, schedule of commissioning tests identified in the plan given earlier, and last but not least the engineering record drawings (i.e., as-built drawings).

As a result of the PIR for BCIT's OASIS microgrid, no special isolation procedures had to be in place to isolate this project when the work takes place on the DC feeder that the solar panels connect to.

In conclusion, in order to synchronize and connect OASIS to the electrical grid, BC Hydro, as the main utility company of the province as well as the local municipal authorities, imposed certain guidelines and technical requirements to make sure that the operation of OASIS would not adversely impact the reliability and the power quality of the interconnected distribution network and would not create risks to the operating and maintenance personnel. BCIT's OASIS microgrid secured an interconnection agreement, which has allowed OASIS to be fully operational since its completion in March 2014.

References

1. CIGRÉ C6.22 Working Group (2012, December) *Microgrid Evolution Roadmap*. CIGRE International Council on Large Electrical Systems.
2. Chris Greacen, Richard Engel, and Thomas Quetchenbach (2013, April) *A Guidebook on Grid Interconnection and Islanded Operation of Mini-Grid Power Systems Up to 200 kW*. Lawrence Berkeley National Laboratory, Berkeley, CA.
3. IEEE 1547.4-2011 (2011) IEEE guide for design, operation, and integration of distributed resource island systems with electric power systems. IEEE, Piscataway, NJ.
4. Paul Sheaffer (2011, September) Interconnection of distributed generation to utility systems: Recommendations for technical requirements, procedures and agreements, and emerging issues. *RAP Energy Solutions*. Available at http://www.raponline.org/document/download/id/4572.

5. BC Hydro (2014, October 17) *Distributed Generation Technical Interconnection Requirements 100 kW and Below (DGTIR-100).* Available at https://www.bchydro.com/content/dam/BCHydro/customer-portal /documents/corporate/regulatory-planning-documents/integrated-resource -plans/current-plan/dgtir100.pdf.
6. Cris Cooley Overdomain, Chuck Whitaker, and Edan Prahbu. *California Interconnection Guidebook: A Guide to Interconnecting Customer-owned Electric Generation Equipment to the Electric Utility Distribution System Using California's Electric Rule 21.* Overdomain, LLC Endecon Engineering Reflective Energies. (2003, September). Available at http:// www.energy.ca.gov/reports/2003-11-13_500-03-083F.PDF.
7. Marcelo Gustavo Molina and Juan Gimenez Alvarez (2011) Technical and regulatory exigencies for grid connection of wind generation, wind farm. *Technical Regulations, Potential Estimation and Siting Assessment,* Dr. G. Orlando Suvire (Ed.). Intechopen, Rijeka, Croatia. Available at http://www.intechopen.com/books/wind-farm-technical-regulations -potential-estimation-and-itingassessment/technical-and-regulatory -exigencies-for-grid-connection-of-wind-generation.
8. IEEE 1547.2 (2008) IEEE standard for interconnecting distributed resources with electric power systems. IEEE, Piscataway, NJ.
9. Ankita Papriwal and Amita Mahor (2012, September) Mitigation of harmonies in inverters. *IOSR Journal of Engineering (IOSRJEN),* 2, 9, 98–105.
10. IEEE 519-2014 (2014) IEEE recommended practices and requirements for harmonic control in electrical power systems. IEEE, Piscataway, NJ.
11. BC Hydro Power Smart (n.d.) *Power Quality: A Guide to Voltage Fluctuation and Light Flicker.* Available at https://www.bchydro.com /content/dam/hydro/medialib/internet/documents/psbusiness/pdf/power _quality_a_guide_to_voltage_fluctuation_and_light_fl.pdf.
12. Galina Antonova, Massimo Nardi, Alan Scott, and Michael Pesin (2012) Distributed generation and its impact on power grids and microgrids protection. *IEEE 65th Annual Conference for Protective Relay Engineers,* April 2012, Texas, USA.
13. S. Chen and H. Yu (2010) A review on overvoltages in microgrid. *Power and Energy Engineering Conference (APPEEC), 2010 Asia–Pacific,* March 28–31, 2010, Chengdu, China.
14. J. Peas Lopes, C. Moreira, and A. Madureira (2006, May) Defining control strategies for microgrids islanded operation. *Power Systems, IEEE Transactions,* 21, 2, 916–924.
15. Minoo Shariat-Zadeh, Ali Palizban, Hassan Farhangi, and Calin Surdu (2014) Analysis and validation of interconnection requirements of a large renewable energy installation with the utility grid. *CIGRE Canada Conference,* Toronto, September 2014.

9

MICROGRID ECONOMIC, ENVIRONMENTAL, AND SOCIAL STUDIES

JOEY DABELL

Contents

This chapter looks beyond the purely technical issues to explore some of the complexities associated with the economic, environmental, and societal aspects of microgrids and brings emphasis to some of the intangibles, such as energy surety, local benefits, and a broader system-wide compatibility, and the issues surrounding them. The chapter discusses economic justification, environmental assessments, community outreach, consumer behavior, and interconnectedness of these topics in the context of renewable energy and microgrids. A case study summarizing the energy awareness and reduction campaign conducted under the campus microgrid initiative at the British Columbia Institute of Technology (BCIT) is included at the end of the consumer behavior discussion.

Making the case for microgrids requires comprehensive and holistic studies of energy use in the context of social, technical, environmental, and economic issues, which are highly interdependent in nature. These interdependencies form a symbiotic socio-techno-enviro economic relationship that needs more study in order to be adequately characterized and understood. Some cost benefit analyses have been done in the United States,[1] Europe,[2] and Canada,[3] although to a lesser degree. However, not enough has been done to the extent needed to understand and characterize the issues, let alone to highlight the benefits that could be achieved with microgrids. In a recent publication by Lund University, in Sweden,[4] the challenges associated with broad scale projects, like those associated with climate change, have been dubbed *wicked problems*. Wicked problems are problems that are so complex they have many causes with a web of interdependencies influencing one another so as to make it extremely difficult to identify and target the causes without triggering unpredictable interactions.

From a techno-economic perspective, it remains difficult to justify the investment in microgrids until they can be integrated into the super grid in which case the benefits, like resiliency, distributed command and control, and security, can be assessed. This is a complex and multifaceted task. Some of the issues include how to quantify the intangibles such as energy surety, local benefits, and a broader system-wide compatibility. From a socio-techno-economic perspective, grassroots movements and behavioral change campaigns can have a huge impact toward influencing energy conservation habits, development and adoption of renewable energy technologies, and development of standards and policies that support these objectives. Yet even at the most basic level, there are complex linkages between our awareness of issues and options, the conservation options we choose, the technologies that are available on the market to help us realize our choices, and the policies and processes that support all these options. The environmental issues to be considered include the substantial amount of greenhouse gas (GHG) emissions produced from burning fossil fuel and the negative impact of these emissions to the local community and our planet. The transportation of fossil fuels has associated economic costs that impact communities, emission costs caused by the transport vehicles, and increased risk of further environmental damage through potential fuel spills, which contaminate the soil, the groundwater, the food chain, and the entire cycle of life. Capturing and quantifying the benefits from all these extremely diverse and yet closely connected perspectives require a holistic vision and cross-discipline collaborative approach that is critical to winning against climate change.

Microgrids have been studied for a number of years, and their potential benefits, for example, to improve power surety and reduce emissions, are widely discussed, but the current status of microgrid projects in general is largely at the prototyping and demonstration phase. Demonstration projects are not intended to be financially viable, but the consideration of eventual viability factors, such as understanding the demand requirements, can influence the design choices and provide more robust options for future deployment. In the last few years, a number of microgrid pilot projects have been conducted. Resolution of remaining challenges such as scaling up and component integration have been successfully demonstrated. In the longer term, these kinds of activities can help to move microgrids toward future commercialization and the integration of microgrid networks system wide.

Case studies based on the demonstration projects have tremendous potential to provide knowledge dissemination and to identify transferable socioeconomic and environmental lessons that may be applicable in other contexts. Identifying and communicating microgrid projects in this way can lead to overall increased awareness, better understanding by individuals of how they can fit into the picture, official mandates and political commitment, and a long-term vision for microgrids and renewable energy. Evaluating the case studies, however, calls for a framework that considers the multifaceted nature of the issues, while providing coordinated identification and selection methodologies, standardized data collection and reporting, and a host of similar coordination and standardization considerations.

The campus Energy Open Access to Sustainable Intermittent Sources (OASIS) microgrid highlighted in this book was conducted as a demonstration project, and it is representative of an urban microgrid. At the outset of that project, the specification for microgrids was a significant missing piece of the puzzle. Specifications of this kind were not well understood, and there was uncertainty among end consumers, utilities, and related stakeholders as to what the specification should look like. The simple and compelling premise of the campus microgrid project was that over the life cycle of the project, by improvising on the initial specification, the project would result in experiential learning and generation of real-world data that could be leveraged to support socio-techno-economic and environmental justification for microgrids. In particular, the Energy OASIS microgrid is going a long way toward demonstrating some of the socioeconomic benefits that may be associated with urban microgrid installations in other contexts, including the ability to support a portion of the campus loads while isolated from the main grid and the ability to contribute energy from a renewable source (solar photovoltaic [PV]) to offset the campus requirements for power from the utility grid.

The high cost of energy and the energy supply issues in off-grid communities can be deterrents to new businesses, limiting future economic opportunities in remote communities. In Canada, there are over 290 remote and first nation communities[5] who rely largely on diesel generators for their power. While the total population of British Columbia's remote communities is smaller than the overall population in other provinces or territories such as Quebec or Nunavut, over 85 of those communities are located in British Columbia, more than any other province in Canada. The significant social, environmental, and economic costs this represent are further underscored with an example from one of the 38 remote communities in the province of Ontario that for 2008 had a reported consumption of 1.2 million liters of diesel fuel and over 3400 tons of carbon emissions.[6] From a socioeconomic perspective, taken on its own, the environmental costs illustrated in this localized example are difficult enough for people to grasp, but for society to understand the multifaceted effects of similar scenarios combined on a global scale is virtually impossible. Establishing microgrids in both remote and urban communities will contribute to increased awareness, optimization of local renewable energy, and acceleration of the the transition to renewable energy system wide.

9.1 Economic Justification

Historically, the management of the main power grid has meant maintaining the same standards for power quality and reliability targets across the entire network of the power grid. This all-things-to-all-people approach means that infrastructure and operational investment and strategies often target a middle ground; the impacts of which are felt as benefits by some but as losses by others.[7] One of the local economic benefits and justification for microgrids is that the source of power is located close to the demand, providing the potential to reduce both the distribution and transmission network capacity and the transmission losses. Across North America, within urban environments, there are residential and commercial pockets that share grid connections with key buildings and infrastructure such as hospitals, schools, data centers, and military bases, where it is critical to match the loads to the energy supply at all times. In contrast, there are many other pocket communities, where it may be less critical to maintain such service levels and where there could be more flexibility to make decisions depending on a series of factors. The current electricity grid was never designed to juggle such complex decisions. Microgrids provide the capability to tailor local requirements, facilitate multiple decision-making, and improve overall reliability. In order to fully utilize these benefits, however, they first need to be quantified and integrated into applicable regulatory frameworks.

For the most part, all microgrids strive to offer the same benefits, namely, to provide reliable, resilient, and secure power on a localized scale. For many parts of the North American grid, the investment has been driven by crisis such as the blackout of the northeast in 2003 affecting Canada and the United States, and Hurricane Sandy, resulting in emergence of new policies, such as mandatory reliability standards. When this is further supported by favorable economics, such as the falling cost of renewable energy technologies, then the cost benefits of improved resiliency, security, and disaster recovery from the integration of microgrids make conventional economic sense and become fairly easy to justify. From a socioeconomic perspective, where people have experienced a crisis firsthand, the prospect of self-reliance for power offered by microgrids becomes an easy sell.

For many other areas including the province of British Columbia, in Canada, the cost of electricity is so low making the economics of urban microgrids extremely difficult to justify.

In regions of low-cost electricity, a strong case also needs to be made for other more intangible benefits of microgrids. Canadian and U.S. electricity grids have many active interconnections[8] and have traded electricity to the tune of billions of dollars. The United States is increasingly engaged in projects to improve resiliency and reliability in the North American grid. This mandate will require the coordination between Canada and the United States for micro- and macrogrid infrastructure, regulatory issues, and communication and related standards. Indeed, concerns over the impact of climate change to the shrinking arctic ice pack, and the needs of northern communities to reduce their reliance on diesel generators, have helped to trigger a program of microgrid demonstration projects in Alaska and other arctic locations. While the location is more remote, this scenario has some fairly tangible benefits too, making the economics justification more straightforward.

Advocates of microgrids are able to envision the many intangible benefits as contributors to a larger picture such as steps toward facilitating the transition to renewable energy sources. While many kinds of intangible benefits have been identified, others can still only be surmised. Furthermore, the full spectrum of the benefits that could be attained from microgrids varies depending on local conditions including end consumer requirements, geographic location, climate, regulations, and others. The intangibles will only become quantifiable and understood as more microgrids are implemented leading to the development and the analysis of case studies and to the broad dissemination of lessons learned from those case studies.

One of the key intangibles is energy surety, which encompasses reliability, resiliency, security, and disaster recovery. Energy surety means having assured access to reliable supplies of energy, the ability to protect and deliver sufficient energy to meet operational needs, and the ability for disaster recovery. The use of microgrid modeling and simulation tools have been proposed[9] as a mechanism for analyzing various options for local scenarios to find the optimal configuration of component technologies that will maximize the economic rate of return for a potential solution. Until such time that we can better put a price to the intangibles, and are in a position to calculate pure monetary costs, the use of simulations could help build an economic justification for microgrids and renewables.

At the local level, the benefits of microgrids can contribute to the deferral of potential infrastructure investments via the reduction or the shifting of peak loads thereby reducing peak demand charges and electrical consumption costs. Energy cost reductions can come from reduced energy use, for example, from increased efficiency and demand response or from reductions in peak charges and consumption costs. In the case of the campus microgrid identified earlier, further benefits could be achieved through the use of the microgrid facility as a living lab research, development, and demonstration environment and as a teaching and learning aide.

From a technoeconomic perspective, a number of studies have been done around how business cases and cost-benefits analysis for microgrids can work, for example, in Canada the Natural Sciences and Engineering Research Council Smart Microgrid-Net project,[10] in the United States, the Lawrence Berkeley National Laboratory studies,[7] and in Europe, the More Microgrids[11] project. Recent large-scale blackouts have made it clear that the top-down architecture and unidirectional power flow of the existing North American electricity grid is becoming less and less sustainable. The comfort level of utilities with new grid-interconnection approaches appears to be increasing, and as the support for new ownership and regulatory models grows, so will the adoption rate of microgrids. In the meantime, cases could be made for microgrids where the development of the super grid would require huge investments.

As discussed elsewhere in this text, microgrids can be categorized as off-grid (i.e., remote communities), grid-enabled (i.e., urban communities), and mobile (i.e., forward-operating bases) microgrids and incorporate a wide variety of technologies, generation architectures, use case scenarios, and business models. Emerging microgrid business models can include any combination of utility-implemented, customer-owned, microgrid-as-a-service or pay-as-you-go approaches. Perhaps one of the most compelling cases for future system-wide adoption can be made by focusing on the islanding capabilities afforded by microgrids. The ability of key buildings or neighborhoods including hospitals and schools to support themselves when isolated from the main grid could be a strong selling point with the community, the utilities, and the policy makers.

In jurisdictions like the province of British Columbia, in Canada, where regulatory pressure keeps the cost of energy low, it can be difficult to justify the investments into microgrids. However, it is critical even in these artificially kept low energy cost scenarios that we change our current way of thinking toward a holistic and future-thinking approach, with less emphasis on the immediate economic payback. If the barriers, which are largely regulatory and social in nature, could be broken, the integration of renewable sources and energy storage into a network of microgrids could not only have a significant impact on the urban microgrids and the renewable energy economy but could also help to better secure the future of our local and global environments.

Society has become more and more inured to hearing terms like *climate change* and *global warming*. The socioeconomic benefits most frequently identified with microgrids such as[12] raising awareness for energy and GHG reductions, creation of new research and job opportunities, and electrification of remote communities have also lost their meaning and impact. It is critical to the economic justification for microgrids that the rationale grows from collaborative partnerships toward diverse interests within our communities.

9.2 Environmental Assessments

An environmental assessment is a means of discerning how a project impacts the environment before the project is permitted to go ahead. Generally, environmental assessments are done for large projects that could harm the environment. An environmental assessment is a planning and decision-making tool that predicts the negative effects a project could have on the environment. It identifies potential ways to avoid or mitigate these effects. The environmental assessment process is important to ensure that major projects meet the goals of environmental, economic, and social sustainability. The assessment process is also needed to ensure that the issues and the concerns of the public, the interested stakeholders, and the government agencies are considered.

In Canada, governments use the information from environmental assessments to help them decide whether or not the project can go forward. Under the Canadian Environmental Assessment Act of 2012, any project may be required to conduct an environmental assessment when there may be adverse environmental impact within the federal jurisdiction. Potential adverse effects include impact on Aboriginal peoples, such as limiting their use of lands and resources for traditional purposes, and changes to the environment that are directly linked to or necessarily incidental to any federal decisions about a project. As part of the environmental assessment process, the government of Canada is obliged to consult and accommodate Aboriginal peoples.

Aboriginal consultations seek to achieve informed consent and early involvement in the process. Information regarding the requirements and the scope for an environmental assessment can be found on the Canadian Environmental Assessment Agency website (https://www.ceaa–acee.gc.ca/).

British Columbia is the only Canadian province to have its own dedicated office to undertake environmental assessments. The province's Environmental Assessment Office was established under the Environmental Assessment Act in 1995. Information can be found on the provincial government's Environmental Assessment Office website (http://www.eao.gov.bc.ca/). A project may be excluded from the Canadian Environmental Assessment Act requirement if it is determined that the province will conduct an equivalent assessment.

Environmental assessments in general share commonalities in the areas that are reviewed. These include examination of the project's regional and national contexts, location and proximity factors, geophysical environment, aquatic and terrestrial environments, atmospheric environment, socioeconomic characteristics, project technology components, and project development and operating activities.

Microgrids by definition include the integration of renewable energy sources. Any form of energy production will have some level of environmental impact. If one considers the full life cycle of a renewable energy resource such as a solar PV panel, the manufacturing process from the extraction of raw materials to the delivery of the panel will have an associated environmental impact. Building a microgrid will require the use fossil fuels through the construction project life cycle and will result in some environmental impact. Still, by most measures, the integration of renewable energy sources is generally acknowledged to have a significantly lower environmental impact than nonrenewable sources. Renewable energy technologies, however, introduce novel characteristics such that the potential environmental impacts are of a different nature. By improving our understanding of the current and potential environmental issues associated with each renewable energy source, we can take steps to effectively avoid or minimize these impacts by incrementally integrating them with the grid. Wind and solar PV systems require large areas for viable energy production. In the case of wind turbines, for example, very little of the land is actually occupied by the turbines themselves. As a result, most of the land the wind farm occupies may still be used for other purposes, such as grazing or crops. Offshore wind farm locations can reduce visual concerns, and the open ocean provides a very good wind resource.

9.3 Community Outreach

Most consumers do care about the use of renewable energy. However, a number of recent conferences and studies, such as a 2011 study commissioned by the National Renewable Energy Laboratory,[13] indicate that the interest is declining, while at the same time changes in behavior are growing. The good news here may be that this seemingly backward finding is generally attributed to new behaviors having become less burdensome to the point of being so fully integrated into daily routines that they have become second nature. Still, in the minds of consumers, terms like *renewable energy* and *microgrid* are lumped into broadly categorized concerns, such as *climate change* and *energy conservation*. As discussed earlier, over time, these kinds of categorizations are increasingly losing much of their appeal with the public and have come to be associated with insurmountable issues leading to disengagement rather than engagement with consumers and within communities. Our attitudes are closely connected with our beliefs, and people generally believe that renewable energy and conservation measures are positive things. However, in the case of renewables, and microgrids specifically, public awareness and understanding of the available options remains very low. People who live in close proximity to a renewable energy facility are generally more likely to have a significant level of awareness and stronger belief in the value of renewables. This information should tell us that while there are many different approaches to community outreach, the outreach strategies that are likely to work best are those that include some form of interaction and develop a sense of ownership with the public.

The Global Learning Forum 2015 (http://forum.renewablecities .ca/) highlighted an outreach project by Greenpeace Brazil to engage with schoolchildren for a renewable energy project to bring solar PV to their school. Among the many tactics available, the project leaders decided that the best way to achieve their objectives would be to use a showcase approach that included increasing awareness and engaging with people in a way they feel touched by or connected with the project, a process for public support, and a crowdfunding campaign. The project team believed that if the stakeholders felt ownership in the project, they would also feel empowered to replicate it elsewhere in their communities. Students were engaged in experiential learning activities including contributing input to the design and right through to helping with the installation work. The project was implemented, reached millions through its social network, brought changes to local tax policies and requests for stakeholders to share their experiences and help with replication of the project in other contexts.

Many cities like Copenhagen, Denmark, and Vancouver, Canada, are adopting 100% renewable energy policies (World Future Council and Renewable Cities programs). Ideally, these initiatives will be supported by open-access and inclusive discussion with all stakeholders in order to inform and educate the public, diversify energy market opportunities, and support long-term energy economic models that enable new business models to emerge.

9.4 Consumer Behavior

Changing the consumers' behavior patterns has a huge potential to contribute to not only how microgrids and related technologies are accepted and ultimately adopted but also to energy conservation and carbon reduction in general. The mind-sets of end users of energy, building system managers, energy regulators, and policy makers have the power to significantly contribute to energy consumption behaviors, environmental impact, and related issues. While technology is also a critical piece of the puzzle, the technology required to make the changes we are discussing already exists. It is the choices made by the consumers at all levels of the energy chain, from the selection of light bulbs in the home, to making technologies available in the marketplace, to selecting and integrating technologies, which have the largest effect on realizing change. The vast majority of citizens, however, do not know how much energy their specific behaviors and choices consume, how much they cost, or what impact they have on socioeconomic and environmental scales. How to engage these different energy consumers in energy-smart behaviors is, therefore, a challenge. At the end of the day, the biggest hope for change is very likely to be triggered from the bottom up, where pressure to change is exerted on governments by individuals through public interest groups.

Supporting renewable energy and reducing the impact of climate change require the promotion of cognitive, emotional, and behavioral changes, through the use of methodologies, frameworks, and tools drawn from a broad range of learning theories from across the education and health sectors. Some of the recent applications of behavior change have some roots in the social learning theory from the 1960s, developed around values of individuals, and what is and is not acceptable behavior. To support energy awareness and behavior change, these tools are being extended and more broadly marketed through the use of information technology and social media.

Behavior change interventions generally include some form of feedback; energy audits; social norms, or nudging. Feedback can take the form of direct feedback, indirect feedback, or combination of direct and indirect feedbacks. Direct or real-time feedback includes consumption data from smart meters received via in-home displays or computer monitors and hand-held devices. Indirect feedback includes information like historical or comparative information on consumption data like the information that comes from electricity bills. Years of research have found that feedback is most effective as an intervention tool when direct and indirect feedbacks are used together. Energy audits provide the information needed to make energy efficiency improvements to an environment and have the additional benefits of including engagement with consumers, which helps to reinforce the behavior changes. In the case of energy behaviors, social norms are sets of energy consumption and conservation behaviors that are considered acceptable by a particular group. A consideration with the use of social norms is the potential for people to feel shunned and isolated if they do not conform. The nudge theory uses positive reinforcement through indirect suggestion to provide a less forced compliance with a concept. For example, to nudge people to public trash bins, a busy pedestrian street in Copenhagen has used painted footprints leading from the middle of the street off to the trash bins.

Approaches for evaluating behavior change include quantitative evaluation such as smart metering and analysis of billing data, quantitative surveys, and self-reporting. There is a lot of appeal and potential for a significant impact through data visualization of the numbers. Among other considerations, a quantitative approach needs to include consideration and measures of effectiveness and testing for the reliability, to guide the selection of the measures that are adopted. Qualitative evaluations include tools such as interviews, surveys, and focus groups. In the case of web-based or paper surveys, both a pre- and a postsurvey are sometimes used. One may expect that a before-and-after snapshot approach could help better gauge the results, but in cases when it is not possible to gauge individual participants' responses between the two surveys, for example, when the postsurveys may not have been completed or returned by the same individuals from the presurveys, the outcomes may not be as expected. Surveys can introduce bias, for example, by asking leading questions or in cases where respondents self-select, and the design requires experienced input to help minimize this kind of risk.

In the case of campus microgrids, many studies have been conducted within student housing in the form of competitions between different residence buildings. These studies generally have similar objectives including the following:

1. Developing awareness in building residents of energy-related issues, impacts, and options
2. Investigating how building residents understand their own energy use patterns, for example, time of day and actual consumption levels, and how this understanding can help change behavior
3. Exploring how flexible building residents are willing to be in terms of the way in which they use their area and overhead lighting, electronic devices, appliances, such as washing machines and dishwashers, and space heating
4. Investigating how the use of tariffs and incentives, such as giveaways and rebates and time-of-use tariffs, could be used and to what effect
5. Investigating how the use of behavioral and related theories could be applied or adapted for energy behaviors and to what effect

9.4.1 Case Study for Behavior Change in the Campus Microgrid Student Residences

Between January 2010 and December 2011, the campus microgrid researchers conducted a research campaign into energy awareness and behavior change in the campus student residence houses. Activities included three short energy savings competitions between the residence buildings. The campus has just under 350 students living in seven residence houses, each house being of approximately the same design and vintage, and all running on electricity. At the time of the competitions, the annual energy consumption in the student residences was roughly 1 ½ MWh, which comprised about 10% of the residences' annual overall budget.

In December 2009, phase 1 of the campus microgrid project was completed, including the integration and installation of smart meters to enable submetering across the campus at the building level, including each of the seven houses. Campus microgrid researchers had developed a basic research energy management system (EMS) to collect meter data to help monitor and manage the campus microgrid technology components. The EMS was extended to include a residence web portal (shown in Figure 9.1), in order to support energy behavior change research activities. Students had access to near real-time feedback about the energy consumption in their own residence house and the neighboring residences. This direct feedback tool supported students and researchers with their goals to increase awareness of energy use, reduce consumption, and conduct research into the behavioral change models and demand-side management strategies, for example, the use of incentives, nudging, social marketing, and the effect of time of use (ToU) and similar tariffs. The residence web portal presented students with tips on energy conservation choices, easy access to near real-time feedback about their electricity consumption and costs, meaningful equivalencies, environmental information, and impact on GHGs. Additional feedback tools integrated with the residence web portal included a leader board with up-to-the-minute rankings enabling students to compare their energy consumption against the consumption of the other residences houses and a messaging tool that enabled students the option to receive customized messages from the EMS when the consumption in their residence house reached the specified level.

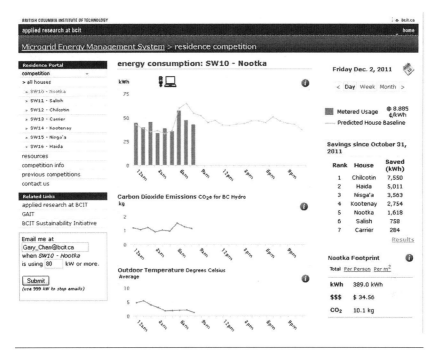

Figure 9.1 Campus microgrid residence web portal. (Courtesy of Joey Dabell.)

Prior to each of the three competitions, the students were invited to a short educational session on energy conservation. Awareness-raising sessions included introductions to common terminologies, local energy conditions and realities, energy consumption and costs, and campus microgrid technologies installed in the residence houses and around the campus. Students and researchers discussed examples of everyday energy-saving measures that would contribute to becoming the winning residence house. Students signed pledges to commit to their own energy conservation targets, were given tips on how much energy was consumed by typical behaviors, and were introduced to examples of nudging and use of prompts with their house-mates. Before and after each of the competitions, the students were asked to voluntarily complete web-based surveys to help researchers gauge the participants' awareness and attitudes. Where appropriate and possible, the survey feedback was applied to the improvements in the residences, such as the installation of low-flow shower heads and adaptation of laundry rooms to include options for cold water-only machines.

Energy conservation competition 1 ran from January 18, 2010 to January 31, 2010. The goal of this competition was education and outreach, to make energy use visible, to see what impact knowledge and visibility could have on energy consumption levels and how long any energy conservation might be sustained, and to identify the peak demand times. During the January 2010 competition, the winning residence house reduced its energy consumption by approximately 20% from the projected baseline. Two weeks following the competition, the average energy reduction for all houses bounced back up to only a 10% reduction, but that 10% savings was sustained for the remainder of the academic term.

Competition 2 was held for two one-month periods, October 2010 and November 2010. Some students would have been living in the residence during the January competition. For those who were not, the second competition provided the opportunity to build on existing momentum while looping back to catch up any students who were new to the student residences as of the September term start. The second round of competitions was designed to test hypotheses and leverage lessons learned from the first competition. It was suggested that the first competition was too short to support the building of new habits and that a longer competition period may result in more sustained energy use reductions. The longer two-month run for the competition was intended to test this theory. The first competition identified two significant demand peaks during each weekday, one in the early morning and one in the early evening. These peaks appeared to coincide with morning showers and after-school dinner and dishwashing. The primary goal of this second competition was to reduce the consumption during the peak demand times, particularly during the morning. The concept of ToU tariffs was introduced to students during the precompetition educational session. It is important to note that the local utility does not currently use any tariffs in their billing process. While the concept is common in other regions, both nationally and internationally, it was a new concept to the students in this study. The concept of ToU tariffs was simulated in the EMS and reflected in the display for the residence web portal. The simulated tariff included different electricity rates for high-peak ($0.20/kWh), mid-peak ($0.10/kWh), and off-peak ($0.05/kWh) demand times. The rate structure was reflected in the web portal by the use of different colored bars. Moreover, in-house designed and built intelligent load control systems were installed on hot water tanks to help optimize their temperature cycling demand (see Figure 9.2).

Over the course of the two competition months, the winning house lowered its peak electricity consumption by 20%. The overall reduction in the electricity consumption for all residence houses was about 14%. This resulted in a significant decrease in the residence's energy bill for this period with approximately $5000 in actual (not simulated) savings.

Competition 3 was held for a one-month period running from October 31, 2011 to November 27, 2011. Like Competition 1, the third competition returned to the basic goal of using conservation strategies to reduce energy consumption. Additionally, competition 3 introduced the use of social media to investigate its potential to broaden energy awareness and engagement. In this case, students were asked to post photographs or videos of their most creative approaches to reducing their energy use.

The competitions resulted in significant savings during the January 2010 competition, although the most savings occurred during the competition in October–November 2010, which carried through into December and even into the next semester (January–May). Figure 9.3 shows the total energy savings over the two-year period in which the competitions were held. The predicted energy consumption for the residences is based on historical data and plotted against actual consumption data. When compared against predicted values, the actual energy consumption during the two-year period where competitions were held represents a total energy savings of almost 350,000 kWh, a reduction of just over 20% when measured against the predicted baseline energy consumption for that period. The results demonstrated for participants that changes in energy consumption behaviors alone can make significant contributions toward reducing energy use and electricity costs. Figure 9.4, charted from the campus microgrid research findings, illustrates the degree to which behavior choices alone can impact energy consumption. The graph charts the savings achieved by each of the seven statistically similar student residence houses, over the course of a one-month competition. The gaps between each line on the graph indicate the difference in energy savings achieved between each house. The different savings can be fully attributed to the different individual energy conservation behaviors and collective strategies made by the students living in each residence house.

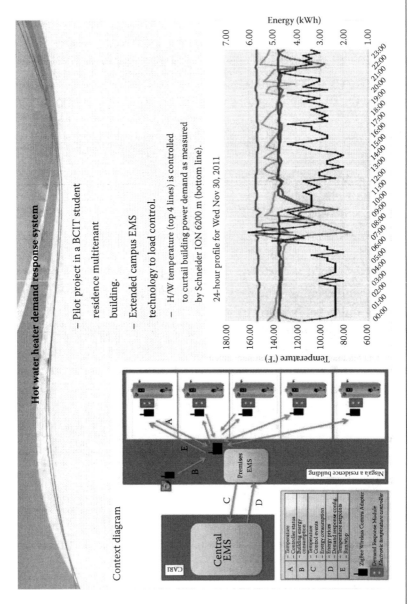

Figure 9.2 Hot water tank demand response system. CARI, Centre for Applied Research and Innovation at BCIT. (Courtesy of Eric Hawthorne.)

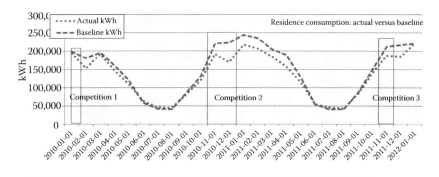

Figure 9.3   Total energy saved from 2010 to 2012. (Courtesy of Joey Dabell.)

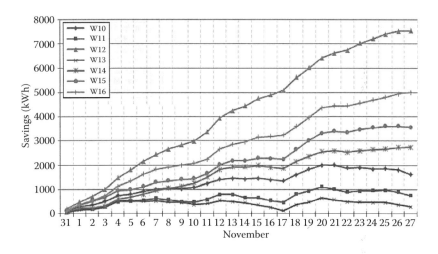

Figure 9.4   Impact of behavior on energy conservation. (Courtesy of Joey Dabell.)

9.5 Lessons Learned

Historically, actions for change are often triggered by crises. In some cases, the writing is on the wall long before the crisis is reached and actions are taken. Every crisis is an opportunity, but, and this is especially true in cases like climate change where the opportunities have been before us for some time, opportunity should not be made to wait for a crisis. Making changes toward choosing renewable energy options, including microgrids, represents the opportunity for building a sustainable future for our planet. University campuses and other communities are integrating local generation and storage assets to create urban microgrids. The combination of rooftop solar panels, power storage packs, electric vehicles, smart meters, and related equipment can make campuses, neighborhoods, and cities more resilient and efficient, for example, enabling communities to reduce peak loads, and support essential services during emergency power outages. Technology exists to knit urban microgrids together for sharing of power and resources. What is needed now is for a wholesale cross-discipline change in how we think and behave toward energy management and use. The legal, regulatory, and social barriers are playing a significant role in limiting the microgrid to more of a concept than a reality in Canada, but all the technologies exist to deliver on its promise. Although there are comparatively few microgrids in Canada, in the United States, it has been predicted[14] that the microgrid capacity could reached close to 2000 MW by the end of 2017.

References

1. Morris, G. Y., Abbey, C., Joos, G., and Marnay, C. *A Framework for the Evaluation of the Costs and Benefits of Microgrids.* Lawrence Berkeley National Laboratory, Berkeley, CA, 2011.
2. Mancarella, P. et al. Business cases for microgrids. *More Microgrids DH3*, April 2009. Accessed at http://www.microgrids.eu/documents/682.pdf (May 2015).
3. Morris, G. Y., Abbey, C., Wong, S., and Joos, G. *Evaluation of the Costs and Benefits of Microgrids with Consideration of Services Beyond Energy Supply.* IEEE, Piscataway, NJ, 2012.
4. McCormick, K., Luth Richter, J., and Pantzar, M. *Greening the Economy: Lessons from Scandinavia.* International Institute for Industrial Environmental Economics (IIIEE), Lund University, p. 7. 2015. Accessed at http://lup.lub.lu.se/record/4986134.
5. Natural Resources Canada. *Status of Remote/Off-Grid Communities in Canada.* Natural Resources Canada, Ottawa, ON, August 2011. Accessed at http://www.nrcan.gc.ca/energy/publications/sciences-technology/renewable/smart-grid/11916.
6. Curtis, D., and Singh, B. M. Northern micro-grid project—A concept. *Proceedings of the World Energy Congress*, Montreal, 2, 1251, June 2010.
7. Marnay, C., Zhou, N., Qu, M., and Romankiewicz, J. Lessons learned from microgrid demonstrations worldwide. LBNL-5825E. Lawrence Berkeley National Laboratory, Berkeley, CA 2012.
8. U.S. Department of Energy. *Quadrennial Energy Review: Energy Transmission, Storage, and Distribution Infrastructure.* U.S. Department of Energy, Washington, DC, April 2015.
9. Arriaga, M., Cañizares, C. A., and Kazerani, M. *Renewable Energy Alternatives for Remote Communities in Northern Ontario, Canada.* IEEE, Piscataway, NJ, November 2012.

10. Natural Sciences and Engineering Research Council of Canada. NSERC Smart Microgrid Network—NSMG-Net Annual Report 2013/2014. NSMG-Net, Ottawa, ON, 2014. Accessed at http://www.smart -microgrid.ca/.

11. Strbac, G., Anastasiadis, A., Hatziargyriou, N., and Tsikalakis, A. Business case for microgrids with economic and environmental evaluation. More Microgrids Annex H3.B to Deliverable DH3, 2009. European Commission, Contract SES6-019864. Accessed at http:// microgrids.eu/documents/684.pdf.

12. Schwaegerl, C. et al. Report on the technical, social, economic, and environmental benefits provided by microgrids on power system operation. More Microgrids DG3 & DG4. December 2009. European Commission, Contract SES6-019864. Accessed at http://www.microgrids .eu/documents/668.pdf.

13. National Renewable Energy Laboratory. Consumer attitudes about renewable energy: Trends and regional differences. NREL/SR-6A20- 50988. National Renewable Energy Laboratory, Washington, DC, April 2001.

14. Glave, J. *Great Grid Shakeup: Microgrids Invite Neighborhoods to Seize Control of Their Electrons*. Clean Energy Canada, Bowen Island, BC, 2014. Accessed at http://cleanenergycanada.org/2014/10/01/great-grid -shakeup-anatomy-microgrid/, May 2015.

Further Reading

Canadian Electricity Association. *Vision 2050—The Future of Canada's Electricity System*. Canadian Electricity Association, Ottawa, ON, 2014.

Electric Power Research Institute. *Methodological Approach for Estimating the Benefits and Costs of Smart Grid Demonstration Projects*. Electric Power Research Institute, Palo Alto, CA, 2010.

Fogg, B. J. *Persuasive Technology: Using Computers to Change What We Think and Do*. Morgan Kaufman Publishers, San Francisco, CA, 2003.

McKenzie-Mohr, D. *Fostering Sustainable Behavior: An Introduction to Community-Based Social Marketing*. New Society Publishers, Gabriola Island, BC Canada, February 2011.

The National Energy Technology Laboratory. *Building a Smart Grid Business Case*. August 2009. Developed for the U.S. Department of Energy Office of Electricity Delivery and Energy Reliability, Washington, DC.

Psychology & global climate change: Addressing a multifaceted phenomenon and set of challenges. *American Psychological Association Task Force on the Interface between Psychology and Global Climate Change*. The American Psychological Association (APA) Science Directorate, Washington, DC. 2011. Accessed at http://www.apa.org/science/about/publications/climate -change.aspx.

Microgrid Use Cases, Testing, and Validation

CLAY HOWEY

Contents

This chapter discusses testing and validation in the context of the campus microgrid development, with a focus on use cases. Since the high-level functional testing of the system was entirely use-case driven, a significant discussion of what use cases are and how they relate to testing is included. It is hoped that where applicable, the approaches discussed herein may be replicated in other application microgrids.

10.1 Microgrid Use Cases

Before diving into the details of testing and validation, it is useful to discuss what use cases are, since they play such a large role in driving the high-level system testing in a microgrid. Simply put, a use case is a list of actions that an actor takes to achieve a goal. An actor can be a human, an external system, or time. Use cases have been employed in software and systems engineering for many years, but they are relatively new to the area of electrical engineering. Before the widespread adoption of use cases, the functional requirements of complex systems were typically composed of exhaustive lists of declarative statements such as "The system shall do X. The system shall do Y." That approach ignores the human in the system, often to the detriment of the functionality of the completed system. It makes it all too easy to overlook requirements. By including humans and external systems in the functional requirements and indeed declaring how the goals of those humans and systems are to be met, the chances of creating a successful system are greatly increased.

As discussed, use cases are essentially narratives capturing the complex web of interactions between stakeholders involved in initiating, conducting, and realizing the system's functionalities and behavior. To document this process, certain tools and platforms have been developed. For instance, Unified Modeling Language notations could be used for documenting use cases. While a detailed study of the development process of use cases is outside the scope of this chapter, it is useful to discuss the basics.

The first step in creating use cases is typically the creation of an actor-goal list. This is a simple list of the actors that will be interacting with the system and what each actor's goal is in using the system. A simplified example of an actor-goal list is shown in Table 10.1.

Table 10.1 Actor-Goal List

ACTOR	GOAL
Microgrid operator	Login to microgrid control system Start microgrid Stop microgrid
Area electric power system (AEPS)	Provide power on demand at the point of common coupling (PCC)
Critical load	Be served power at the expense of noncritical loads in the microgrid

The actor-goal list serves as the starting point for each use case, and each use case is then further refined to a "fully dressed" use case, which can include actor definitions and roles, specific information exchanged, preconditions and assumptions, step-by-step description of how the goal is to be achieved, postconditions, etc. Alistair Cockburn defined a use-case template in his popular book *Writing Effective Use Cases* that includes the following fields:

- Title (an active-verb goal phrase that names the goal of the primary actor)
- Primary actor
- Goal in context
- Scope
- Level
- Stakeholders and interests
- Precondition
- Minimal guarantees
- Success guarantees
- Trigger
- Main success scenario
- Extensions
- Technology and data variation list

Use cases are often modeled in diagrams. The Unified Modeling Language visually expresses the relationships between actors and use cases in use-case diagrams. Figure 10.1 shows a simple use-case diagram that expresses the use cases from our actor-goal list example.

The actors in Figure 10.1 are displayed as stickmen figures, use cases are displayed as ovals, and lines indicate which actors are related to which use cases.

10.2 Electric Power Research Institute Use Cases

The Electric Power Research Institute (EPRI) has published many use cases related to smart grid on their website located at http://smartgrid .epri.com/Repository/Repository.aspx.

Of particular interest is the microgrid use-case category. Table 10.2 shows the actor roles for some of the EPRI microgrid use cases.

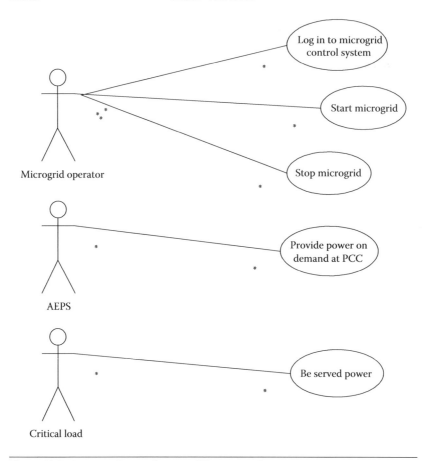

Figure 10.1   Use-case diagram. (Courtesy of Electric Power Research Institute, Palo Alto, California.)

EPRI currently has 10 use cases related to control and operations between the AEPS and advanced microgrids in connected, transition, and islanded modes. These 10 use cases are as follows:

- Frequency control
- Voltage control (grid-connected and islanding)
- Grid-connected to islanding transition—intentional
- Grid-connected to islanding transition—unintentional
- Islanding to grid-connected transition
- Energy management (grid-connected and islanding)
- Protection
- Ancillary services (grid-connected)
- Black start
- User interface and data management

Table 10.2   Actor Roles for EPRI Microgrid Use Cases

ACTOR NAME	TYPE	DESCRIPTION
AEPS	System	The electrical power system that normally supplies the microgrid through the PCC.
Asset switch	Device	Has the capability to disconnect assets within the microgrid (e.g., Non Critical Load [NCL]) from the microgrid for control purposes. The asset switch can receive control signals from the microgrid controller (MC) and can inform the MC of its status.
Centralized protection controller	System	A central control that is able to communicate with protective devices. It can operate to update settings or coordinate the operation of protection in real time. This can be a stand-alone function, or it could be a part of the microgrid control center (MCC).
Critical loads	Device	The highest-priority loads within the microgrid.
Local electric power system	System	The electrical power system on the customer's side of the PCC.
Market operator (MO)	System	Accepts bids from assets, such as a micorgrid (MG), in its AEPS and dispatches these assets to provide energy and ancillary services to ensure reliability for the AEPS. The MO may be part of the AEPS or may be a separate entity.
Microgrid controller	System	The MC control system that is able to dispatch the microgrid resources including opening/closing circuit breakers, changing control reference points, and changing generation levels, and it coordinates the sources and loads to maintain system stability.
Microgrid supervisory control and data acquisition (SCADA)	System	Provides the data acquisition and telecommunication required for the MC functions. It collects real-time data from each microgrid actor and executes control actions such as economic dispatch commands and circuit breaker controls/status.
Microgrid switch (MS)	Device	A switch at the PCC of the microgrid and the AEPS. The switch has the capability to detect the loss of power from the AEPS and disturbances in the AEPS. The MS can open and close automatically and on command from the MC and can inform the MC of its status.
Noncritical loads	Device	The lowest-priority loads within the microgrid. These loads may be left unserved in favor of the critical loads.
Other resources	Device	
PCC	System	The interface substation between the AEPS and the microgrid.
Primary DERs	Device	The distributed energy resources (DERs) participating in voltage regulation. Primary DERs could be a generator and energy storage.
Protection relay	Device	Can detect and clear a fault. With communication channels, it can communicate with other devices or the MCC.
Switching device	Device	Can disconnect DER within the microgrid. The switching device can receive control signals from the MC and can inform the MC of its status through SCADA.

Let us look at a couple of examples of these microgrid use cases. The following is the EPRI use case for intentional transitioning a microgrid from grid-connected to islanding.

USE CASE NAME	INTENTIONAL ISLANDING TRANSITION
Brief description	This use case describes the function when a microgrid disconnects from the area power system (APS) (AEPS) in a planned manner when the AEPS is grid connected and in a normal operating mode. The process by which the microgrid transitions from grid-connected operation to islanded operation is described.
Narrative	A microgrid needs to be capable of disconnecting itself from the AEPS for reasons such as economic operation, foreseen AEPS disturbances, maintenances, and testing. The microgrid needs to obtain permission from the AEPS for intentional islanding. The microgrid EMS and microgrid SCADA initiate the process of intentional islanding transition by dispatching islanding transition commands to the components in the microgrid. The microgrid EMS will estimate the microgrid load level and the available generation capacities, shed or reduce the loads with lower priorities, and redispatch the real and reactive power outputs of each generator and energy storage unit so that there is no import/export of real/reactive power between the microgrid and the AEPS at PCC and the microgrid components are managed in the islanded operation as well. After the islanding transition dispatch commands are executed, the power flow at the PCC is close to zero, and there is minimum impact on both the microgrid and the APS when the microgrid switch disconnects at this condition. After the microgrid is disconnected from the AEPS, it continues with the islanded operation. The microgrid EMS updates the islanded dispatch commands to manage the microgrid in the islanded operation. The microgrid SCADA and the primary sources perform the real-time control and operation to maintain microgrid system stability. The microgrid EMS can continue to participate in market activities by bidding into the daily/hourly-ahead energy market if it is known that the microgrid will be in grid-connected operation at that time.

The EPRI Use Case Repository also details the information exchanged in the use case. The information exchanged in the Intentional Islanding use case is shown in Table 10.3.

The EPRI Use Case Repository also has a section to indicate any contracts or regulations that a use case must adhere to and the impact of those contracts and regulations on the functioning of the system within the context of the use case (Figure 10.2). The section on intentional islanding use case contracts/regulations is shown in Table 10.4.

The real heart of a use case is the step-by-step description of how the goals of the actor(s) are met. EPRI calls this the "step-by-step analysis of function," and this is shown in Table 10.5. This is preceded by the

Table 10.3 Information Exchanged in EPRI Intentional Islanding Microgrid Use Case

INFORMATION OBJECT NAME	INFORMATION OBJECT DESCRIPTION
Microgrid bid	The microgrid's bid for energy and/or ancillary services sent from the microgrid EMS to the MO. It also contains information about the microgrid's availability to participate in the energy market when the microgrid is in different operation conditions.
Market dispatch	The dispatch from the MO to the microgrid EMS. The microgrid incorporates this dispatch information into its optimization.
Microgrid economic dispatch	The dispatch signal sent from the microgrid EMS to the microgrid SCADA. It incorporates both the microgrid operation conditions and the market dispatch when the microgrid is available to participate in the energy market or considers only the microgrid itself when it is unavailable to do so.
Measurements and status	Includes voltage, current, and/or power measured at each actor and the status of the actor, including on/off status, operation modes, and other actor operation status indicators.
Microgrid control commands	The control commands sent from microgrid SCADA to individual microgrid actors, including sources, loads, MS, and protection devices. The commands dispatch the economic dispatch from the microgrid EMS and send control signals to the actors between the two economic dispatches to maintain the system stability during islanded operation mode. The commands include the microgrid source control mode commands, real and reactive power dispatch commands, and load levels for controllable loads. The source control mode commands determine if a microgrid source is operated as a primary source that controls the frequency and/or voltage of the microgrid during islanded operation condition or as another source. It also includes the frequency and voltage setting point.
Islanding request	A signal sent from microgrid SCADA to the APS requesting permission for intentional islanding.
Islanding request response	The response of the APS to the islanding request. It can be yes (allow intentional islanding) or no (do not allow).
Islanding commands	The commands sent by the microgrid SCADA to microgrid actors to control the microgrid so that the power flow is minimized to specified ranges at the MS for the intentional islanding transition.
Islanding command response	The confirmation signal sent to the microgrid SCADA after the actors have executed the islanding commands to indicate that intentional islanding conditions have been met.
MS open command	A command sent by the microgrid SCADA to the MS to open the switch so that the microgrid is disconnected from the APS.
MS status	A signal sent by the MS indicating the status of the MS.

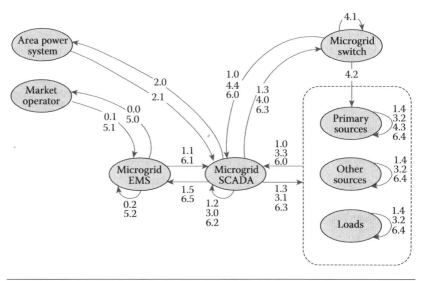

Figure 10.2   EPRI intentional islanding microgrid use-case diagram.

preconditions and assumptions, shown in Table 10.6, and succeeded by the postconditions and significant results, shown in Table 10.7.

Since use cases describe exactly what goals the system is trying to achieve, have step-by-step descriptions of how they achieve those goals, and describe what results are expected, we can see how well they lend themselves to testing. Each use case translates directly into one or more test cases where the completed system is put through its paces to ensure that expected results are achieved.

Table 10.4   Contracts/Regulations in EPRI Intentional Islanding Microgrid Use Case

CONTRACT/REGULATION	IMPACT OF CONTRACT/REGULATION ON FUNCTION
IEEE 1547 standard series	Standard for interconnection to the AEPS at the PCC
Interconnection agreement	Typical provisions include construction, interconnection, operations, safety and maintenance, access, exterior AC disconnect switch/isolation device, conflicts in agreements, disconnection, customer generator billing and payment, insurance, customer-generator indemnification, limitation of liability, termination, permanent disconnection, survival rights, and assignment/transfer of ownership of the customer-generated facility
Public utility net metering regulations	As applicable, where the microgrid exports to the AEPS
ISO market rules	As applicable, where the microgrid participates in markets

Table 10.5 Step-by-Step Analysis of Function in EPRI Intentional Islanding Microgrid Use Case

NO.	EVENT	PRIMARY ACTOR	INFORMATION PRODUCER	INFORMATION RECEIVER	NAME OF INFO EXCHANGED
0.0	Bid submission	Microgrid EMS	Microgrid EMS	MO	Microgrid bid
0.1	Receive market dispatch	Microgrid EMS	MO	Microgrid EMS	Market dispatch
0.2	Calculate microgrid economic dispatch	Microgrid EMS	Microgrid EMS	Microgrid EMS	Microgrid economic dispatch
1.0	Update measurement	Microgrid SCADA	All microgrid users	Microgrid SCADA	Measurements and units
1.1	Update microgrid economic dispatch	Microgrid SCADA	Microgrid EMS	Microgrid SCADA	Microgrid economic dispatch
1.2	Update control commands	Microgrid SCADA	Microgrid SCADA	Microgrid SCADA	Microgrid control commands
1.3	Send control commands	Microgrid SCADA	Microgrid SCADA	All microgrid users	Microgrid control commands
1.4	Execute control commands	All microgrid actors			
1.5	Update measurements	Microgrid SCADA	Microgrid SCADA	Microgrid EMS	Measurements and status
2.0	Send islanding request	Microgrid SCADA	Microgrid SCADA	APS	Islanding request
2.1	Receive islanding request response	Microgrid SCADA	APS	Microgrid SCADA	Islanding request response
3.0	Calculate islanding commands	Microgrid SCADA	Microgrid SCADA	Microgrid SCADA	Islanding commands
3.1	Send islanding commands	Microgrid SCADA	Microgrid SCADA	Primary sources, other sources, loads	Islanding commands
3.2	Execute islanding commands	Primary sources, other sources, loads			
3.3	Islanding commands response	Primary sources, other sources, loads	Primary sources, other sources, loads	Microgrid SCADA	Islanding commands response
4.0	Send MS open command	Microgrid SCADA	Microgrid SCADA	MS	MS open command
4.1	MS opens				

(Continued)

Table 10.5 (Continued)   Step-by-Step Analysis of Function in EPRI Intentional Islanding Microgrid Use Case

NO.	EVENT	PRIMARY ACTOR	INFORMATION PRODUCER	INFORMATION RECEIVER	NAME OF INFO EXCHANGED
4.2	Send MS status to primary sources	MS	MS	Primary sources	MS status
4.3	Voltage and frequency control	Primary sources			
4.4	Confirm MS open	MS	MS	Microgrid SCADA	MS status
5.0	Bid submission	Microgrid EMS	Microgrid EMS	MO	Microgrid bid
5.1	Receive market dispatch	Microgrid EMS	MO	Microgrid EMS	Market dispatch
5.2	Calculate microgrid economic dispatch	Microgrid EMS	Microgrid EMS	Microgrid EMS	Microgrid economic dispatch
6.0	Update measurement	Microgrid SCADA	All microgrid actors	Microgrid SCADA	Measurements and status
6.1	Update microgrid economic dispatch	Microgrid SCADA	Microgrid EMS	Microgrid SCADA	Microgrid economic dispatch
6.2	Update control commands	Microgrid SCADA	Microgrid SCADA	Microgrid SCADA	Microgrid control commands
6.3	Send control commands	Microgrid SCADA	Microgrid SCADA	All microgrid actors	Microgrid control commands
6.4	Execute control commands	All microgrid actors			
6.5	Update measurements	Microgrid SCADA	Microgrid SCADA	Microgrid EMS	Measurements and status

Table 10.6 Preconditions and Assumptions in EPRI Intentional Islanding Microgrid Use Case

ACTOR/SYSTEM/INFORMATION/CONTRACT	PRECONDITIONS OR ASSUMPTIONS
MO	Logged into microgrid EMS
APS	Power is available at PCC

Table 10.7 Postconditions and Results in EPRI Intentional Islanding Microgrid Use Case

ACTOR/ACTIVITY	POSTCONDITION DESCRIPTION AND RESULTS

10.3 Planning and Design

The testing and validation of a microgrid is guided by planning. In the case of the Open Access to Sustainable Intermittent Sources (OASIS) system, there were several planning stages, the first of which began during the system design phase due to the compressed timeline of the project.

Two design charettes were conducted at the start of the project to introduce partners, discuss very high-level concepts as design candidates for the system, and identify communication protocols for integration. During that process it was agreed that an aggressive approach to testing was required due to the short project timelines and geographical separation of the project partners. This led to the decision to have project partners collaborate on pairwise integration testing to test communication integration remotely.

The key planning considerations for testing specific to this project were as follows:

- Compressed timeline for the completion of the project
- Components coming from different partners had never previously been integrated
- Need for integrated components to be remotely tested to ensure that on-site integration went smoothly
- Need to ensure that project partners understood the overall objectives and goals of the entire system rather than just the particulars of their own components

Testing of individual components was typically done by partners at the factory according to their own factory acceptance tests (FATs).

The results of these FATs were provided upon request. Components from different partners that were required to communicate with each other require factory integration tests (FITs) to ensure that the components work correctly when shipped to the job site. Site acceptance tests were conducted once the components were shipped to the job site to ensure that they were not damaged in shipping and that they met design specifications. Finally, high-level use-case testing was conducted to ensure that the system met the overall project objectives.

In the case of the OASIS project, testing was made more difficult due to the language, cultural, and time zone differences between the partners involved. Commissioning and integration was very time constrained due to the cost of travel and accommodation of personnel from the various partners.

10.3.1 Detailed Design and Specification

Test plan documents for the system were developed early on and shared with all project partners. In the case of the OASIS system, this was done via a wiki. It took considerable efforts and time for the design team at the British Columbia Institute of Technology (BCIT) to draw the attention of partner personnel, who were assigned to implement the solution, to review the tests plans on the wiki and provide BCIT with their feedback. Ordinarily, and as the case is in many engineering projects, such personnel tended to focus on their own individual projects, rather than being concerned with the solution as a whole. This was one of the major issues that had been discussed between partners during the initial planning charettes, and the management in each partner organization was well aware of such risks and had taken the necessary steps to reduce its impacts.

10.3.2 Partner Factory Acceptance Testing

FAT was done by the partner at the factory to ensure that the component complied with the partner specifications and was ready to ship. Moreover, and as expected, there were cases in which certain FATs could not be shared across all partner teams due to intellectual property considerations.

10.3.3 Pairwise Factory Integration Tests

FITs were performed by partners at their factories to ensure that their components would communicate properly with other partner components. Pairwise refers to two components coming from different companies that need to communicate with each other. FIT was necessary due to the compressed timelines of the OASIS project. BCIT could not afford the time to debug communication problems as the components arrived on site, so this process needed to be done ahead of time.

Moreover, there were technical challenges getting virtual private networks in place and firewall demilitarized zones set up to allow different partners to conduct remote testing of components. Such arrangements had to address the rightful concerns that some partners might have had in opening up these communication channels to other partners who might have been perceived as competitors in some areas.

Despite rigorous planning, FIT between some of BCIT partners was not completed as their respective components were not ready at test time. To address this, BCIT created software that emulated the signals that such components would generate and tested them remotely with the rest of the system.

10.3.4 Partner Site Acceptance Testing

All partners were required to conduct the agreed-upon site acceptance tests to ensure that their components arrived undamaged and performed according to specification. However, despite careful planning, delays on one partner's part affected other partners, which created difficulties in completing all testing on time.

10.3.5 Use-Case Testing

The solution functional testing, or use-case testing, focused on verifying that the Energy OASIS system's control system and electrical power components could operate in the modes that demonstrate the defined objectives of the system development project, that it can be configured to operate with the system behavior defined by the objectives, and that it responds safely and in a manner that reduces risk of damage to faults in any subsystem and actively notifies remote system operators of faults.

The specific use cases tested were as follows:

- Storage and later use of PV for EV quick-charging with no impact on grid
- Support loads during power outage
- Support loads until unable during power outage
- Intentional islanding—EV charging using BESS storage
- Intentional islanding until unable to continue
- Optimal dispatch of energy in a microgrid
- Fault handling at the system level

Each of these use cases is discussed in plain language in the next sections. It is useful to note that these are the highest-level use cases, representing the major goals of the project. More trivial use cases such as system log-in and log-out are of less interest and beyond the scope of this book.

10.3.6 Storage and Later Use of Photovoltaic Generation for Electric Vehicle Quick-Charging with No Impact on the Grid

This test used stored PV generation only to charge two EVs. To ensure only stored PV generation was used, the battery system was discharged to its lowest allowable state (20% state of charge [SOC]), then allowed to charge using PV only (i.e., not via the grid) to at least 30% SOC. The test took place while the grid was connected, but the system was not allowed to draw power from the grid. The two EVs were then charged using the battery system only—PV was disconnected during the EV charging.

10.3.7 Support Loads during Power Outage

This test used manipulation of the point of interconnection (POI) breaker state to simulate grid power failure and restoration. Prior to the invoked grid power failure, PV generation capability was removed from the OASIS system so that OASIS was forced to use battery energy storage system (BESS) battery energy to support loads during the outage. EV charging (two vehicles) and canopy lights were used as OASIS system loads during the grid outage, and the test assessed whether OASIS supported those loads during the grid outage. The test also assessed whether the OASIS system operated normally in grid-connected mode after grid power was restored. An EV charge after grid power restoration was used to verify this.

10.3.8 Support Loads until Unable during Power Outage

This test was very similar to the previous test with the main difference being that the test was run until the system was no longer able to support the loads. This test used manipulation of the POI breaker state to simulate grid power failure and restoration. Prior to the invoked grid power failure, PV generation capability was removed from the OASIS system so that OASIS was forced to use BESS battery energy to support loads during the outage. EV charging (two vehicles) and canopy lights were used as OASIS system loads during the grid outage, and the test assessed whether OASIS supports those loads during the grid outage.

This variant of the test allowed only a small amount of energy to be stored in BESS batteries prior to the simulated grid outage and kept using loads (EV charging) until the system had insufficient energy to support those loads. The test assessed the control system's and electrical system's response to that energy shortage. The decentralized energy management system (DEMS) and BCIT software (EV charging load manager) collectively acted to deny or cut off EV charging due to low available energy.

The test also assessed whether the OASIS system operated normally in grid-connected mode after grid power was restored. An EV charge after grid power restoration was used to verify this.

10.3.9 Intentional Islanding: Electric Vehicle Charging Using BESS Storage

This test involved scheduling a period of intentional islanding with the operator portal human–machine interface (HMI). The ability to use PV during islanding was removed, so that only BESS stored energy could be used to support the loads during the islanded period. The system was expected to automatically precharge the BESS to support this islanded period. Two EV charges were conducted during the islanded period. The system reconnected to grid on schedule, and an additional EV charge was used to verify normal grid-connected operation.

10.3.10 Intentional Islanding until Unable

This test was very similar to the previous test with the main difference being that the test was run until the system was no longer able to support the loads. This test scheduled a very long period of intentional islanding with the operator portal HMI. The ability to use PV during islanding was removed, so that only BESS stored energy could be used to support the loads during the islanded period. At the start of test, the BESS batteries were fully discharged. The system automatically precharged the BESS to support this islanded period, but only a small amount of energy was allowed back into the BESS batteries. Two EVs were charged during the islanded period. The system ran out of energy during the intentional islanding period, and the DEMS also predicted running out of energy. The DEMS commanded an early return to grid-connected mode, and the system executed that command. The DEMS recommended islanding once enough power was stored in BESS to support some more islanding and that the system islanded again.

The system reconnected to grid on schedule, and an additional EV charge was used to verify normal grid-connected operation.

10.3.11 Optimal Dispatch of Energy in a Microgrid

This test comprised the prescheduling, using the operator portal HMI, of three successive periods: the first being a grid-supported mode in which the system was allowed to and expected to draw power from the grid, followed by a grid-neutral period when the system was not allowed to draw grid power but could contribute PV power to the grid if excess was available, followed by a period when the OASIS system was actively grid-supporting, that is, had been directed to generate power to the grid at 250 kW.

At the start of the test, the BESS batteries were fully discharged and the ability to use PV power was removed, so that the DEMS was compelled to demonstrate charging the BESS batteries from grid input power during the first grid-supported period.

There were two additional aspects of the test. During the middle, grid-neutral period, the DEMS HMI was used to command generation of reactive power to the grid to counteract prevailing low power factor.

The last aspect of the test was that during the grid-supporting period, an EV charge was attempted, but the control system and user interfaces of the system rejected that EV charge initiation, due to the fact that the system had been asked, at higher priority, to generate 250 kW to the grid and 250 kW is the maximum allowed power flow out of the inverter system toward grid and loads combined.

10.3.12 Fault Handling at the System Level

This test consisted of generating a fault/fault indication in each major subsystem, verifying safe system response, and exercising restart. The tests were carried out with a fault injected into each of BESS, PV, PCS, EV charger, Substation breaker, BCIT software, and MEM subsystems.

The general procedure for the test of each fault was generate fault, observe fault indication in HMI, operators to be notified of fault by e-mail, verify OASIS automatic system safing, carry out simulated diagnosis and actual fault clearing procedure, restart OASIS system, and verify normal operation.

10.4 Lessons Learned

BCIT learned that despite early agreement among partners that testing was a high priority, when it came time to perform particularly the FITs, some partners were reluctant to work with other partners due to the competitive nature of the private industry.

Technical challenges relating to this included difficulties with a certain partner's choice of virtual private network product that made it challenging to get other partners, and BCIT, connected to perform the testing.

Unforeseen challenges relating to this testing included cultural differences between partners from different countries. For example, employees of a partner could be very blunt and direct in identifying an issue or problem, which can offend those of another partner who culturally prefer a much milder approach and interpret such directness as being rude.

Operational challenges with this testing were the reality that different partners were in different time zones, which made interoperability testing very difficult. Some partners had union rules around working hours for their employees, which made it difficult to coordinate times for testing.

11

CAMPUS MICROGRID LESSONS LEARNED

JOEY DABELL AND CLAY HOWEY

Contents

This chapter discusses the lessons learned in the context of the campus microgrid research development and demonstration activities, which can be replicated in other broad-reaching applications microgrids. Achievements versus expectations, as well as unforeseen challenges, will be discussed using experiences from the campus microgrid. Moreover, the opportunities for leveraging these lessons in other microgrid contexts will be presented. The chapter examines the lessons learned during the operation of and the ongoing research activities in the campus microgrid, including the discussion of the role of microgrids in education, and concludes with a summary of recommendations and next steps toward broader-based applications of microgrids.

11.1 Learning by Doing

It should be noted that at the outset of our endeavor to build a microgrid, the end point was not completely clear. We had ideas about what a microgrid should look like, but its exact specifications, features, capabilities, and integration with the larger grid had to be further developed. In that regard, we capitalized on our close working relationship with our local utility company, BC Hydro. As the major stakeholder of this initiative, BC Hydro assigned its experts to work with us and define the framework of a joint BCIT/BC Hydro smart microgrid. This was done through a series of retreats, bringing experts from BC Hydro and the British Columbia Institute of Technology (BCIT) together to discuss overlapping interests and opportunities.

Given the fact that at the time when these discussions began (March 2007), the concept of intelligent microgrids was in its infancy; in early retreats with BC Hydro and BCIT, there was much debate about the definition of a microgrid. Was it simply a diesel generator and load? Was islanding required? What exactly made a microgrid intelligent? These discussions over a period of six months resulted in a joint strategic technology road map for smart microgrids. Detailed discussions about the structure of that road map were included in Chapter 3, Section 4 of this book. Suffice to say here that despite the clarity and the sense of certainty that such road maps tend to provide, we have gone through a great deal of learning since then, and that learning was accomplished simply by doing. Our specifications gradually came into focus as we moved along and were shaped by what was feasible, regulations in place in our jurisdiction, availability of willing partners to join us, and our deeper understanding of the requirements of an intelligent microgrid.

We found that anyone interested in microgrids purely from a return on investment (ROI) perspective is misguided. The application of a microgrid determines the ROI. For example, at University of California in San Diego (UCSD), natural gas-powered generation is used to displace loads where the tariffs run roughly 30 cents/kWh. Here in British Columbia, the cost is closer to 7 cents/kWh where a BC Hydro feed is available, but it is much higher in isolated off-grid communities that rely on diesel gensets. That is why UCSD's microgrid focus (which began almost at the same time as ours) was on addressing the energy costs of the campus, and as such was championed by UCSD's facilities department. In contrast, given the extremely low electricity tariffs in the province of British Columbia, investments in a microgrid could hardly be purely justified through an operational ROI. For that reason, BCIT/BC Hydro's microgrid focused on research and creation of know-how around microgrid technologies, and as such was championed by researchers and faculty. Moreover, the microgrid was further developed as a test facility to enable researchers and entrepreneurs alike to generate ideas, develop and test novel approaches and products, and understand the merits of microgrid concepts and components and their relationship to the larger smart grid.

11.2 Achievements vis-à-vis Expectations

In a small microgrid, large load swings and renewable generation uncertainties (i.e., deviations from forecast) are common and occur in subsecond time frames. As such, a microgrid energy management system (EMS) for small microgrids should be capable of reoptimizing energy use and power flow at subminute timescales and should be capable of adaptive power flow control on timescales no longer than several seconds. The EMS technology employed in the Energy Open Access to Sustainable Intermittent Sources (OASIS) microgrid was more suited to balancing large regional electricity networks with large renewable energy farms. The EMS was initially required to perform once-per-day power flow planning, which was soon changed to once per 15 minutes. This planning granularity was insufficiently agile to keep up with spontaneous unexpected load or unexpected drop in PV generation, so the saliency of the EMS power flow plan was limited.

In a small microgrid, detailed energy models of power sources, sinks, and losses are needed by the EMS, to allow true optimization of energy cost and power flow control. EMS planning and power flow control in a small microgrid should account for losses such as AC/DC and DC/AC conversion losses, battery climate control, battery self-discharge, and standby losses of power subsystems and microgrid loads. The EMS developed for the Energy OASIS was not configured to account for such small microgrid concerns, but rather assumed a simplified energy balance model without modeling of losses. The use of power in the microgrid has to be modeled more accurately in the next iterations of our EMS. Further accuracies in this area shall lead to more optimal energy optimization and power flow control.

As a side benefit of a detailed energy and energy losses model in the EMS, the EMS energy cost optimization logic could seek to minimize the standby power losses (phantom load) by techniques such as following:

- Switching off load feeders upstream of the transformers if possible.
- Turning smart power systems (such as bidirectional inverters) down to their lowest standby stopped operating mode during planned intervals during the day when the power conversion is not needed.

The Energy OASIS system will benefit from more refined EMS models and optimization logic, which may further reduce standby power losses through smarter and more agile equipment control decisions.

11.3 Unforeseen Challenges

Complex projects of this nature will typically encounter a number of unforeseen challenges and deviations across their life cycles. These kinds of challenges are by their nature impossible to predict and can severely impact their success. These challenges occur even in projects that use proven technologies, clear specifications, and mature components. In the case of microgrid projects, some of the factors contributing to these challenges can be attributed to the novel ways in which novel technologies may be required to integrate and operate to provide a solution for unique locations, consumers, and other seemingly disparate requirements. Challenges are further exacerbated by the lack of regulatory and technical standards, and government policies. This section summarizes some of the unforeseen challenges encountered and mitigated during the campus smart microgrid project.

11.3.1 Project Planning, Coordination, and Management Challenges

The design and realization of a complex system, using a consortium of diverse partners with different corporate cultures, workflow processes, and technologies is extremely challenging. Aside from technical challenges in integrating such diverse technologies, the development team learned the following valuable lessons:

- It is extremely important to ensure a smooth transition and handover between various groups and teams within partner organizations. For example, in some cases, commitments made by the technical design teams were not properly communicated with the implementation teams within the same organization.
- The need to negotiate and conclude a role and responsibility matrix upfront; any ambiguity in who is responsible for what in the early stages of the development can cost the project valuable time and efforts later on to elaborate and identify.
- More time spent at the system design phase will help with a smoother transition between various stages of the development. In particular, a detailed specification of each and every component upfront can be extremely beneficial to the overall project schedule later on.
- It is critical to enquire with each and every partner the specific definitions that different companies have for the same objects, implementations, and flavors of the same standards. Confusions that can arise in the debugging phase due to seemingly similar but different definitions for the same parts of the applicable standards could be extremely time consuming.
- Discussion about partnerships and different agendas make it difficult to focus on the selection of most appropriate technologies and needs versus wants.

11.3.2 Site Selection, Approvals, Preparation, and Construction Challenges

- Original plan for rooftop photovoltaic (PV)
  - Seismic and space requirements.
  - In general, need to consider regional codes, standards, and similar requirements.

- Approvals
  - Timelines for permitting and related approvals underestimated. In the campus microgrid, one of the rooftop solar PV systems had to be installed in such a way as to not penetrate the roofing membrane. The engineers designed a ballasted mounting system in which the solar PV panels were mounted on standard racks, which were held in place with concrete ballast blocks. The design was new to permitting authorities and required additional time and consideration in order to receive approval.
- Construction timelines generally include contingencies. In the case of the campus microgrid, a number of unanticipated issues ranged from hidden boulders impeding foundation work, to difficult cable pulls, to delivery delays for components. These contributed to delays beyond the planned contingencies and have underscored the importance of planning and contingencies, for example, in the context of remote community microgrids, where such delays could become extremely amplified due to location-related issues such as transportation of materials and crew assignment.

11.3.3 Unforeseen Design Challenges

The campus microgrid experienced a significant unforeseen design challenge resulting in the need to redesign the racking system for the battery modules in the storage system. This resulted in project time and cost overruns. The original design called for the use of a readily available, off-the-shelf rack system. Because it was one of the first battery installations of this size, the requirements for scaling up the number of battery modules in the storage container were not fully understood. During the testing in the detailed design phase, it was determined that the original layout of the battery modules led to the modules overheating. The layout design was changed, resulting in more complex racking requirements, which necessitated customized design, manufacture, and testing of a new solution. While the new racking system proved successful, due to project time and resource constraints, the manufacturing of the new system was largely supported by the design engineers. In this case, the use of design engineers in the build phase was a necessary step, but one that incurred unplanned project costs. Mitigating this issue also resulted in time delays.

The lessons learned from this issue resulted in a novel racking system design that can be applied to future projects and has provided engineers with the knowledge to facilitate subsequent builds with lower cost labor.

11.3.4 Component Commissioning Challenges

- Unanticipated noise

    In general, a number of components used in microgrids have historically been placed inside substations or in locations with no noise impact on the neighboring community. With the OASIS system, the power conversion system (PCS) and the container heating, ventilating, and air conditioning created noise levels exceeding local city bylaws and caused complaints from nearby residents, and a noise mitigation strategy had to be developed after commissioning.

- Manufacturer out of business

    The campus microgrid has suffered from manufacturers of various components going out of business or simply dropping a component from their catalog, leaving that component unsupported.

- Certification of components

    For insurance purposes, BCIT required that all electrical components be certified by an independent body such as Canadian Standards Association (CSA) or Canadian Underwriters Lab (CUL). Many utilities do not have this requirement, and this can lead to misunderstandings with vendors and to procurement and commissioning delays.

11.3.5 System Integration and Testing Challenges

The ideal situation for a campus microgrid, and indeed for microgrids in general, is to be built using proven technologies. However, given the novelty of microgrids, that is not always possible. The design team was often left with two hard choices: compromise on the design objectives in favor of using off-the-shelf components or stay true to the design objectives and expose the design to technologies with potentially novel integration considerations and requirements. That level of customization of major components, particularly the battery energy storage system (BESS), the PCS, and the EMS, but also the DC fast charging (DCFC) units, cost the design team a lot of time and resources.

The control integration process for each particular microgrid system must be rigorously managed with central technical integration decision authority and contingency budget allocation authority. Protocol standard adherence is not enough to ensure the interoperability of complex power subsystems and smart loads.

During the project, intersubsystem interface specifications were not respected in any detail by some subsystem partners, and the interface specification refinement agreement process was not prioritized by the subsystem partners, in an apparent belief that the interface being formatted according to a certain communication protocol would be sufficient to achieve interoperability. An interoperability incompatibility crunch therefore occurred near the end of the project, resulting in less time available for overall system use case testing.

As a side effect of the lack of interface specification and refinement process rigor, the boundaries of control logic responsibility between one major subsystem and the EMS remained unclear throughout the system development project. This resulted in a number of control logic gaps remaining until very late in the system build, and in some control logic gaps, remaining after initial commissioning. For example, which microgrid power subsystem or controller or EMS is responsible for an orderly multistep startup logic; which subsystem is responsible for setting submodes of operation within a key subsystem; which subsystem is responsible for setting operating limits; which subsystem is responsible for battery group charging coordination; and which subsystem is responsible for battery capacity learning, cycle logic, and initiation.

A specific lesson about the integration of smart power subsystems into a unified microgrid control system is that each monitoring and control interface specification (between a pair of interacting subsystems) must be treated as the entire allowable interface between those subsystems. It came to light that one major subsystem offered a control and monitoring interface that included the two control set points and four monitoring data points specified in the interface specification but also offered (and required knowledgeable use of) dozens of other control settings and hundreds of monitoring data points. This was seen by the partner as offering flexibility, but the system integration consequence was that that subsystem was not self-managing and required another external supervisory control system to understand its internal details. That external supervisory control system did not exist, because the other system's designer assumed (as they were entitled to) that the specified interface was the entire interface. In an integration of complex control subsystems, one subsystem offering (and requiring use of) more control options and monitoring detail than specified in the intersubsystem interface specification is not a benefit but a significant problem.

The project on-site testing timeline included component commissioning, system integration, system functional testing, and use case testing. The intent was that all partners be present on site for the duration of all these activities, requiring members of the technology provider technical teams to be on-site for over two months. At various points during this timeline, some of the technical teams were in sit-and-wait mode, while other teams were actively testing. From a practical perspective, this kind of commitment was an impossible sell. Partner support teams hailed from North America, the Far East, and Europe. It was extremely difficult to get buy-in from partners to stay on-site past the component commissioning, through the system integration and use case testing. The feeling was that the technologies were installed and integrated and should work. The reality was that implementing the system use case tests would test the components in ways they may not have been previously tested. Indeed the first year of operations has proven this to be true.

11.3.6 Early Integration Testing

Early integration testing (over virtual private networks over the Internet if necessary) of intersubsystem monitoring and control interfaces is essential, before power subsystem hardware and EMS are on site. The Energy OASIS project's use case testing period was burdened because serious incompatibilities in the control and monitoring interface protocol details and operating logic were being discovered and addressed in the very last scheduled commissioning period of the system. The smart power subsystem partners and the EMS partner did not allocate sufficient time to the midproject integration testing, having an overreliance on their adherence to a communication protocol standard, and the consequence was a significant reduction of time available to exercise, refine, and validate the overall microgrid system use case operation.

11.3.7 Managing Final Integration Testing

Regardless of the reasons for the delayed use case testing of an overall microgrid EMS and control system, such integrated system use case testing (also known as solution-functional testing) must fully take place, and the tests must pass in order for subsystem partners to be considered complete in the performance of their commitments. Subsystem partners would prefer the complete performance to be attached to passing an individual site-acceptance test (commissioning test) of their individual subsystem, but overall system integration and function problems are certain to occur in a complex smart subsystem integration, and the subsystem supply performance should include successful discovery, negotiation, and resolution of whole system, scale control and operating deficiencies.

Ultimately, the system integration testing was completed; some partners remained on site through the use case testing phase, and others provided support remotely from their home location. OASIS has been operating, with some exceptions, since March 5, 2014. An ongoing operation has uncovered deficiencies that are addressed as they arise with support from partners via e-mail exchanges. Future projects will benefit by securing partner commitment through a longer system integration and use case testing phase and by ensuring that the development of operational and maintenance support agreements is explicitly scoped during project planning, and that the development of these agreements includes appropriate stakeholder representation.

11.4 Campus Operation and Research

11.4.1 Campus Microgrid Operational Learning Curve

The campus microgrid represents the addition to a living campus of new technologies and processes and on a fairly significant scale. Operating the campus microgrid requires the introduction and the integration of new skills and processes. There are many operational processes under existing campus infrastructure maintenance routines, but these often require the integration of new skills, practices, and procedures to match the new technologies. In the case of the campus microgrid, new skills and processes were developed by the research team through hands-on activities over the life cycle of the project, and while tackling operational challenges throughout the campus microgrid startup and system commissioning phase. Future projects could benefit by applying mitigation activities such as the following:

- Incorporating an appropriate transition and operational plan with stakeholders, during the early planning and conceptual design phase of the project. (This should include developing a shared understanding of current operations and processes, what changes may be required to accommodate the new technologies, and a clear delineation of roles and responsibilities for ongoing operation and maintenance.)
- Incorporating a project transition phase at the end of the project that includes knowledge transfer overlap between the resources from campus facilities and operations and the experts from the technology providers.

11.5 Role of Microgrids in Education

While microgrids can be tools for education in a variety of roles, there is also a need for awareness and education around subjects relating to microgrids themselves. A microgrid educational subject matter targeting designers, practitioners, utilities, and related stakeholders will promote a working understanding of the design options for microgrids, how microgrids can be operated and managed, particularly under emergency situations, and how to identify threats and manage security incidents such as cyber or physical infrastructure attacks. Street-level education around microgrids will promote awareness and understanding at the community level, highlighting the benefits of microgrids such as modernization and reduced dependency on energy sources that require lengthy transportation, improved energy security and reliability during emergencies, conservation and reduced carbon footprint, and enhancement of local economies.

11.6 Conclusions, Recommendations, and Next Steps

A key feature of microgrids is that the technologies applied are appropriate to the requirements of its loads. Demonstration projects are not intended to be financially viable, but the consideration of eventual viability factors, such as understanding demand requirements, can influence the design choices and provide more robust options for future deployment.

The campus microgrid has shown how soft and firm sources of energy could be integrated in a distribution environment to provide reliable service for unplanned loads, such as electric cars. In the process, OASIS demonstrated the viability of battery energy storage technologies as a means to counteract the intermittent nature of soft power, as well as the role an EMS can play in ensuring the dispatchability of a diverse portfolio of energy sources.

The strong potential for solar PV as a generation source has been demonstrated. In general, the grid-scale energy storage must be increased from present-day levels, in order to balance the expected increase in intermittent clean renewable energy sources and to balance and stabilize the grid.

A combination of grid-scale energy storage, microgrids with local storage, efficient DC power transmission capable of spanning weather systems, and demand response control is likely needed to maintain grid stability in the face of the needed significant penetration of intermittent clean electricity generation into the electrical power grid.

As alluded to in Section 11.1, certain factors will always need to be considered when broadening the reach of microgrids. Climate, loads, location and access, behaviors, standards, and regulatory factors are all important factors that will have an impact on the ROI and the ultimate success of a microgrid.

Index

Note: Page numbers ending in "f" refer to figures. Page numbers ending in "t" refer to tables.